The Last
RESORT

The Last
RESORT

A CHRONICLE OF PARADISE,
PROFIT, AND PERIL AT THE BEACH

SARAH STODOLA

An Imprint of HarperCollins*Publishers*

HarperCollins books may be purchased for educational, business, or sales promotional use. For information, please email the Special Markets Department at SPsales@harpercollins.com.

Ecco® and HarperCollins® are trademarks of HarperCollins Publishers.

Parts of the chapter on Waikiki originally appeared in the article "Climate Change Drowns the Beach Vacation," in *Culture Trip*, and the essay "Among the Very Tall," in *Flung Magazine*.

All illustrations are courtesy of the author unless otherwise noted.

FIRST EDITION

Designed by Angela Boutin

Library of Congress Cataloging-in-Publication Data has been applied for.

ISBN 978-0-06-295162-5

22 23 24 25 26 LSC 10 9 8 7 6 5 4 3 2 1

CONTENTS

The Last
RESORT

PROLOGUE

I grew up, as you probably did, with an ingrained concept of the beach as shorthand for paradise. Life's a beach, the beach is great, and so is life, if you're at the beach. I accepted that there was no more coveted environment than 82 degrees, with a light breeze tousling the leaves of a palm tree as it provided sun-dappled shade for a lounge chair and a piña colada, a soundtrack of lapping waves underscoring the vibe. Still today, I can think of no more surefire way to elicit expressions of envy from another person than by mentioning a recent trip to such a place. This person will "hate you." "Tough life," she will say, enjoying the sarcasm. Such is the position the beach resort has attained today. It plays host in our collective imagination to the highest form of leisure.

It's a phenomenon that has always struck me as thorny. The envy is unexamined, almost compulsory. It treats loving the beach as an innate human characteristic, although before the late eighteenth century, the oceans mostly instilled fear in general populations the world over and were avoided altogether if possible. Even at the first seaside resorts, the beach and ocean were not cherished, but tolerated in service of one's health.

A couple of centuries later, the allure of the beach resort came to be considered self-evident, a truth seldom questioned. The presumed universal appeal of beaches has been mirrored back to us by the media, leaving little room for serious consideration of the major global industry that has bred economic and social inequalities in many a locale, as well as contributed to the climate crisis while coming under existential threat from it—a paradise both threatening and threatened. With regard to these lapses, *The Last Resort* is meant as both corrective and warning.

I consider my relative newcomer status to resort life to be an asset in this pursuit. Mine is not a family historically concerned with the beach. My parents grew up in small towns in Wisconsin, where the oceans were irrelevant to everyday life. As a child, my mom took an annual family road trip in the 1950s to Florida, on two-lane Highway 41 all the way. The journey took three days in each direction. Once in Florida, she tells me, the family spent more time inland than at the shores. My dad saw the ocean for the first time at age twenty-two—the Indian Ocean, as it turns out, after he arrived in Tanzania with the Peace Corps. I grew up with their view of the beach as incidental, although I did recognize its elevated role in the culture at large, from movies and television to the aforementioned envy I saw when classmates traveled to beach destinations during school holidays.

When I finally began traveling to beach destinations regularly, as a concession to a relationship with a surfer, I came to the culture as an outsider. By this time, I was publishing travel journalism, which familiarized me with the always-sunny disposition required of destination coverage. After so many hours spent endorsing places as a default position, I knew I wanted to look at them through a more critical lens.

This aligned with my tendency to approach my beach breaks analytically, and anthropologically. I often enjoyed the sun and the snorkeling and the views, but I found the sanitized bubbles in which resorts existed curious. Their common culture, so widely treasured, necessitated further examination. To be honest, beach resorts weirded me out a little—their insistence on indolence, and on forgetting the world outside, both the one back home and the one immediately beyond the property; their soundtrack of Bob Marley and Jimmy Buffett; the amount one has to fork over for a margarita. I've often found resorts' peculiar brand of utopia more disquieting than relaxing. At the same time, I've seen economies and cultures transformed by them. Sometimes for better, and sometimes for worse, but always in ways that seem coated with ambivalence.

I've traveled around the globe to destinations that have been singularly affected by beach tourism, to understand who goes where and why, to document resorts' underreported role in economies large and small, and to contend with climate change's impact on them. I've chatted at the pool bar with honeymooners and hedge funders and spring breakers. I've visited once-remote villages that have been altered completely by the arrival of a resort. I've seen how the explosion of the global middle class is forcing travel companies to evolve and creating new ones to compete with them. I've seen prominent resort areas going to great lengths to preserve the eroding shorelines that buttress their prosperity, even as their behavior contributes to an unsustainable carbon footprint via air-conditioning, excessive water consumption, golf courses, coral reef damage, and persistent emissions generated by importing food and drink to remote locations. My hope is that, together, the stories in *The Last Resort* will create a nuanced understanding of the beach resort industry where none currently exists.

To see the locations necessary in completing the research, long-haul flights were often required, making me an accessory to the industry's growing carbon footprint. I purchased offsets for all flights taken in service of writing this book, while acknowledging that doing so is not enough to rationalize the emissions.

Unease with the concept of the beach as paradise may be sinking into our psyches. In 2021, despite the promise of revived international travel during the waning days of the COVID pandemic, we largely sat on our sofas, presented with a string of TV shows and movies in which things go sideways at the beach: In *White Lotus*, guests and staff at a five-star resort in Hawaii grapple with their place on the spectrum of white privilege and inequality. In M. Night Shyamalan's *Old*, a family on vacation heads to a beach that compresses their entire lives into a single horrifying day. And *Nine Perfect Strangers*, filmed in Byron Bay, Australia, starred Nicole Kidman as a wellness guru with sinister undertones running a resort for troubled wealthy folks. Even *Bachelor in Paradise*, the stalwart show putting former contestants on *The Bachelor* and *The Bachelorette* together on a beach in Mexico, documented the cast being evacuated in the face of an approaching tropical storm. The beach resort became a de facto setting for stories probing our contemporary fears and concerns.

"The Last Resort" on one hand implies an end to the beach vacation as we know it. With sand that can't be relied on to stay in place, and water threatening to inundate properties, developers may eventually find the current resort model untenable. It's happened before: There was a last resort in Baiae, ancient seaside escape of the Roman elite, and a last resort in Rockaway, New York, once the preeminent beach destination in America. On the other hand, we are unlikely to see the global beach resort's definitive demise in our lifetimes. We may instead have a last resort of another kind, one that comes when all other options have been exhausted, when we've failed to curb climate change and have no choice but to accommodate its directives. This book aims to find out where the beach resort is headed, as a last resort.

I'M NEVER COMING HOME

Thailand and England

When I first encountered Railay, a small peninsula of unreasonable beauty protruding into Thailand's Andaman Sea, I was wallowing in the demise of the major relationship of my twenties. The timing compounded my mood—2009, the thick of the financial crisis, when I'd wake up, open my laptop, and read another email from another laid-off editor who would no longer be hiring me. My formerly live-in boyfriend had returned to his native England, and my state of mind was such that for several months I took up smoking, not in earnest, but melodramatically, sitting in the pocket window of my apartment, glass pushed open into the dead of winter.

By the time I booked a flight to Thailand in April, the smoking phase had ended, replaced by one in which the cultivating of distance became my preferred diversion. The other side of the world appealed in its polarity to home. I found Thailand recommended as a good place both for first-time Asia travelers and solo women, and that settled it.

I wasn't anticipating a beach vacation, but after a couple of days in Bangkok, I understood for the first time that not every major world city would be for me—too many beer-swilling backpackers and brazen sex tourists for my taste. I got a bus south and when I got off at Krabi, Railay emerged as a nearby option. Cliffs and jungle rendered it inaccessible by land, so I took a wooden long-tail boat—the kind featured on every promotional material for Thailand ever. The half-hour ride introduced me to a landscape of tropical waters and high limestone cliffs, some of them jutting out of the water to form unearthly, multi-colored vertical islands, something like if Gaudi had built them.

After landing at Railay East, an inferior beach used mostly for transport, I set out to find a place to stay, heading up a paved jungle path and renting a cabana for five dollars a night at a ramshackle spot that would take its place atop the list of the most revolting places I've ever slept—bugs, stained sheets, a toilet that potentially was cleaned once. Immediately after checking in, I dropped my bag off and headed back into town for a meal, without even a glance at my bed or the bathroom.

Phra Nang Beach, on the Railay peninsula in Thailand.

The town arranged itself around a path bisecting the peninsula from Railay East to the magnificent Railay West Beach, with its fine white sand flanked by more karst limestone cliffs. Next to town, the sprawling, five-star Rayavadee Resort seemed to monopolize a bigger chunk of land on the peninsula than the town itself. No matter—one could easily walk around the perimeter of the resort to arrive at Phra Nang Beach, the best of them all.

After the nightmare maze of Bangkok, where I was never not lost, Railay presented a small and faultless world unto itself. It was a place made for walking; there were no cars, and only a handful of motorbikes. The beers and the pad thai were priced right for my financial situation. I couldn't afford to stay on the beach but that didn't matter here, because every part of the place felt so accessible. I was just getting to the age when New York no longer promised an adventure down every block, and here I was on this tiny peninsula where everywhere I looked I found something new or beautiful or exhilarating.

Certain details would stick in my mind: the young Thai Rasta men who worked behind the bars. The jet lag that woke me up at 5 a.m. in my wretched stained bed, leading me on a walk to Phra Nang Beach and a swim with all of Railay to myself, the breakfasting monkeys notwithstanding. The seawater, almost too warm in the heat of the afternoon, that felt just right in the morning calm. How good the cold beers tasted in the late afternoon.

I checked out of my cabana and found a clean room in town with AC for twenty-five dollars a night, from which the next couple of days rambled by in a contented haze. I'd go swimming every morning, and then, after a few drinks, again at night, lured by the bioluminescent waters. I'd never even heard of bioluminescence, so to jump into the dark sea and find my every movement trailed by incandescent fairy dust was a shock of delight, if not an act of downright magic.

One afternoon, as I was sitting on the sand in the shade of a tree, two German guys struck up a conversation with me. I hung out with them for the rest of the day and for dinner. They were heading to Thailand's eastern islands the next day and invited me to join. I would do so, after a couple more days in Railay, meeting them just in time for a half-moon party on Ko Pha Ngan that would get busted by the cops half an hour after we arrived. Still, the adventure represented just the kind of serendipity that Railay seemed to produce endlessly.

On my final afternoon, I signed up for a snorkeling trip—I had snorkeled only once before, off a beach in Baja California with little in the way of underwater ocean life. This time I was gobsmacked. Afterward, the guides took us to an empty sandbar for dinner and beers. At a distance of maybe one thousand feet, a much larger, hilly island loomed with nary a sign of human activity.

And then, the sunset. It did not present itself to us as a spectacle in the distance. It didn't contain itself to the horizon in one direction. We were *in* this sunset. It subsumed us. The sky and water in every direction lit up with the intensity of melted iron. Toward the end of this show, just when the sun dipped below the horizon entirely, from the much larger island rose hundreds of giant bats. *Giant* bats, like you've never seen, creating solid black silhouettes against the sky's lingering glow.

IN AN ESSAY FOR THE *NEW YORK REVIEW OF BOOKS* TITLED "FIND YOUR Beach," Zadie Smith recalls a two-story ad for beer on a building outside her Manhattan window, bearing those three words. The ad works thanks to our widely held understanding that "your beach" equals your happy place; the beach is contentment. Just saying "beach" can work as shorthand for the best place to be in life. Drink this beer and you'll get there, to the beach.

Think how entrenched a concept has to be in a culture for that phrase—find your beach—to be effective unto itself as an advertisement. Somehow, we came to love the beach so much that the word ceases to mean the beach and comes to mean something else entirely, so that Smith can write of her home country, "In England even at the actual beach I cannot find my beach," and have us know what she means.

With its beauty and spectacle, Railay became an ideal for me against which all other beachfront locations were to be measured. I remember my five days there as a saturnalia of new and amazing occurrences. The cumulative effect was one of wonder. I found my beach in Railay.

THE RAILAY BEACHES MAY HAVE BEEN THE FIRST ONES I LOVED, BUT I don't know if I learned to love the concept of the beach, truly, on that trip. It's a suspicion about myself that is brought into relief as I'm poking around one day on the website of *Coastal Living*, a magazine dedicated to beachfront lifestyles in or near the United States. Partway through a slide show of America's historic beach resorts, including the Breakers in Palm Beach and the Hotel del Coronado in San Diego, a pop-up window prompts me to sign up for the magazine's email newsletter. I want to decline, but instead of a simple *No Thanks* button, I am presented with a declaration I must own if I want to wriggle free of *Coastal Living*'s emails in my inbox: *I don't like the beach*.

It's funny, I understand, because it's implausible. Nobody doesn't like the beach. Who could possibly click on that. I click. There is a small pang of . . . shame? *I don't like the beach*. I wonder if it's true. And if it is, how did I find my beach?

It wouldn't be without precedent if I didn't love the beach. Before the Enlightenment, humans mostly wanted nothing to do with the ocean. In the opening sentence to his widely regarded 1994 book, *The Lure of the Sea*, Alain Corbin states right up front that "with few exceptions, the classical period knew nothing of the attraction of seaside beaches, the emotion of a bather plunging into the waves, or the pleasures of a stay at the seaside." Although the Greeks and especially the Romans had been smitten with the oceans and seas, by the time Europe emerged from the Middle Ages, the ancient resort areas along the Mediterranean had fallen into the well of history.

Corbin rightly points out that throughout the Bible, the ocean generally represents chaos and evil. In one of the book's most famous stories, God basically overruns the entire surface of the Earth with ocean, sparing only the creatures on Noah's Ark—this is the ocean as agent of destruction. In another biblical tale, the sea monster Leviathan provides an early example of the horrifying creatures used to represent the fury of the ocean in cultures around the world.

But then Europeans began to tame the oceans. The Ferdinand Magellans and Amerigo Vespuccis sailed into the great beyond and returned to tell the tale of previously unknown lands. In 1719 Daniel Defoe published *Robinson Crusoe*, arguably the first-ever novel in English, an immensely popular tale of a shipwrecked sailor who survives on an island beach for years on end—Defoe presents the ocean as the setting for a riveting adventure with a triumphant conclusion. In the three centuries since its publication, the novel has never gone out of print, and it still today ranks among the most famous English novels of all time.

Later in the 1700s, the Romantic Era arrived, during which European philosophers, poets, and artists took a renewed approach to their relationships with nature, the ocean especially. They found in its vastness a medium through which the self could be lost to something bigger, then reconsidered and reclaimed. In doing so, the inherent terror inspired by nature could be overcome. The philosophers called this the sublime. An early-nineteenth-century painting by Casper David Friedrich, *The Monk by the Sea*, depicts a single faceless figure lost in self-reflection next to a monastic, slightly menacing seascape, and encapsulates the period's moody, solitary search for the sublime. The painting shows the ocean becoming, rather than a source only of fear, a place for contemplation, and even self-improvement. "There is a rapture on the lonely shore," Lord Byron wrote a few years later.

We see the ocean differently today, but echoes of the primordial fear remain, expressed in pop culture phenomena like 1975's *Jaws*, which opens on a classic beach scene of teenagers around a late-night bonfire during the run-up to the Fourth of July. A pretty girl entices a boy away from the group for a skinny-dip, and is terrorized by a great white shark. The following day, a young boy is similarly killed during a busy beach afternoon, and panic sets in.

More recently, *The Beach*—both the 2000 film and the novel by Alex Garland on which it's based—presents the beach as a utopia that inevitably devolves into a nightmare. In it, a young, white American man named Richard heads to Thailand and (paralleling my own trip) leaves Bangkok after a few days for the beaches in the south of the country. He's in search of a rumored secret community, and he finds it—filled with Westerners. "It was just a beach resort for people who don't like beach resorts," says the on-screen version of Richard, played by Leonardo DiCaprio. What seems like paradise quickly turns sour after a shark attack leads to the same kinds of power struggles you'll find in any society, and the same disregard for those in need. Throughout, the community ignores the inherent imperial nature of the paradise they've created in a nonwhite country that they presume is theirs for the taking.

These fictional stories, it turns out, are no match for the devastation that can be wrought by the ocean in real life. The Boxing Day Tsunami in 2004 killed more than 225,000 people, among them staff and beach vacationers at resorts from Thailand to the Maldives to Sri Lanka. Recent hurricanes have caused untold destruction to beach resorts in the Caribbean, East Africa, Southeast Asia, the Pacific Islands, and on North American coasts. Sunny-day flooding brings chaos even when the weather is good. Sea level rise echoes the great flood in the book of Genesis. These natural events keep the fears of centuries past relevant. In their presence, we don't enjoy the beach at all. *I don't like the beach* becomes more reasonable. We find our beach only where the ocean is friendly, and still today this happens at the ocean's discretion, not ours.

Scrolling through my Instagram feed, I come across a post from a Bay Area nurse named Nicole Elgin, who posts under the handle @wheretopeanut. In it, she's in an infinity pool overlooking the ocean, incidentally the same pool featured in *Bachelor in Paradise*. In her caption, Nicole says that "as much as I love the beach, I gotta say an infinity pool overlooking a beach is second to none."

I write to ask her why. "I think it's primarily about the view from the pool," she tells me. "Without waves or sand to contend with, I truly can allow my mind to open and to allow wonder to enter, uninterrupted. It's a meditative space for me, even more than having the sea wash over my feet. Mother nature and I are not contending with one another, I am observing as an outsider from a vantage point that mimics nature."

Mimicking nature. This seems central to the concept of the beach resort, and connected to the Romanticists' sublime. Paradise is not nature; paradise is nature conquered, nature tamed. The infinity pool erases—visually at least—the demarcation between nature and civilization. It gives us the illusion of the sublime, without the part where we confront the terror inherent in nature.

Last New Year's Day, as we were sitting around a bonfire on an island beach in Florida, my dad commented, *There's infinity in the ocean.* He meant it as a compliment, a nod to the sublime. And it's true, there's a lot of room in infinity for awe, but also for things to go terribly wrong. Wallace Stevens, in his 1937 poem "The Man with the Blue Guitar," writes: *The sea is a form of ridicule.* We haven't really conquered the sea, as it likes to remind us. The beach resort only works as well as our ability to pretend otherwise.

CRITICS OF ALAIN CORBIN POINT OUT THAT IN SOME PARTS OF THE world, including northern Africa and southern Europe, people were jumping into the waves well before the eighteenth century. In Polynesia, people were surfing at least as far back as the 1700s. This is true, but these were not the swimmers around whom resort culture sprang, and no line can be drawn from them to the beach industry as we know it today. The English lie at the start of that line. More specifically: the English upper classes.

As early as the late 1500s, they'd begun retreating, or "resorting," to inland spa towns for the treatment of various physical ailments, real or perceived. There, they'd developed a keen affinity for the apparent power of water to address all manner of conditions. The spa trips proved so enjoyable that the leisure classes started spending entire seasons at Bath or Tunbridge Wells, often only nominally for their health.

Then in 1660 a doctor named Robert Wittie came to Scarborough, on England's northeastern shore, having heard about a mineral spring there being used by the locals for its supposed restorative powers. He soon published *Scarborough Spaw*, in which he promoted the town as a curative destination. Scarborough became the world's first modern seaside resort on a technicality—the ocean was incidental until Dr. Wittie, in a bid to distinguish his spa business from all the others, thought to promote the health benefits of ocean water in addition to the waters from the spring. By the beginning of the eighteenth century, the idea that submersion in cold ocean water could produce positive health effects had taken hold at Scarborough, and it soon spread.

In 1736, a reverend named William Clarke spent a month on the southern coast of England, in a small trading and fishing town called Brighthelmstone. His letter to a friend became perhaps the first written account of beach resort life: "My morning business is bathing in the sea, and then buying fish; the evening is riding out for air, viewing the remains of old Saxon camps, and counting the ships in the road, and the boats that are trawling." Brighthelmstone, an unwieldy name for a place, soon shortened to Brighton.

In *A Dissertation on the Use of Sea Water in the Diseases of the Glands*, published in 1750, the English doctor Richard Russell prescribed, among other "cures," bathing in cold seawater, drinking seawater, and even washing the eyes with seawater. His recommendations reached an amenable public. Initially published in Latin, as was standard for medical literature at the time, the book created a sensation and was quickly translated into English for mass consumption. In 1753, Russell moved to Brighton and built a seaside house for himself and his visiting patients. In Brighton and other towns along the English shores, the resort concept took hold.

Around this time, someone invented the first bathing machine, not so much a machine as a horse-drawn dressing room that brought a lady some distance into the ocean for her salubrious swim. She'd enter through the land-side door in her standard clothes, change into a bathing costume or simply strip down while being hauled out into the water, then jump into the sea via the sea-side door, completing her dip in privacy. The bathing machine became a hallmark of beach resorts throughout northern Europe, and held on into the early twentieth century.

Visitors to the ocean engaged in all kinds of unpleasant activities for the sake of their health. They drank seawater just before bed and again just after rising; they drank seawater mixed with wine, seawater mixed with milk; they dipped into cold seawater for some ailments, and into hot seawater for others. People didn't yet love the beach. They endured it for their well-being, egged on by doctors set to profit from the "cures." Eighteenth-century Gwyneth Paltrow would have been all over it.

Soon the first true seaside resorts were built to serve this wellness industry. These early hotels prioritized not proximity to the beach itself, but the creation of a self-contained atmosphere for "polite society." Only as people began to consider the beauty, the infinity, and the awe-inspiring qualities of the ocean did hotels reorient themselves toward it over the course of the nineteenth century.

SOMETIME BETWEEN THE FIRST BATHING MACHINES AT BRIGHTON AND the all-inclusive resorts of today, the beach softened into an ideal.

The ascetic painting of a monk in contemplation gave way to relaxed Impressionist seascapes full of light and color. Dips into the gray English waters gave way to frolics in the blue Mediterranean. The seawater beverage gave way to umbrella-festooned cocktails. Lord Byron's "rapture on the lonely shore" gave way to Philip Larkin's "miniature gaiety of seasides," in his poem "To the Sea."

The great literature of the early twentieth century often used beaches and beach resorts as its setting, especially in depicting the upper classes—the Lido in *Death in Venice*; Balbec, modeled on the Norman resort town of Cabourg, in Proust's *In Search of Lost Time*; Newport in *The Age of Innocence*; Long Island's North Shore in *The Great Gatsby*; the Isle of Skye in *To the Lighthouse*.

The beach entrenched itself as a cultural phenomenon, bigger in a way than its physical self. We started to refer to the beach, and only the beach, as paradise, a loaded word stemming from an ancient Iranian word for the walled gardens popular with Persian nobles. Like its Persian forebear, the original Christian paradise—the Garden of Eden—existed near no body of water. Paradise's relocation to the shore is a twentieth-century phenomenon.

Not all beach destinations qualify. People love the Hamptons, but I've never heard anyone refer to them as paradise. They don't even have palm trees there. The beach of paradise has to be somewhere far away, preferably another country. The sand must be white and fine. The water must be a superior shade of turquoise. It must give the visitor the feeling of having the place—to some extent—to herself. It must be a good place for newlywed couples to wrap themselves in romance for a week or two.

I think about my favorite beach experiences. There's the Octopus Resort in Fiji's Yasawa Islands, where the front steps of my bungalow led me directly onto the sand and, beyond that, onto a great coral reef ten or so feet into the water. There's the island beach house off the coast of Florida where I sat around a bonfire on New Year's Day. And there is, of course, Railay. Difficult places to get to, all of them. Paradise is also—and this is important—a finite resource. If it weren't, we might not covet it so intensely.

The beach of paradise removes us from our frenzied contemporary daily life, harking back to what we perceive as a simpler and, by implication, better time. In other words, more primitive. This approach is of course selective in its conception. The beach of paradise is simpler in that there's no rush hour traffic or PowerPoint presentations, but surely not simpler in the infant mortality rate or suppression of women's rights or the widespread starvation during a drought that may be the reality of the place for those who live there permanently, and who are likely to see the beach as a place where they must cater to outsiders. In an essay for *The Nation*, Marilynne Robinson captures the foundation on which the beach of paradise is built:

> I was in college when Margaret Mead was in her glory and anthropologists could still claim to find societies untouched by the modern world. The idea was that in such places human nature would have been preserved in a purer form than in the rationalist and technological societies of the West. By observing these societies we could learn what we are essentially and how we ought to live. These societies were gentle, violent, uninhibited, and so on, depending, it came to seem, on the preferences of the anthropologist. . . . In any case, the "primitivity" of these populations could in general be called poverty.

Paradise is only paradise when we have travel insurance that includes medevac.

THE FIRST BEACH TRIP I REMEMBER CARING ABOUT CAME AT AGE NINE, when after an edifying few days spent ticking off the monuments of

Washington, D.C., my family drove on to Hilton Head, South Carolina, where my parents had rented a condo with lots of mirrors and mauve carpeting. Hilton Head was a place where the overtly privileged kids I knew vacationed. The condo was a five-minute or so walk from the ocean. This was typical—mine were vacations to be enjoyed always at least one street removed from the beach.

As a child of flyover country, the beach and the ocean for me fell into the realm of things that belonged to an exciting, cultured, almost mythical world beyond my reach—that of cosmopolitan cities and great art and actual castles. The beach was where Daryl Hannah emerged as a mermaid and also where she emerged in a wetsuit at Gordon Gecko's Hamptons place. It was where Dylan and Kelly consummated their summer affair. It's where Danny and Sandy started theirs. The beach vacations of my youth were different—strictly regional affairs within driving distance of home, and never to destinations that might qualify as glamorous. I would not take a flight to a beach until my mid-twenties, when a brutal New York City winter drove me to book a four-day trip to Miami Beach, where I stayed in a small hotel two streets removed from the beach.

When I recall these beach vacations, I remember hotels and meals and bars. I remember, especially during the Hilton Head trip, caring a lot about my outfits. I don't remember what I did at the beach. Perhaps because what people are doing at the beach doesn't tend to be of interest. Look around today and they are taking photos of their own legs, with the ocean beyond. They are texting with boyfriends back home. At the resort today, there is always one young couple engaged in Instagram creation, the woman posing, the man snapping. People are reading books. They are lounging at the pool instead. They are showing off the body they've been working hard on, or positioning themselves strategically to best exhibit the one they haven't. They are wondering how much fun they are having. They are eating air-temperature french fries. They are wondering whether they will forget about the broken dishwasher back home before they have to get back to it. They are having their first drink at noon. They are, against all medical advice, working on their tans. They are trying to corral their children away from the shady haven of their air-conditioned rooms. They are getting bored. They are getting hungry. They are getting hungry because they are bored.

This is the reality that exists parallel to paradise, and it is nothing new. Henry James visited the English seaside town of Hastings in the 1880s and reported: "Four or five miles of lodging-houses and hotels staring at the sea across a 'parade' adorned with iron benches, with hand-organs and German bands, with nursemaids and British babies, with ladies and gentlemen of leisure—looking rather embarrassed with it and trying rather unsuccessfully to get rid of it."

The English photographer Martin Parr began shooting local beach scenes in the 1980s, and eventually documented beach culture throughout the world. I recently bought a small book of his work, titled *Life's a Beach* in shiny gold cursive over a pink background with green leaves and red and yellow flowers—an intentionally retro design, and a cheeky introduction to the contents within, which is beachgoing at its least glamorous. Images of women lying out on a concrete seawall in Ireland. Plastic lawn chairs and commanding beer bellies and a local child hawking knickknacks to a sunbather. Elderly people dozing in chairs on the boardwalk, their mouths slack.

Because the beach is paradise and paradise is perfection, travelers understandably arrive to it with heightened expectations. Despite evidence to the contrary that they will inevitably encounter, they hold on to the idea that they have reached paradise, if only for the four vacation days they have left this year. If actually we were feeling restless lying there on that lounger, or the hotel room itself was kind of depressing in its similarity to all other midrange hotel rooms in the world, or the wind coming in off the water was perpetually too strong, is beside the point. That's not the story we tell when we get home, to others and to ourselves.

I look at the listing for Parr's *Life's a Beach* on Amazon. One review complains that the book is "too 'warts & all' for me. A slice of life at beaches around the world, but I guess I like the romanticized version better!" Here we have the sentiment upon which a major global industry has been built.

WHERE ALL PASSIONS COMBINE

Monte Carlo, the Jersey Shore, and Cap d'Antibes

MONTE CARLO

It was the mid-nineteenth century and Monaco was nearly broke. The small principality along Europe's Mediterranean coast had recently lost the towns of Menton and Roquebrune to secession (both would end up part of France), amounting to 80 percent of its territory and nearly all of its farmable land, gone. In the wake of the loss, attempts to establish a manufacturing industry—a perfumery, a distillery, a lace factory, a false-teeth production plant—had all failed. Prince Florestan, head of the ruling Grimaldi family, sold off royal paintings and jewels to stay afloat, leaving his palace hollowed out. An 1852 guidebook noted Monte Carlo's general state of "sad abandonment and decay."

Florestan had little interest in the minutiae of running things, content to squander what was left of his wealth and influence in the swirl of Paris. Instead, his wife, Princess Caroline, devised a scheme for the principality's survival. A former stage actress with a commanding presence who was known for taking political matters into her own hands, Caroline got wind of a lively scene in the German spa town of Bad Homburg. The brainchild of a self-made Frenchman named François Blanc and his twin brother, Louis, Homburg offered a welcoming extravagance that travelers couldn't get enough of—full orchestras, complimentary horses and guns for hunting, famous chefs manning the kitchens. These offerings functioned as loss leaders, keeping patrons in town another day for Homburg's true moneymaker, the gambling tables. In 1855 Princess Caroline sent an operative to gain a better understanding of the resort's success.

Gambling in the spa towns had until recently enjoyed a gentler reputation as a pursuit for the rich—losing money in good spirits being the ultimate display of wealth. In Homburg, Blanc had recast the pastime as something aspirational, selling the possibility of sudden riches to those who didn't already possess them. If the visitor's get-rich plan failed, which it usually did, there was the consolation prize of a few days spent in a sumptuous hotel, mimicking the life of the aristocrat. Blanc understood before anyone else how readily the emergent middle classes could be motivated to splurge in order to appear more like the upper classes.

Caroline's operative returned with tales of outrageous spending sprees by the rich and not-quite-rich alike, and the princess saw an opportunity. All around Monaco, gambling had become illegal. Venice's great gambling establishment, the Ridotto, had been outlawed back in 1774, sending gambling into unofficial "casini." France outlawed gambling on New Year's Day 1838, leaving Parisian bettors adrift and willing to travel to get their fix. The German spa towns had been reaping the rewards of their predicament up to now, but rumors abounded that Germany, too, would soon ban gambling (it would come to pass on the last day of 1872). The timing felt fortuitous. Within weeks, Caroline convinced Prince Florestan to legalize gambling in Monaco.

Monaco took other cues from nearby Cannes, Nice, and even Menton, towns that had turned their mild weather and invigorating Mediterranean air into the bedrock of an early wellness industry. The locals gave their winters over to the sick and could-be-sick of northern Europe, where the dreariness of the colder months might convince anyone of means that his health felt off enough to justify an escape to sunny climes.

The towns of the future French Riviera in turn took their cues from the aristocratic Brits and their early seaside resorts. But the English seas were generally cold and gloomy. It didn't take long for some English health-seekers to go on the hunt for a more forgiving climate. First, they jumped the English Channel to establish resorts at Dieppe and Trouville. Then they began taking to the warm sea air of the French Mediterranean, thanks in no small part to the author Tobias Smollett, who in 1765 published the widely read *A Journey through Italy and France*, which chronicled his time spent in Nice and Cannes. Afflictions reported cured by the air in Nice included consumption, weak nerves, obstructed perspiration, languid circulation, scurvy, chest pain, general weakness, faintness, low spirits, fever, and loss of appetite. It can't hurt that Smollett also described the climate in Nice as producing "less rain and wind . . . than in any other part of the world that I know; and such is the serenity of the air, that you see nothing above your head for several months together, but a charming blue expanse, without cloud or speck." At the time, poverty pervaded the South of France, thanks to increasingly outmoded agricultural practices and its isolation from the commercial centers—making it ripe for commandeering by rich northerners.

By the early nineteenth century, visitors had a selection of hotels and "lodging houses" in Nice to choose from and an English Quarter was well established. While diversions emerged to keep them occupied, at its core the fledgling tourism industry of the French Riviera focused on improving health. Guidebooks of the time listed the best English doctors in all the Riviera towns as a matter of course.

Monaco decided to incorporate its neighbors' health resort concept. In addition to the casino, Princess Caroline envisioned a bathing facility on a spot along her tiny country's 2.4 miles of shore. In 1856, its government released initial plans for turning the principality into a Bad Homburg by the sea. The plan described a "fine sandy beach" tucked into the deep, calm bay at the foot of the cliffs that housed the main town. The bathing facility would go here, a colonnaded sanctuary backed by the flower farms of the Condamine district. Two small prototype casinos were opened quickly, both also in La Condamine. In 1858, work on the bathing facility got under way. Meanwhile, plans moved ahead for a more permanent casino in Les Spelugues, a rocky plateau of undeveloped shorefront land named for the grottos that lay underground there, considered up to now nothing more than arid, empty, undesirable land.

The early resort struggled to draw crowds. Work on the bathing house slowed and then nearly ground to a halt thanks to shady management and financial difficulties. As for the casinos, they were far from town. Their décor was lackluster, the grounds unsightly, leisure activities nonexistent, and transportation from the target market of Nice unreliable at best. Rooms meant for a café or lounge had yet to be furnished. The house held little in reserve, meaning that only low-stakes wagers were possible. The whole enterprise felt uninspired, and possibly doomed.

But it didn't die. The bathing building finally opened in 1861, making Monaco the first place in the world to combine the diversions of the German mountain spa towns with the pleasures of the seaside. In February 1863, the new, bigger casino opened in Les Spelugues. Then, later that year, François Blanc, the impresario responsible for Bad Homburg, agreed to take over in Monaco. Unlike the string of past managers, he was ready to spend money in order to make money.

Blanc built the grand Hotel de Paris next to the casino, which he also filled with sumptuous furnishings, Italian paintings, marble columns, crystal chandeliers, silk curtains, a grand entrance, and a see-and-be-seen terrace. He added a second level to the bathing house, in which he installed another hotel. He improved the nearby roads and harbor, implemented consistent ferry service from Nice and Genoa, and imported exotic vegetation for the grounds. Not just palm trees, but those, too. He hired a famous doctor to practice hydrotherapy at the spa. Next to the casino and across from the hotel, he opened the Café Divan, soon to be renamed the Café de Paris. Blanc convinced Prince Charles, who had assumed the throne after his father Florestan's death, to change the name of the casino area from Les Spelugues to something more reflective of the grandeur he was going for. The prince named it after himself—Monte Carlo.

Blanc did this all just as the French Riviera was coming into its own. A decade before Monaco launched itself as a tourist destination, the 1847 edition of *Handbook for Travelers in Northern Italy* stated, "Almost all of the hotels in Nice are deficient in cleanliness, and are indifferently furnished." (At the time, Nice was part of Italy.) By the 1852 edition, the hotels there were "much improved of late years, as regards furnishings, cleanliness, and domestic comfort." By 1858 they were "as good as in any other part of the Continent," and finally in 1866, Nice's hotels have "become of late years as expensive as those in the largest capitals of Europe." The conditions were right if Monaco could capitalize on them, by replicating the success of a place like Nice with its own hotels, and by luring Nice's hotel guests over for a day at the tables.

Blanc advertised Monte Carlo heavily throughout Europe, ensuring that people would have a romanticized idea of Monaco before ever seeing it firsthand. It worked; visits increased and so did gambling receipts, although not enough to save a country, even a tiny one. Blanc knew that a crucial piece of the puzzle was still missing. In 1868 he succeeded in adding a train stop at Monte Carlo along the new rail line from Nice, which had been connected to Paris by rail in 1864.

The floodgates were open. The year before the train to Monte

Carlo began service, fewer than 30,000 people stayed at the new resort. The year after, that number shot up to almost 170,000, with 345,000 visits to the casino. The casino, hotel, and café now comprised a sort of overstated town square, with a backdrop of Mediterranean blues and a foreground of fountains and gardens sweeping up toward the Maritime Alps. With a few additions and alterations, this square would endure straight into the twenty-first century. Just down the shore, the bathhouse took full advantage of the era's craze for water-based therapies, and also provided moral cover for the casino visitors.

All of a sudden, Monaco was drawing the world's most prominent travelers during the winter season, along with those minted in the new middle classes, who arrived and assumed if only for a few days the position of someone occupying a higher lot in life. By 1873, the *New York Times* was writing that the man who arrived at Monte Carlo "has left the ordinary life and the countries of reality to enter into that brilliant region where all passions combine to obliterate the mind and obscure the reason."

Just beyond the casino and bathhouse, the seas of the Mediterranean had newly risen a fraction of a centimeter. It was imperceptible, but the start of something big. The advance of the oceans would continue over the next century, then pick up terrifying speed as we approached the twenty-first, and it is no coincidence that it really got going alongside the Industrial Revolution, which had human activity releasing carbon dioxide into the atmosphere in abnormal quantities for the first time. Between the 1880s and 2020, the temperature of the oceans rose 1.8 degrees Fahrenheit. The new trains bringing those hundreds of thousands of tourists to Monte Carlo relied on coal to power their steam engines. In this and other ways, coal literally powered the Industrial Revolution, which increased standards of living and led to a world population explosion. The burning of coal would send more carbon dioxide into the atmosphere than any other human behavior. Its mining would release trapped methane, a gas even more harmful than carbon dioxide. More humans meant more demand for coal, a compounding cycle with seemingly no natural endpoint.

But no one could have been expected to notice that minuscule rise in the sea level. Of more immediate interest: Monte Carlo had created a template that would soon be replicated along the French Riviera. Seeing the success of Monte Carlo, France eventually caved and legalized gambling at seaside resorts in 1907. Cannes, Juan-les-Pins, Deauville, and Le Touquet were soon running their own casinos, and playing host to crowds that no longer pretended they were there for their health. The entirety of the French Riviera embraced high living, well on its way to a reputation as "a sunny place for shady people."

For the first time, travel was less an immersion in some edifying experience and more an escape from the day-to-day drudgery at home. Before Monte Carlo, there was travel as education, as in the Grand Tour, and there was travel to inland spas and seaside health resorts as convalescence. But unlike the English tradition of seaside resorts that preceded it, and which Nathaniel Hawthorne described as having a "well-to-do tradesmanlike air," Monte Carlo invented travel as unadulterated diversion. The age of the glamourous, hedonistic beach resort was upon us.

Monte Carlo's new resort format soon expanded beyond France to the rest of Europe, and from there to the Americas. In many places, the casino faded away as the sea itself became ever more central to the resort experience, but the notion of escapism would remain, as would the grand hotel on the shore, the place where all passions combined.

UNLESS YOU ARE ARRIVING IN ONE OF THEM, A MODERN-DAY EVENING spent at the Monte Carlo Casino usually begins with a lengthy gawk at the parade of luxury cars valeting out front. Ferrari after Bentley after S-Class after Rolls. Mere upper-middle-class Americans and

Brits and Chinese and Germans form a band across the street from the casino, that same one opened in 1863, just to watch the valets in action. I am no exception, and I take my place one evening among the crowd. While I'm no car person and haven't even owned one in the current millennium, the extremes are fun to watch.

At this time of night, entering the casino can be intimidating, not so much because the door staff might reject you—although they will if you haven't adhered to the dress code—but because a large crowd will watch you ascend the stage-lit stairs and get your bags checked and your attire looked over. In other words, you'll have an audience.

More transfixing for me than the cars, and harder to dismiss as mere showboating, is the woman sitting at the front corner table of the Café de Paris in a slim-fitting dress and a pillbox hat with a bird-cage veil shrouding her eyes. As I walk by, I take in the flash of her laugh, bellowed in response to something said by one of her two companions. At a table behind her, a thirtysomething couple—I presume, without any good reason, that they are American—takes a seat at one of the round café tables. This is an attractive couple, but they lack that intangible sheen of the superrich. From the woman in the pillbox hat, actual light emanates. The thirtysomething couple by comparison looks tidy but dull, like a perfectly fine living room in need of a good dusting. This is how Monte Carlo works. If you can pay the 22 euros for a cocktail, you are welcome to a seat at the Café de Paris, but that doesn't mean that light will emanate from you.

With this nightly scene of urbanity, Monte Carlo might at first glance seem a strange place to contemplate the origins of the beach resort. The chief reason would be that at Monte Carlo today, there is no beach. That "fine sandy beach" mentioned in the original plans for Monaco's bathing facility has long since been replaced by a functional marina for mega-yachts. The principality is dominated by glassy high-rises cascading methodically up the mountains, having supplanted a previous era's villas with buildings that multiply available square footage in Monaco's 0.78-square-mile footprint many times over. Monte Carlo spawned the modern formula for the beach resort, then realized that on its list of priorities, the beach ranked low, actually. The original bathhouse closed in 1904 as the marina took precedence. When the beach became more central to the concept of leisure in the postwar years, Monaco created an artificial sand beach on its eastern end, at Larvotto, where pleasure and even hedonism would overtake somber "cures" for good. It is as good as any along the Riviera. Nevertheless, I don't know of anyone today who heads to Monaco first for its beach.

Instead, tourists come here for the concentrated wealth, and the ways in which the country accommodates it. Almost a third of Monaco's residents are millionaires, and its residential real estate is the world's most expensive. It is the first country to have remade its fortunes via seaside tourism. A generally acknowledged fact holds that had Monaco not opened its resort and casino back in the nineteenth century, it would by now be another department of France. Instead, it became the proof of concept for a country wishing to achieve prosperity by luring pleasure-seekers to its shores. Countries around the world have been trying to repeat its success ever since, from Thailand to Fiji to the Bahamas to, much more recently, St. Kitts and Nevis, after its sugar industry shut down in 2005. These nations see the possibilities in pivoting from an underdeveloped economy, usually relying on agrarian practices, into precisely the kind of place where a woman wears a veil-accented pillbox hat out for an early-evening cocktail; governments look at their countries' miles (and sometimes hundreds of miles) of beachfront, and they see a workable economic vision.

In a more direct copy of Monaco's approach, Atlantic City turned to gambling in the late 1970s in an attempt to revive its economy—like Monaco, Atlantic City would offer casinos in a region of the world with no other legal gambling options, and combine that offering with an equal emphasis on seaside diversions.

Other beachy locales have emulated Monte Carlo's tax haven status—Prince Charles abolished the income tax in Monaco in 1869, to appease citizens' frustrations with so many jobs going to foreigners. It proved an irresistible draw for the superrich. In the decades since, places like the Cayman Islands, Mauritius, Bermuda, the Bahamas, and even the state of Florida have happily and prosperously followed suit.

THOSE PASSING THROUGH MONTE CARLO IN THE NINETEENTH CENTURY included English ladies, Russian grand dukes, American industrial tycoons, French actresses, Brazilian emperors, and German barons, along with the strivers, hucksters, dandies, and members of the emergent bourgeoisie from throughout Europe. While the English seaside resorts were the first of their kind, they served a domestic clientele—not even the nearby French were lured across the English Channel for Britain's beaches. Here on the Riviera, however, an unprecedented petri dish for the international exchange of culture and ideas flourished. For beach resorts, this role would prove resilient into the twenty-first century, and even become formalized in the out-of-all-scale convention centers of many oceanfront resorts, from Miami Beach to Cannes. (The first-time visitor to Cannes, in fact, may be taken aback to find that all the glamour of the Cannes Film Festival takes place in a rather depressing circa 1982 structure; during my recent visit it was hosting the Duty Free & Travel Retail Global Summit.)

A more informal global intermingling takes place one afternoon on the terrace of Hotel de Paris's Bar Americain, with its view of the casino but not the sea. The bar is just off the lobby, which has recently been fully renovated to shiny effect, all the hard-earned patina of a splendid history buffed away. I overhear an English guy—or is he Dutch—complain to his party of four, who seem all to be from different places, about some business prospect turned complicated. As he grows more animated, two twentysomething women walk in and past him, performing practiced walks in what look to be brand-new

Louboutins. I order a Campari and soda. My waiter, who is so professional in his niceness that it hits me as genuine, leaves the entire small bottle of soda with me. I take a first and second sip as three more women walk in, two of them in sneakers, though the sneakers are Chanel. After they sit, one puts on a red sequined blazer. They chat in what sounds like Russian. The blond one lights a very skinny cigarette. Then, out of nowhere, a waiter appears and drapes fleece blankets over their laps because the wind has kicked up a little.

A little later, I sit near the bar in the casino with a glass of rosé. This is nothing like the other casinos I've been in, in Vegas and Atlantic City, or even those on other seafronts in Europe. This is gambling as museum piece. There is no tacky carpeting, no flashing lights, no questionably attired cocktail waitresses. The room is spacious and grand, and features just a few gaming tables, with generous amounts of space between them. Half of the gamblers are Chinese, and if anything signifies the winds of change in global tourism today, there it is. As a group, international Chinese tourists now outspend even their American counterparts, a phenomenon that would have seemed impossible just a decade or two ago, and one with wide-ranging implications for beach resorts around the world as they pivot to accommodate a new set of expectations.

THE JERSEY SHORE

Across the Atlantic during an early-nineteenth-century August, residents of New York City and Philadelphia were sweltering. Women sat fanning themselves in the putrid air of their drawing rooms. Men dispensed with the wigs they normally wore. Most residents dared not move if they didn't have to between the hours of 11 a.m. and 4 p.m. If there could be an escape from this misery, they were ready to embrace it.

At the southern tip of the Jersey Shore, every ship en route to

Philadelphia had to pass by the state's southernmost town of Cape May, where the Atlantic Ocean meets Delaware Bay and from there, the Delaware River. Some of those ship passengers noticed Cape May's large, gently sloping sand beach and the cooling breezes blowing onshore there. Though it was settled by the English in the first half of the seventeenth century as a whaling village, over the course of the eighteenth century locals and visitors had bit by bit begun to see the waters off Cape May differently, especially during the high heat of summer. By the turn of the nineteenth century, rudimentary rooming houses were popping up along the beach. An 1801 ad in the Philadelphia *Aurora and General Advertiser* for one such accommodation beckoned city dwellers with its description of a shoreline with a slope "so regular that persons may wade out at a distance. It is the most delightful spot the citizens can retire to in the hot season."

After the War of 1812, Philadelphians of means could be found enjoying August at the Atlantic Hotel, Cape May's first, opened by the man who placed the 1801 ad in the *Aurora*, Elgin Hughes. The Atlantic's offerings were sparse at best, with mostly dorm beds and little privacy, but they filled up, despite the two-day trip from Philadelphia required to reach them. Then, in 1816, Hughes's son Thomas built a boardinghouse on the ocean that could welcome one hundred guests at a time. He called it the Big House. People thought he was nuts. But visitors booked rooms there, too, no matter the crude amenities. The Big House burned down after only two years, but Hughes built it back even bigger.

In 1825, steamboat service from Philadelphia to Cape May began, shortening the trip significantly. A year later, Hughes sold the Big House and the new owners gradually added to it, while its luxury quotient inched upward. By 1853, it could accommodate 800 guests and was known as Congress Hall, in honor of Hughes's election to the U.S. House of Representatives. By this time, Cape May boasted a number of world-class accommodations. In the latter half of the century, Congress Hall competed with major hotels like the Tremont

House, the Columbia Hotel, the Ocean House, and the United States Hotel for clientele. All could welcome many hundreds of guests at a time. In 1853, the partially completed Mount Vernon Hotel opened one wing. It was meant to eventually offer 3,500 rooms and stake its claim as the largest hotel in the world. But in 1856 it burned to the ground, set afire apparently by a former employee trying to cover up a robbery and murder of the hotel's proprietor. Nevertheless, its sheer scale reflected the nascent American taste for bigness. Why have a hundred guests when you could have a thousand—and why stop there?

The achieved combination of beach, breeze, comfort, and culture had the attention of heat-exhausted city dwellers. In its August 1859 issue, *The Knickerbocker* magazine, the cultural arbiter of the day, covered "that most charming of ocean summer resorts and watering-places, that famous refuge from the heat and dust of the weary city—the beach at Cape May." The lengthy feature detailed the "gay whirl of the merry dance," yachting parties, a "moonlight stroll by the side of the solemn sea," and the "infinite tail of restaurants." It also made note that the shoreline hotels, which were up to the standard of any in the country, "standing close upon or not far removed from the shore, present a bold front, and surprise the unexpecting voyager as he sails."

AT THE OTHER END OF THE JERSEY SHORE, JUST ABOUT AS FAR NORTH AS one can go before hitting New York City, two men in the town that would become Long Branch built a few bathing houses on the shore in the last decade of the eighteenth century. By the end of the following decade, three basic boardinghouses had gone up on the beach, each able to hold a hundred or so guests. After a lull thanks to the War of 1812, steamboat service began from Manhattan in 1828, with many city dwellers happily following a doctor's orders to take some rest along the five miles of beach there. New Yorkers joined the increasing number of Philadelphians arriving by a regular stagecoach line during the hot months, and Long Branch seemed destined to become a "health resort" in the European mold.

But the health resort atmosphere would soon give way to a livelier setting. In 1834, one writer pointed out the "much and fashionable company" as the best thing about Long Branch. By the 1840s, small accommodations were giving way to grand hotels like Conover House, which could take in 175 guests at a time, and the Allegheny House, which could handle even more. These establishments catered to travelers who were beginning to emphasize enjoyment over health—card games, beach drives, and dancing became part of the summer scene, even as a lingering air of propriety kept it somewhat subdued.

In August 1861, Mary Todd Lincoln stayed in Long Branch for ten days, kicking off an era of visits by presidents, actors, and other celebrities. The opening of the nearby Thoroughbred racetrack in 1870 provided an element of licentiousness that made Long Branch into the most popular beach resort in the United States. The *New York Times* considered this consensus, with a correspondent writing: "No one can be surprised that Long Branch has become the favorite watering place of the United States. It can boast of a fine cliff, a magnificent beach, and a beautiful country at the back; and besides these natural advantages, it always presents a gay and animated spectacle." In a nice bit of symmetry, the Jersey Shore resort soon enjoyed a reputation as "the American Monte Carlo."

While some New Yorkers and Philadelphians established their summer getaways on the Jersey Shore, others headed to Rockaway and similar Long Island spots. Farther up the East Coast, Bostonians established their own resort for cooling off during the summer months. On Nahant, a rocky island connected to the mainland by a two-mile strip of sand, boardinghouses began cropping up in the first years of the nineteenth century. Just in time for the summer season of 1823, the Nahant Hotel opened, and over the years got expanded until, by 1854, it could welcome 600 guests at a time. Nahant's run as a resort was short-lived, and when the hotel burned down in 1861, it wasn't replaced. But by then it had kick-started a beach resort culture up and down the New England coast.

By the turn of the century, the northeastern edge of the United States from New Jersey to Maine had been remade as a summer refuge from the cities. Americans had found a way not only to tolerate summer, but to indulge in it. The way Americans were now using the beach practically required temperatures north of 80 degrees. While Europeans escaped the cold to the temperate French Riviera, Americans honed an affinity for the heat. There was a resort for every type, from Ocean City, founded by four Methodist ministers and alcohol-free, to Atlantic City, a resort catering to the working classes that soon showed up even Monte Carlo in terms of debauchery.

"Every type" did not in this case include people of color, even though Blacks who recently relocated from the South comprised the majority of resort employees in many Northeast resort towns. As workers, African-Americans participated in the new beach resort culture. As guests, they were banned. In Atlantic City, they lived in an appointed neighborhood, segregated from both tourists and white residents. Even with Atlantic City as their home, access to the ocean proved difficult—the whites in charge allowed Blacks to swim only at a designated place and designated time. In the following century, middle-class Black populations would establish their own resorts, especially in the South, where the collapse of coastal land prices after the Civil War had enabled them to buy property and build communities along the Atlantic Ocean. Even as Jim Crow endured, the resorts sprang up in what Andrew W. Kahrl describes in his book, *The Land Was Ours: How Black Beaches Became White Wealth in the Coastal South*, as "the ironic fruits of segregation for elite black Americans." In places like Highland Park, Maryland; American Beach near Jacksonville, Florida; Atlantic Beach, in South Carolina; and Gulfside Assembly in Waveland, Mississippi, African-Americans were able to develop their own oceanfront enclaves. Even in the North, a couple of notable summer resort towns eventually took hold—Oak Bluffs on Martha's Vineyard and the northern section of Sag Harbor on Long Island.

But in the North of the nineteenth century, coastal land wasn't generally available to Blacks. Mary Todd Lincoln stayed at Long Branch—a symbolic marker of progress there, perhaps, but her husband's fight to abolish slavery didn't translate into opportunity or access for African-Americans at the resort town's beaches.

TO WANDER THE STREETS OF CAPE MAY TODAY IS TO OVERDOSE ON quaintness, thanks to the largest extant collection of Victorian houses in the country, their colorful trim, picket fences, and front porches suggesting some lost, idyllic version of American life that never really existed. Their continued presence is a by-product of Cape May's two major misfortunes. The first came in 1878, when thirty square blocks of the city burned in a fire started in the Ocean House hotel. The town rebuilt, remaking itself using the well-established Victorian architecture of the day. The second misfortune came as more of a slow burn, when over the decades of the early twentieth century, Cape May fell out of favor, along with much of the Jersey Shore. Since there was no longer money to be made, no one tore down the Victorian manses in favor of new developments.

Most of those Victorians now operate as bed-and-breakfasts, and I've come to Cape May with my partner, Scott, to stay in one of them for my April birthday. We ride bikes along the beach and take photos of the houses. We eat a fancy dinner at the Ebbitt Room, paying Manhattan prices to do so. We wander in and out of the shops on Main Street, knowing we will be disappointed by the beachy décor for sale but looking anyway.

We spend one afternoon sipping French 75s in Congress Hall's lush Brown Bar, listening to a spectacular guitarist play rock hits from the seventies. That Congress Hall is still here is a feat, and an exception. In his fantastic history of New England's coast resorts, *Summer by the Seaside*, Bryant F. Tolles Jr. counts more than 150 major resort hotels built on New England's shores between 1820 and 1950, not including, then, hotels in New York and New Jersey, nor the thousands of more modest establishments. Of those Tolles counts, fewer than ten remain standing today. In Cape May, there is only Congress Hall, still thriving and advertising itself as America's first beach resort, and although the claim may or may not be strictly true, it enhances its allure.

A two-hour drive north in Long Branch, the diverging fates of the two seminal Jersey Shore resorts of the nineteenth century come into sharp relief. Long Branch lies twenty-seven miles from my apartment in Brooklyn—fewer as the crow flies—yet the name hardly rang a bell. After its late-nineteenth-century turn as *the* resort, Long Branch entered a steep, startling decline that by the 1920s had rendered it a slum. A major part of its draw had been the racetrack, which closed in 1894 after the state outlawed gambling. The society set soon decamped to Newport, Rhode Island, while the partygoers headed for Atlantic City.

At the northern end of town, an oceanfront park has been named after the seven U.S. presidents who summered in Long Branch at one point or other. Its southern border hits the spot that once held Ulysses S. Grant's summer home, though there is no marker there. South of the park, among condo high-rises and retirement communities, a couple of new hotels near the shore mark the effort to return to Long Branch its lost status as a beach destination. It's a pleasant enough place, but destination remains a reach.

Between Long Branch and Cape May, there are dozens of other towns along 140 miles of barrier-island sand. On a meandering drive home from Cape May, Scott and I set out to see as much of it as we can. I've popped into the Jersey Shore before—to visit Atlantic

City, Asbury Park, and Manasquan over the years—but I don't have a sense for its scale. I haven't experienced the full expanse.

We come first to Wildwood, where 1950s motels with pools in their parking lots hang banners advertising prom packages to New Jersey's high schoolers. We continue north along Ocean Drive, through Stone Harbor, Avalon, Sea Isle City, and Strathmere, then over the Strathmere Bascule Bridge, with its cash-only tollbooth. To the right, the Atlantic Ocean, to the left, a marshy grassland. On this first day of May, its desolation arouses a novelistic lonesomeness. We descend from there into Ocean City. In yet another bit of transatlantic symmetry, Grace Kelly summered here in her youth before becoming the princess of Monaco.

Like the other towns along Ocean Drive, Ocean City boasts the same wan blocks of beach houses, their palette unbroken by trees or landscaping. The beach houses here soon give way to boardwalks and amusement parks. None of it could be called beautiful, exactly, until we park and walk out onto the beaches themselves, where the dunes soften the panorama of sand, water, and sky. Rather than any one town taken in isolation, it's the sheer number of them, each with its hundreds of summer-house blocks, that impresses upon one passing through how thoroughly the concept of the beach resort defined entire regions.

Then we hit Atlantic City, its casinos rising out of nowhere like they're crashing a party. We stop for lunch at the recently opened Ocean Resort Casino, in the property once known as the Revel Casino, which cost $2.4 billion to build and closed barely two years after it opened. On the boardwalk, I can't see the ocean for the sand dunes, placed there in 2004 to protect the boardwalk from the next big storm. Almost fifteen feet high when built, they're dotted with beach grass to help secure them in place. They separate town from ocean in a way that shifts focus from the shore altogether.

We end the day in Seaside Heights, with its boardwalk and

amusement park rides mostly empty. The town derives its fame from two sources: the bird's-eye photo of its roller coaster askew in the ocean after Hurricane Sandy, and the MTV reality show *Jersey Shore*. We track down the house where the cast members lived, tucked in just behind the boardwalk with a vibe of haphazardness, forgotten there amid a lot of concrete and old motels. The roller coaster has by now been replaced. Next to it is a chairlift to nowhere.

CAP D'ANTIBES

The most expensive cocktail I have ever ordered takes the form of an old-fashioned on the terrace of the white stucco Hotel du Cap Eden Roc, at the tip of Cap d'Antibes on the French Riviera between Nice and Cannes. It costs 30 euros. It is excellent, but more importantly it comes with a generous enough presentation of bar snacks that I can pretend this is a meal. I'm a couple hundred yards from the shore, a distance at which tourists preferred their hotels back in the nineteenth century, when this one was built. A meticulous lawn and pebble path lead the way down to the water and ensure an unobstructed view of it.

An older couple at a nearby table sips from glasses of champagne, but otherwise the terrace is empty. The sun beats directly onto us, and I note how odd it is that an awning has never been installed. My waiter makes no pretense of speaking French. There's a counterintuitive rightness to this, considering that from exactly this spot, a smattering of Americans once remade the seaside holiday in Europe, bringing their summer-centric version of it from the Jersey Shore, Rhode Island, and Connecticut back to the former health resorts of the French Mediterranean.

The Americans at the center of the smattering were Sara and Gerald Murphy, an American couple of means and creative proclivities who knew and charmed all of the most artistic people in interwar Paris. John Dos Passos noted that in their company "people were always their best selves." In the summer of 1922, the Murphys visited Gerald's college friend Cole Porter for two weeks at the chateau Porter had rented for the season on Cap d'Antibes. Around them, the cape was deserted. For Europeans, traveling to the shore was a strictly wintertime pursuit; as the temperatures crept up, the scene wound down. In Antibes, the summer months saw the little movie theater open only once per week and telephone service come to a halt at 7 p.m. It was just what the Murphys were looking for after the whirlwind of Paris.

Gerald and Sara returned the following summer to buy a place of their own. During the search, they convinced the owner of the nearby Hotel du Cap, open since 1889 but never past May 1, to keep the place running over the summer for them. They'd do the same thing the following summer while the renovations on their hillside villa ground on, and invite F. Scott and Zelda Fitzgerald to join them. The Murphys, with their beauty and glamour and unearned wealth, were just the types that most intrigued Fitzgerald. In 1926, he and Zelda would move into a villa close to the Murphys' in nearby Juan-les-Pins as Scott worked on the novel that would—years of creative struggle later—follow *The Great Gatsby*.

Tender Is the Night opens on a newly famous Hollywood actress named Rosemary Hoyt as she arrives to "Gausse's Hotel," then heads to the beach and sees Dick and Nicole Diver, a dazzling couple with a home nearby, throwing a beach party. A couple of days later, Rosemary more properly gets to know the Divers. Sitting with the group at yet another beach party, she asks Nicole if she and Dick like it here at the beach. "They have to," their friend Abe North breaks in. "They invented it."

Nicole elaborates: "This is only the second season that the hotel's been open in summer. We persuaded Gausse to keep on a cook and a garcon and a chasseur—it paid its way and this year it's doing even better."

F. Scott Fitzgerald immortalized the international beach culture
phenomenon at La Garoupe Beach in his novel *Tender Is the Night*.

Fitzgerald scholars understand Gausse's to be a version of the
Hotel du Cap (Fitzgerald changes it from white to "rose-colored")
and Dick and Nicole a version of Gerald and Sara Murphy. The conversation between Rosemary and Nicole recalls the actual events of
the Murphys' summer of 1923, when they first lived in the Hotel du
Cap and passed their time with Pablo Picasso and his ballerina wife,
Olga. Gerald spent much of that summer and the next clearing the
seaweed from tiny La Garoupe Beach—he would later tell the *New
Yorker* the seaweed had been four feet deep, evidence of a beach never
yet used, especially for leisure.

Sara sometimes brought her new Kodak camera to the Murphys' beach outings, documenting their hours spent at La Garoupe.
There's Picasso holding Olga's raised hand as she strikes a dance pose
in full tutu, point shoes digging into the sand. Here's the Count-
ess de Beaumont, her swimsuit and hair covered in elaborate bead-
work. There's Picasso wearing an enormous white top hat. An *Alice*

in Wonderland quality infuses the photos, and I suspect their existence has played no small role in cementing the French Riviera as a place of whimsy, suited to people unconfined by conventionality. They made the beach into, as a friend described it to me once, the modern picnic.

Fitzgerald re-created in his novel the moment when Americans brought their beach culture, originally borrowed from Europe and now altered, back across the Atlantic. A handful of European resorts beyond the French Riviera had already established a summer season, with city dwellers trading the stifling summer heat at home for sea breezes and 75 degrees at places like San Sebastian in Spain, Biarritz on France's west coast, the Lido in Venice, and Ostend in Belgium. But even in these spots, the beach itself remained a place to improve one's health, and a place to behave. Until the Murphys and their band of outsiders came along, it was not a place for fun.

In the summer of 1923, both Sara Murphy and Coco Chanel, who ran in a circle with Sara's sister, got deep brown suntans on the French Riviera. Against her skin, Sara tended to drape a long, contrasting string of pearls, a fashion quirk that Picasso painted and Fitzgerald fictionalized. Just like that, getting sun became something you have the leisure to do instead of something that happens to you while you're out toiling in the fields.

On La Garoupe, the beach itself was turning into a place of frivolity, and the French Riviera started taking its cues from the brazen young United States. To wit: In 1924, a Nice restaurateur named Edouard Budoin watched a film that featured a Miami beach party scene, and found himself inspired to do up the frayed casino in Juan-les-Pins in a similar vein, with a cabaret and an air of decadence. The Murphy crowd descended immediately.

ONE MORNING ON CAP D'ANTIBES, I WALK DOWN TO LA GAROUPE, ANTICI-
pating something idyllic. When I get to it, I think I've taken a wrong

turn somewhere, because La Garoupe today is not only as small as it ever was, but covered rather aggressively in the lounge chairs and dining tables of beach clubs and restaurants. A couple of businesses have built relatively substantial piers out into the water, one holding more loungers, the other more dining tables. There is very little exposed sand on this coveted sand beach, and I'm reminded again of the underemphasized fact of the French Riviera—that it is pretty terrible at doing beaches, actually. They tend to be either rocky or tiny or both. Or they are manufactured entirely, as sandy stretches in both Cannes and Monaco have been. The beach at the Hotel du Cap, for another example, is so bad that it doesn't exist—Fitzgerald relocated La Garoupe to the property in *Tender*.

Nevertheless, the beaches of the French Riviera were where the modern beach resort became an international phenomenon, evolving as it traveled from England to France to America, and then back to France again. On both sides of the Atlantic today, beachgoers chase hot weather, heading far south in the winter and to more northerly locations in the summer. The beach resort has shed its original purpose of convalescence and transformed leisure time. It has proven that it can reshape an economy. It has served as a catalyst for globalization and an economic driver of it. All the while, those rising waters have been inching oh-so-gradually up over the beach, unnoticed in their ascent.

THREE

AMONG THE VERY TALL
Waikiki

The ride from the Honolulu airport into Waikiki, the famous beach on the Hawaiian island of Oahu, takes us first along the city's notoriously clogged freeways, victims initially of bad design and later an underpredicted influx of people and cars. Stopping, then going, crawling then picking up speed, the torture-device boredom of automobile travel finally sedates us and we sink into the cacophony of Waikiki itself, along the streets of which there is no sign of the ocean, only a concrete and brick milieu that could easily stand in for the business district of a midsize midwestern city, Hermès and Chanel stores and throttling crowds notwithstanding.

The van we're in turns and passes through a walled entrance, to what is not exactly clear. Buildings loom on all sides with a very modern confidence. We ride past a thirty-nine-story, 1,600-room Sheraton. Just beyond it the grounds of the Royal Hawaiian Hotel stand preserved as they have been for nine decades, tucked in at the end of the way through a low-slung gate, the passage to the other side of which feels like the switch from black-and-white to color; into what Waikiki might have been, or once was.

Starting with its opening in 1927, The Royal Hawaiian presented an almost impossible-to-believe delight. Guests called it the Pink Palace for obvious reasons, with its blushing stucco façade popping against the blues of the sky and ocean, its luxury enabling easy appreciation of the white sands and long slope of the bay, the dramatic Diamond Head mountain marking its far end. All of this lay on a relative speck of earth so remote in the Pacific Ocean that beyond the archipelago at hand, the closest piece of land stood 2,400 miles away, in California.

The Royal Hawaiian is also the place that spawned one of Joan Didion's best sentences. "We are here in this island in the middle of the Pacific in lieu of filing for divorce." The essay that contains it, "In the Islands," covers Hawaii more broadly, its history and its problems, but the passages in which Didion considers her more personal memories of Hawaii are the ones that make the essay transcendent.

It's these passages that lead Scott and me, decades later and on the final night of a trip to Hawaii otherwise spent avoiding Waikiki, to book a room at the Royal Hawaiian. We get a deal because of a family connection at Starwood, the corporation that operates the hotel. I tell the connection I have my heart set on a room in the original building. *Won't be a problem*, she says. *Everyone wants to be in the new tower.*

That tower and all the others that now line Waikiki's shore collectively comprise the vast majority of Oahu's 27,000 hotel rooms, anchoring the Hawaiian Islands' $18 billion tourism industry. The Royal Hawaiian alone accounts for 528 of those rooms, although compared to the Sheraton next door, not to mention the Hilton Hawaiian Village just down the shore, with its 3,386 rooms and status as the largest hotel in the United States outside of Las Vegas, it barely makes a dent.

These hotels sit on the front line of the battle against rising seas.

They exist on a beach that is not only perpetually disappearing but artificially created in the first place, on an island where sea level rise is expected to occur faster than the global average. They are representative of similar challenges on shores around the world, just as the beachfront vacation is exploding in worldwide popularity on an unprecedented scale.

The battle against the tides is being lost on some fronts already, including in Hawaii. Whatever dazzling notions the word *Waikiki* brings to mind, a walk along the coastline in person quickly dispels them. As Chip Fletcher, head of the Coastal Geology Group at the University of Hawaii, summed up its current state to me, "In some areas, the beach is completely gone, you just have a seawall. In other areas you have a very thin beach. In three areas, there's a fairly wide beach." It's a dirty secret of Waikiki tourism that notable stretches of the shoreline there resemble not a tropical paradise but the industrial stretches of a declining port town. No expert can assure me that in a hundred years, the Waikiki beaches will be here at all.

LONG BEFORE THE ROYAL HAWAIIAN MADE ITS MARK ON TOURISM, WAIKIKI was a playground for royalty. In the nineteenth century, the beach was more or less a barrier island, with wetlands taking up the area between it and mainland Oahu. Hawaiian royals and other members of the nobility celebrated its utterly consistent, idyllic climate; the gentle waters were ideal for swimming, and offshore reefs and the slope of the bay created perfect waves for surfing on boards or canoes. Earth had provided humans with few more perfect nautical playgrounds. When the Royal Hawaiian opened, its first guest was Abigail Kawānanakoa, the woman who would have been queen of Hawaii had the monarchy survived, and hints of the former royal presence remain today—the stretch of Waikiki known as Kūhiō Beach, for example, was the site of Prince Kūhiō's beach home. He'd inherited the property from Queen Liliʻuokalani.

Later in the 1800s, a trickle of adventurers from the United States began making their way to Hawaii. Leisure travel from the American mainland to Hawaii became a reasonable proposition with the advent of the steamship in the mid-1800s, and in 1866, what was meant to be the first regular service between San Francisco and Honolulu began. The *Ajax* steamship threw in the towel after only two profitless round trips, but that was enough to get a thirty-one-year-old Mark Twain over, where he stayed for four months, reporting on the islands for the *Sacramento Union*. Back in the States, he gave popular lectures on "The Sandwich Islands" (the name given to Hawaii by Captain Cook when he landed there in 1778), subsequently providing Hawaii with the kind of publicity that money can't buy.

By that time, the islands' location in the middle of the Pacific Ocean had made them a natural stopover—and one with no competition—for ships needing to restock provisions and undergo repairs as they traveled from America to Asia, and vice versa. At the same time, Hawaiian sugar production was becoming the prime economic driver in the islands, dominated by white American plantation owners who would eventually feel entitled to take Hawaii as their own.

A group of Americans with interests in Hawaii succeeded in toppling the already weakened Hawaiian monarchy in 1893. That year, upon his return from the islands on an exploratory visit, William Libbey, a professor at Princeton College, told the *New York Times* of the recently deposed Queen Lili'uokalani, "She is living very quietly at a little place called Waikiki." The queen, of course, was onto a secret that would soon get out. The U.S. government officially annexed Hawaii in 1898, and the islands became a U.S. territory in June 1900. Plans to develop its tourism industry were already well under way by prominent local businessmen, many of whom became players in the new government there.

Meanwhile, over in California a man named William Matson bought his first steamship in 1882 and began transporting sugar from Hawaii back to the mainland. He soon expanded both his fleet and his business offerings, bringing travelers over from California to visit the islands. The Matson Navigation Company opened the Royal Hawaiian and also ran Waikiki's first major resort, the Moana. In an early example of what we now call vertical integration, he built the hotels in order to give customers a reason to get on his ships. His company's hotels, the Royal Hawaiian especially, became legendary draws, and its ships the primary means of reaching them.

By then, the idea of Hawaii as a gracious paradise had taken root. Mark Twain, for one, never got over the islands, writing to a friend in 1881, "What I have always longed for was the privilege of living forever away up on one of those mountains in the Sandwich Islands overlooking the sea."

WHILE WAITING AN UNREASONABLY LONG TIME TO CHECK IN CONSIDERing the high room prices, we take in the Royal Hawaiian's open-air lobby, which some executive at some point during some renovation acknowledged would not be improved by air-conditioning. The outdoors are right there, streaming in through a line of enormous arched doorways. Our turn comes up and, in what seems to be the current fashion for high-end resorts, we approach not a counter but an extravagant desk, where we sit down across from an attendant. For no reason that we are aware of, we are upgraded to a suite. We will learn only later that it has no ocean views.

From her own room on an eerie afternoon in some bygone decade, Didion was "watching the long translucent curtains billow in the trade wind and trying to put [her] life back together." Today those windows open only a couple of inches, and the Royal Hawaiian is no longer an appropriate backdrop for that kind of crisis. After a brief attempt at re-creating the billowing, I opt to leave the windows shut, submitting to a climate control that no executive would have vetoed and that negates the splendid things Hawaiian air does to a person's hair and skin.

We go downstairs and sit in rocking chairs on a swollen veranda, its black-and-white stone floors solid beneath our feet, the pink stucco columns holding up a roof that protects us just this moment from a brief afternoon rain. In front of us sprawls a sort of imperial lawn, green grass dotted with palm trees that give way abruptly at the edges to tropical foliage. It would feel like a scene from another era were it not for the high-rise hotels crowding into view at its far end. This swath of lawn is known as Coconut Grove and is said to be the site of nineteenth-century Hawaiian queen Ka'ahumanu's summer palace.

THE BEACH RESORT ON A GRAND SCALE MAY HAVE BEEN A NINETEENTH-century invention, but in the twentieth it became a true cultural phenomenon. The Royal Hawaiian helped usher in the new era of the densely developed resort area, and Hawaii gave beach vacationers a first taste of what they considered the exotic—in proximity to a culture unlike their own, among people who didn't look like them. In places like Waikiki, Acapulco, the Amalfi Coast, Atlantic City, and Miami Beach, resorts represented a new way to experience leisure time, and people all over the Americas and Europe aspired to join this party. In many cases, the resorts were massive, with hundreds of rooms and expansive spaces for social events. No longer presented primarily as a place to bolster one's health, they became aligned with Hollywood, cocktails, dinner clubs, and an escape from the banalities of real life back home. Silent film mega-stars Mary Pickford and Douglas Fairbanks helped set the tone when they stayed at the Royal Hawaiian in 1930.

For Waikiki, the new decadence meant hula shows and mai tais, "beach boys" and "mahalo." Popular culture took notice, and a foray into exotic Hawaii became something for the masses to aspire to, especially after World War II, when the combination of a booming economy and the novel concept of paid vacation time emerged for white-collar workers. Resort towns grew more densely developed in order to accommodate first a larger pool of affluent sunseekers and later a wider range of budgets (which eventually led these resorts to lose their glamour—a story for another chapter).

By the time the Royal Hawaiian opened in 1927, the beach at Waikiki had already suffered at the hands of overdevelopment by humans. As ever more enormous buildings were built as close to the Waikiki water as possible, their developers learned the hard way that these types of structures interrupt the natural flow of sand, causing it to wash away. Property owners on Waikiki almost immediately began efforts to keep their treasured waterfront property in place. An article in the *New York Times* from October 1928 described Waikiki's upcoming beach improvement project, possibly the first of its kind in Hawaii, modeled on previous projects on the New Jersey shore.

The article is striking in its portrayal of a beach ruined by development: "Waikiki as it exists today is generally a keen disappointment to the visitor, viewing it for the first time in the light of the romantic glamour which poets and others have cast over a famous spot. It is a white crescent, hardly a mile across, almost completely suffocated by the buildings of private owners." In addition to their houses, these owners constructed seawalls to protect their properties—"which hemmed in home sites, but which spelled destruction to the natural sand formation." In other words, the sand had begun to disappear from the Waikiki shoreline, and with naturally narrow beaches to begin with, the result was quickly understood. Officials concluded that the sand had relocated to a sandbar offshore, and a plan was developed to build a series of groins, or perpendicular walls, jutting out into the water (the *Times* described them as "semi-dams") that would result in the sand's return to the Waikiki shore. By around 1930, eleven such groins had been constructed.

Months after the Royal Hawaiian opened, one of those groins went up in front of it, keeping the sand from moving on down the shore. It worked, but in almost no time it also caused the shoreline on the other side of the groin to lose sand completely. Today there is no beach there.

Scott and I don't know this when we set off for a stroll from the Royal Hawaiian. We come out on the sand, look out to sea, and decide spontaneously to head to our right. When we come to the groin, the scene changes from one step to the next, from one of idyllic beach paradise into something akin to wasteland. Sandbags had been stacked in an apparent effort to compensate for the now-crumbling groin. We climb past them, then walk down a staircase onto the top of a concrete seawall with metal railings, the water lapping right up against it—on Google Maps, this is generously labeled the Sheraton Boardwalk, after that 1,600-room hotel which abuts it. This is not a scenic stroll, and it does nothing to invoke the concept of paradise as it is commonly understood.

Groins, seawalls, jetties, offshore breakwaters, and other permanent structures are known as "hard" solutions in beach preservation

The old groin at the Royal Hawaiian held the beach fronting the resort in place, but caused the sand on the other side to disappear.

Courtesy of Scott Rosenstein

circles. Most often, hard solutions serve to protect buildings but intensify the problem of sand erosion. "Natural coastal erosion . . . does not take away beaches, it just moves them," Robert Young, a coastal geologist and director of the Program for the Study of Developed Shorelines at Western Carolina University, explained to me. Sometimes this means that a beach gradually migrates down the shore; other times it means that the flow of sand continually replenishes a beach in one place. Either way, hard solutions interrupt that natural cycle. "Beaches disappear when you put a road, a seawall, a bulkhead, or a big building in the way of that movement," says Young. The issue is not that the sand is moving—that's what nature intended, in fact—but that we insist it stay in one place.

As a result of this realization, hard solutions gradually lost favor to "soft" solutions—namely replacing lost sand, euphemistically known as beach nourishment, and building sand dunes, which can both protect coasts and draw more sand to accumulate. The world's first beach nourishment projects were completed in the early 1900s, and Waikiki was engaging in it at least by 1939.

IN WAIKIKI, THE USUAL PLAYERS IN MANAGING BEACHES—GOVERNMENTS, hotels, plus an assortment of engineers, scientists, and local community efforts—are joined by another group. Surfers hold more sway here than in many other beach locations around the world, thanks to Waikiki's entrenched and legendary surfing culture. Indeed, the entire history of surfing runs time and again through the waters off Waikiki. It started with the native Hawaiians, of course, who began surfing here as an unofficial national pastime well before Captain Cook's ship brought the first Westerners to the islands. In those times, men and women alike rode on boards made from the wood of local trees. Members of Hawaiian royalty got the best beaches, which included Waikiki. They surfed using not only boards but also canoes.

Then, in the early twentieth century, native Hawaiian and Olympic swimmer Duke Kahanamoku did more than anyone to popularize the sport beyond its Polynesian roots. While not a royal, Kahanamoku came from a noble family and grew up in Waikiki. After his Olympic days (he was by now an American citizen), he toured the world putting on swimming exhibitions and, in a less formal capacity, surfing shows, helping introduce surfing to both California and Australia. In 1920, he took the Prince of Wales (Edward, the future king) out into the Waikiki surf.

Beginning with Duke, surfers became pioneers of beach tourism. Like the artists who move into cheap spaces in a run-down urban neighborhood, only to see twenty years later that they've been followed first by other creative types, and finally by the moneyed classes who enjoy proximity to creativity, surfers proved willing to explore unnoticed coastlines in search of their ideal break. Once they would find one, they'd set up camps, the locals would start to offer them basic services, and then word of the place would begin to trickle out. It's a phenomenon that's continuing today from Mexico to Indonesia.

Waikiki still boasts the seven or so breaks that originally drew surfers to this bay, and today surfers command a respect here as the historic guardians of the waves. They are also a remarkably well-organized local political force, opposing beach nourishment out of a not-unfounded concern that additional sand will, as Chip Fletcher describes it to me, "change the characteristics of the breaking waves," potentially rendering one or more of the breaks unsurfable. Save Our Surf, an organization founded in 1964 to protest the widening of some Waikiki beaches, was seminal in this regard. Since then, surfers have consistently wielded influence over the fate of the shore here.

"There's a tension between the surfers and the people that want a beach," Fletcher says, although "even the surfers want a beach, they recognize that." Still, their objection to the continued engineering of Waikiki's shoreline highlights the counterintuitive conflict between keeping beaches in place and truly preserving a waterfront ecosystem.

Surfers have also been instrumental in ensuring that sand no longer ships in from other areas. To keep Waikiki as it is, sand has to be found within the system—or littoral zone—of that beach's natural sand flow. The problem, Fletcher tells me, is that there's not a ton of sand on the ocean floor near Hawaii, in contrast to a region like the northeastern United States, where plentiful offshore sand makes dredging for beach nourishment a relatively sustainable practice.

Further complicating matters, Waikiki's calcium carbonate sand is notably fragile. When it is being dredged from offshore, Fletcher said, the grains of sand can fracture into even smaller pieces, sometimes so small that they become silt, which remains suspended in the water instead of falling to the bottom. The Waikiki sand can also take on some cement-like properties when pressure is placed on it, becoming compacted to form a dense matter that hardly resembles sand at all, as happened during the 2012 beach replenishment, when large trucks drove over existing sand in order to deposit more.

After decades of beach nourishment, the 1928 groin in front of the Royal Hawaiian not only remained in place, it became crucial to maintaining the beach at Waikiki as we know it. However, the groin itself was poorly maintained, and after it fell into a state of disrepair that threatened the integrity of the beach, a $1.5 million restoration and expansion was proposed. The surfers organized to protest the groin being rebuilt bigger than before, and in the end the largest proposed version of the new groin did not come to fruition, as it was revised from a "T-head" to an "L-head" design.

THE ROYAL HAWAIIAN AND ITS ENVIRONS ARE PUT INTO THEIR CONTEMPORARY context later in the evening, as the boat we are on leaves behind the beaches of Waikiki, spawning a moment of visual trickery as the shoreline panorama compresses in front of our eyes. The once-grand Royal Hawaiian is now chastened by the many-windowed behemoths surrounding it. A doll-size pink dot among the *very* tall.

The sun sets, and looking back to the shore we see the gray slabs of buildings become twinkling hemispheres. The Royal Hawaiian melts into the larger sparkling picture. *It looks like a real city*, Scott says, observing the skyline of high-rises crowding up against the water.

The next day back on shore: *Just another day in paradise*, our waitress says when we ask how's she doing. *Just another day in paradise*, says the surfer sitting next to us on the beach. *Just another day in paradise*. It's what people in Hawaii say to you instead of saying *fine*. It's a phrase always spoken with a hint of sarcasm, confessing in the subtext certain connections between leisure and perfection and despair.

We sit on the hotel's terrace, eating our lunch and staring out at the ocean through a procession of pink umbrellas. What is most remarkable, we observe, is the complete absence of elements. Neither too hot nor too cold nor whipped by a breeze nor suffocated by a stillness, the water is as turquoise as possible without becoming a cartoon. Beachgoers wade hundreds of yards out with their surfboards or paddleboards or just their own bodies and a loved one or two. They dot the bay like pleasure-seekers in a Seurat painting, and I think it's no wonder members of Hawaiian royalty chose to spend their leisure time here. And no wonder that the richest Americans chose to do so too, as soon as it became feasible from the mainland.

"The Royal Hawaiian is not merely a hotel but a social idea, one of the few extant clues to a certain kind of American life," Didion wrote in 1969. That "certain kind" of American life can be easily translated as the most privileged kind. The beach vacation, especially one to a remote place like Hawaii, started as an activity for the rich exclusively. In the early decades of the twentieth century, before affordable air travel made far-flung vacations possible for the American middle class, a stay at the Royal Hawaiian required not only a surplus of money but also of time. Guests arrived by steamship, and they stayed for months. In 1885, a round-trip ticket on a steamship between San Francisco and Honolulu cost $125, or somewhere in the neighborhood of $3,500 in today's dollars. The journey each way took a week. It wouldn't have made sense to go through all that and not spend at least a few weeks in Hawaii once you got there.

Commercial air travel arrived between the continental United States and Honolulu in 1936, via a weekly Pan American Airways flight that carried eight or nine passengers in addition to cargo and mail. The first passenger on the plane's inaugural flight in October 1936 was Richard F. Bradley, a manager at Standard Oil. A few years ago, a curator at Washington's Air and Space Museum came across Bradley's "Passenger Identification Coupon" from the flight, which included the price paid for his flight to Honolulu and then on to Manila: $3,000, more than it would cost you today without accounting for inflation, or about $53,000 if you do.

The financial barrier to entry made for a specific lifestyle at the Royal Hawaiian, involving the leisure class and conspicuous consumption. Women showed up in fur coats for reasons having nothing to do with the need to keep warm. Dances in the hotel's ballroom brought out diamonds and pearls and elaborate drop-waist dresses. After Pickford and Fairbanks, another silent film star, Dorothy Mackaill, came to the Royal Hawaiian and stayed for decades—she died in her room there in 1990. After her came Elizabeth Taylor, Dean Martin, and others in the original Hollywood jet set. After World War II, air travel put a trip to a place like Waikiki within reach of the American middle class, but its aura of glamour remained. It was entirely appropriate that the creators of *Mad Men* sent Don Draper and his second wife, Meghan, on vacation to the Pink Palace.

The social idea at the Royal Hawaiian today is different and no longer distinctly American; just ask the scores of guests at any given time who have flown in not from Los Angeles or Portland or even, like me, New York, but from Tokyo or Taipei, and who insist on a room in the new tower, which went up in 1969, during a regrettable era for architectural projects, in order to increase the total capacity of the resort. The seventeen-story tower, incidentally, was reimagined in 2015, with rooms now costing nearly double those in the original building.

Today's Royal Hawaiian clientele is a reflection of the emergent global middle class, which now numbers well over 3 billion people, the majority from East Asia and India. In 1950, by contrast, the "global" middle class numbered a mere 321 million people, almost all of them from Europe and the United States. There are more members of the middle class today than there were people in the world in 1950, and the hotels have grown accordingly. In 2017, a third of visitors to Hawaii came from outside the United States, with a full 17 percent coming from Japan, according to data from the Hawaii State Department of Business, Economic Development, and Tourism. This number may be in part due to a surprising twist in the story of Waikiki's hotels: Since 1974 the Royal Hawaiian has been owned by a Japanese company, Kyo-ya Hotels and Resorts, LP. Under this ownership, the property was operated first by Starwood, then by Marriott after its acquisition of the former, but neither has ever owned the hotel itself. Kyo-ya also owns the Moana Surfrider, the Sheraton Waikiki, and the Sheraton Princess Kaiulani along Waikiki's shoreline. Perhaps to some visitors, a trip to Waikiki still offers clues to a certain American life, but only in the same way that Manhattan's Lower East Side today offers clues to the immigrant experience.

THE SEAS LAPPING UP AGAINST WAIKIKI ARE RISING, AS THEY ARE ON most beaches around the world. They will continue to do so, likely by somewhere between two and six feet by the end of the century. In 2013 the Intergovernmental Panel on Climate Change (IPCC), a group of roughly two thousand scientists assembled by the World Meteorological Organization and United Nations Environment Programme to periodically produce assessments on the outcomes of global warming and the closest thing we have to a consensus on sea level rise, put the worst-case scenario at more than one foot of global sea level rise by midcentury.

Sea levels rise at different paces in different locations, thanks to a number of factors, including land subsidence, or sinking, and regional ocean flows. Chip Fletcher pointed out one curious effect on Hawaii and Waikiki: As the Greenland Ice Sheet melts, its gravitational pull will diminish. As a result, ocean water that had been pulled closer to Greenland will move away from it, causing sea levels to rise even more than the global average in places that had previously benefited from the sheet's gravitational pull. Hawaii is one of those places, and thanks to this phenomenon, combined with other factors, the islands will likely see sea levels rise 25 percent faster than the global average. In fifty years, Fletcher says, "I think it will be a very different place, unless there's something with the climate system that we don't understand, and that very well may be the case."

Rising seas are having secondary effects as well. In Waikiki, the most urgent of these may be what is known as sunny-day flooding, or nuisance flooding. There's only about two feet of room between the surface and the groundwater—the water you're looking for if you dig a well—in Waikiki. The city receives just seventeen inches of rainfall per year but is prone to heavy downpours and also absorbs runoff from steep slopes just inland. This makes the risk of flooding significant even without rising seas. When the estuary between Waikiki Beach and mainland Honolulu was filled in in the 1920s, engineers conceived of the Ala Wai Canal to catch the area's overflow of water and direct it toward the ocean. The canal never solved the flooding problem completely, but in recent years it's proven an entirely insufficient match for the rain and rising tides. Add to this the fact that the groundwater itself may be rising thanks to rising seas—shrinking that two feet of wiggle room—and it becomes clear that flooding will be a major concern sooner than later.

Lest we continue to think of sea level rise as an event lying fifty years in the future, consider these facts: In the twentieth century, global sea levels already rose somewhere in the vicinity of six inches. Since 1960, sea level in relation to the shoreline has risen between two and six inches at any given spot in the Hawaiian Islands. In April 2017, Waikiki experienced its highest-ever tide. In 2015, flooding from heavy rains sent 500,000 gallons of wastewater into the Waikiki waterways, shutting the beaches down for several days. There's a thing about any extreme weather event being dismissible as a freak occurrence, and then there's our current deluge of extreme weather events that makes it harder to ignore that the center is not holding, to borrow a phrase from Didion, who borrowed it from Yeats—both writers who had the luxury of seeing the "center" as something existential. It was not flooding their hotel rooms. Consider again that the Greenland Ice Sheet has the fate of Hawaii, more than five thousand miles away, partially in its hands, and it's hardly a leap to contemplate other, equally bizarre repercussions of a phenomenon we still barely understand.

In Hawaii, there is no denying the ocean. Perhaps because of this, the players involved here have been quicker to act against global warming and rising seas than many other locations around the world—a low bar to clear, but still. In 2014 the state created the Interagency Climate Adaptation Committee (ICAC), renamed the Hawai'i Climate Change Mitigation and Adaptation Commission in 2016. The Climate Commission coordinates county, state, and federal efforts along with those of external bodies. In 2017 Hawaii also became the first state to write adherence to the Paris Agreement into law, just a week after President Trump withdrew the United States from the accord. And at the beginning of 2021, Hawaii became the first state to ban the sale of sunscreens believed to contribute to the catastrophic bleaching of coral reefs.

Hawaiian hotels, too, have been less likely to stick their heads in the figurative sand than hotels in other locations, where so far hospitality companies have been able to rely on local, state, and federal governments to fund necessary beach replenishments and other sustainability efforts. A major Waikiki sand replenishment project in 2012 cost $2.4 million, paid for by a combination of public and private entities—with $500,000 coming from the state-funded Hawaii Tourism Authority; another $500,000 from Kyo-ya Hotels; and the remaining $1.4 million from the State of Hawaii Beach Restoration Fund, which generates revenues from fees on landowners who encroach on state-owned land (primarily all underwater land in Hawaii).

Larger hotel companies like Marriott and Hilton so far seem to be content to ignore the problem of sea level rise, at least publicly. Both declined to speak with me on the topic of climate change. Why would they, when so far governments are footing the bill to maintain their beaches? A public relations rep for Hilton did direct me to the company's Corporate Responsibility section on its website, which I checked out. I couldn't find a single mention of sea level rise.

MIDWAY THROUGH OUR SECOND DAY IN WAIKIKI WE CAN NO LONGER head off a panicky ennui. There is no relief between us and 10 p.m., when we go to the airport to fly home to New York. The pressure to spend money cannibalizes leisure and sunshine. At every turn, there's no escaping the smothering crowds, unless one is willing to pay for the seclusion, in an overpriced bistro or overpriced pub or overpriced boat ride, none of which are convincing in their intimation of experience. Back in the hot tub at the Royal Hawaiian, a waiter comes by with a tray of pineapple slices, toothpicks sticking up. This small gesture provides such satisfaction, such momentary escape, that we hate it almost immediately, for reminding us in contrast about everything else. I want to present this unsavory afternoon as proof that Waikiki has passed peak tourism, except then how to explain the tens of thousands of occupied hotel rooms within eyesight.

Yet, since our return, I've squandered more than one afternoon chasing down old photos of the Royal Hawaiian online. A postcard bearing an image of the hotel in 1928 now hangs framed in our bathroom, the new groin having already altered the beach considerably. My own memories still mingle with the ones I have only read about. Looking at the postcard, I marvel at the bird's-eye views of the Waikiki shoreline, looking empty but for the two great resorts. I marvel that once there were single-family houses on Waikiki Beach. I marvel at the untouched land behind the shore. I marvel at how obvious it is that Waikiki was once truly far flung. Then, how obvious it is that decades later, when I made my visit, the Royal Hawaiian has become the backdrop for a very different kind of crisis, indeed.

FOUR

INTO FAR-FLUNG PLACES

Fiji

THE KOROLEVU BEACH HOTEL

I'm standing at the terminus of a dirt drive on the southern coast of Fiji's main island, Viti Levu, with a man named Chris Clark. In front of us, the Pacific Ocean. To our right, a softly bending bay with a fantastic beach running the length of it, the odd palm tree leaning out from the foliage as if straining to get a look at us. Behind us, several horses loiter in a ditch full of stagnant water. I assume they belong to someone, even though I spot no potential owner. In the distance, green hills. I feel it's important to emphasize the green of these hills, so full-bodied it seems liquid. This is December, the beginning of Fiji's rainy season, and the air contains the kind of soupy heat that a breeze can make bearable, but otherwise feels like something that might slowly kill you.

Nicola Thomson, a Fijian friend who introduced me to Chris, arrives and together we all make our way down the sand, which surrenders to dense vegetation on our right. Above it, the tops of long-abandoned concrete buildings peek out. Up ahead, two kids splash around at the water's edge. At a clearing, we turn inland and greet the man we find there. Chris knows him, says hello, and explains that he's showing us around. The man is the property's caretaker, hired by the magnate who now owns this land. He's set up living quarters in a hollowed-out room in one of the concrete buildings—the room closest to the water, incidentally.

I head farther into the clearing and find the concrete shell of another two-story building. On its outer wall, still intact and clear as day, in muted blue lettering that would fit in fine on the awning of a present-day Brooklyn restaurant, reads "Korolevu Beach Hotel." This is Fiji's first beach resort. It is also the place where Chris spent his childhood.

Chris's parents, Bill and Kathy Clark, both of whose families had come to Viti Levu from Britain after Fiji became a colony, moved onto this land in 1940 from a city on the western side of the island. At the time, sugar production dominated Fiji's economy, and as a British colony, Fiji's significance was seen in terms of agriculture. They planned to farm, but, in addition, Kathy opened a rest house by the dirt road for travelers making their way between the eastern and western ends of the island. Demand was high, which got the Clarks thinking about shifting their focus away from farming.

Tourism to Fiji existed already but didn't include the beaches. Instead, cruise ships would stop off in the capital of Suva on their way to or from Hawaii. As in Hawaii, the Matson Navigation Company played a role, bringing the biggest cruise ships into the port by the 1930s. The Union Steamship Company built Suva's Grand Pacific Hotel in 1914 to accommodate its high-end cruise guests, who disembarked to find a town populated mostly by Europeans.

The Clarks opened the Korolevu Beach Hotel in 1949 with just a few bungalows, or bures, as they'd come to be known. By 1956, they'd built thirty-seven of them and a large common building housing a bar and restaurant. They'd cultivated grass lawns, flowering bushes, and well-placed palm trees. In the early days guests lounged directly on the grass, taking a catnap against a pillow, perhaps, or sitting in a small group enjoying cocktails. (The pool would come later.)

In the 1950s, the Korolevu Beach Hotel represented—perhaps unwittingly—the future for Fiji's economy. It also helped pioneer a new global wave of beach tourism to "exotic" locales that would captivate travelers in the second half of the twentieth century.* In the nineteenth century, resorts were built in the West, for a Western clientele. Now Europeans and Americans were ready to take their beach vacations beyond their own borders.

ALSO IN THE 1950S, THE KOROLEVU OPENED ITS OWN AIRSTRIP ON THE land behind the resort, enabling quick transfer from the island's main airports in Nadi and Suva—a serious amenity for a beach resort, even a high-end one. For Chris, those plane landings were a childhood highlight. They approached over the water, disappeared behind a dewy mountain, then reappeared just in time to land, hurtling toward the resort but coming to a stop with plenty of space to spare. It seems likely this experience played a part in his ambition to become a pilot for Fiji Airways, where he spent a career flying travelers to his home country from lands far and wide.

As it did in Hawaii, the advent of transoceanic flights like these made the modern beach tourism industry here possible. Freed up from supporting the war effort—during which there was virtually no leisure air travel—airlines pivoted to commercial service in the postwar years. On the ground, former army installations became airports. In Fiji, a former U.S. Air Force base near the city of Nadi became the country's major international airport. In 1958, Pan American Airways offered the first commercial direct flight over the Atlantic

---

* Another resort opened on Viti Levu, called the Beachcomber, around the same time as the Korolevu. But the Beachcomber's location on the island's rainy eastern coast doomed it, and its influence never approached that of the Korolevu.

Ocean—with no stops for refueling—from New York City to Brussels, marking a new era of convenience. Before long, an airline could get a person from New York to Fiji in a day or two rather than the weeks that a ship would have required.

Back on the ground, change had been afoot for travelers in other ways. In 1936, France guaranteed its citizens two weeks of paid vacation every year. In 1938, British workers gained one week. Those countries and many others offer far more time off today, and while the United States didn't then and still doesn't mandate paid time off for its workers, by the 1950s it had become standard for both white-collar and blue-collar employees to receive paid vacation days. At the same time, unemployment was consistently low, and thanks to strong unions and other worker protections, wages were robust. In the States between 1940 and 1970, GDP would rise ten times over, kicking off an era of innovation, optimism, and entitlement. "Average" families in countries with advanced economies now had disposable income, and disposable time during which to spend it. The entire West seemingly found itself on the cusp of long-term prosperity—in the States first, followed by Europe as it rebuilt after the war. As other countries saw the potential of tourism, they began to ease the visa process for tourists from these chosen developed nations.

At the same time, advances in science and technology heightened the appeal of tropical locations. Mass availability of air-conditioning brought a new level of comfort to hot, sticky places. Without it, one can imagine more moderate climates having outmaneuvered the tropics for beach resort supremacy. Air-conditioning also made the economics of running a resort easier by enabling a year-round season, or close to it, and not one limited to the most pleasant months.

Back in the final years of the nineteenth century, a British doctor named Ronald Ross built on the work of his predecessors to prove that mosquitoes transfer malaria from one human to another. For his discovery, Ross received the Nobel Prize in medicine in 1902. In 1901, another doctor, Walter Reed, confirmed that mosquitoes similarly transmit yellow fever. Immediately after, mosquito nets went into widespread production, and landowners began draining the marshes that provided breeding grounds for the malaria vectors. In the postwar years, vaccines for yellow fever and other tropical diseases became available to travelers, as did malaria prevention pills. The lowered risk of serious illness opened up large swaths of the globe to vacationers who previously would have been wary. For Europeans, this often meant heading to the current or former colonies of their respective countries.

Island nations especially began to see beach tourism as a viable alternative to agricultural industries that were losing profitability. The Hotel Bora Bora opened on the island of the same name in 1961 with eighteen huts, introducing resort tourism to French Polynesia. The world's first overwater bungalows opened in Tahiti in the 1960s—another twist on the "bure" format in Fiji. Today they're considered the height of resort luxury and honeymoon goals, but in the beginning the overwater bungalow was conceived in order to attract tourists to shorelines lacking in beaches. The Maldives, with its 1,200 islands, opened its first resort in 1972 and soon became the global poster child for overwater luxury. The way a reserve of oil could shape a country's destiny in the past, now so too could a good long stretch of coastline.

As Western tourists fanned out to the world's new renowned beaches, seaside tourism became a key driver of the extraordinary growth of international tourism. In 1950, just 25 million international arrivals were logged. By 2019, that number had grown to nearly 1.5 billion. The number of total airline passengers globally increased from 31 million in 1950 to ten times that number just two decades later. Tourism is now the third-largest export globally (classified as an export when it caters to international travelers), behind chemicals and fuels and ahead of automotive products and food. It provides more than one in every ten jobs worldwide, and accounts for about 10 percent of global gross domestic product (GDP), according to the World

Travel & Tourism Council's research. One UN report has gone so far as to call it the biggest industry in the world.

The Korolevu found itself on the front end of this exploding industry. At its peak in the late sixties and early seventies, it boasted a global reputation among the jet set. All kinds of distinguished people stayed here—Noël Coward and James Michener and Burt Lancaster and Robert Wagner, and a few for whom the last name is all you need, like Hitchcock and Disney and the entire Von Trapp family. By this time, resorts were opening up and down the shore from the Korolevu, in an area that came to be called the Coral Coast, although no one I talk to remembers exactly when or by whom. (Educated guess: It was the marketers.) From there Fiji beach tourism exploded, expanding to many of its more than three hundred smaller islands, especially in the Mamanuca and Yasawa chains. By the early 1980s, it had surpassed sugar as Fiji's biggest industry.

THE CARETAKER'S TWO KIDS JOIN OUR TOUR AS WE WALK INTO THE Korolevu Beach Hotel's shell of a building, its concrete skeleton still solid. The little boy has long hair and an endearing unruliness. He doesn't speak a word of English and has no idea what we're up to, but he's into it. His older sister, a girl of about eleven, is home on holiday break from a boarding school in one of Viti Levu's bigger towns. She's fluent in English and hangs on our every word.

We climb the stairs to the second floor, where despite the lack of flooring, paint, furniture, or windows, it's easy to make sense of the rooms. The first one we enter would be small by today's resort standards, with just enough space for a bed, dresser, maybe a couple of small armchairs. We walk into a larger room, a suite, Chris says. Standing where the wall once separated the room from the balcony, I feel the breeze coming off the water and can see exactly why the better rooms were on the second floor.

This is where the honeymooners stayed, I venture.

Yes. Thick walls, Chris says, and pounds on one to prove it.

Before we leave and when no one is looking, I tuck a loose bathroom tile into my bag as a souvenir.

Outside one of the second-floor suites, the boy cuts his foot on the glass of a broken bottle. He tries to exhibit that he's fine, but Nicola tells him in Fijian that we're sending him home to get it cleaned up—his banishment clearly pains him more than the cut itself. We walk down a different stairwell back to ground level and follow Chris along the beach as he points out where the pool used to be, where the bartender once served cocktails. Maybe because I'm looking at things through his eyes, memories seem scattered around the place, and they make it pulse with a past that is still present.

In the 1950s, Chris's parents visited Honolulu and Waikiki and returned home filled with ideas to apply at Korolevu, "to do Hawaii, but Fijian," as Chris puts it. Inspired by the hula dances they enjoyed in Hawaii, the Clarks began hiring Fijians from the nearby village to put on traditional war dances on Saturday nights, and brought in fire walkers from a neighboring island once a month. These performances soon became a signature offering. As Hawaiian hosts offered leis, the Clarks began placing shell necklaces around guests' necks on arrival.

In the postwar era at the Korolevu and elsewhere, most conceptual roads in beach tourism led back to Hawaii, from which a standardization of global beach resort culture took root. Hawaii represented the transitional stepping-stone from a Western-centric beach resort culture to a global one—it was a place rooted in what Westerners considered exotic but as part of the United States provided a certain familiarity. Many fads originating there became staples of beach resorts—a bartender at the Hilton Hawaiian Village resort in Waikiki popularized the cocktail umbrella in the late 1950s, for one example. The surfboard itself made its way around the world thanks to Hawaii, for another. The colorful block prints common in resort attire stem from the Hawaiian shirt, invented in Honolulu in the 1920s or 1930s. The alignment of "beach" and "paradise" took hold as Hawaii's influence expanded.

The Korolevu's own contribution to resort culture came from its layout. I've been told, and seen it claimed in news articles, that the Korolevu was the world's first beach resort to feature individual bungalows—guests stayed in bures with bamboo walls and thatched roofs extending down to the top of the doorway—inspired by the local architecture instead of a single grand building in the European mold. The idea was to re-create the appearance of an entire native village, which soon caught on elsewhere. In a further departure from the Western model, the Korolevu's buildings were often placed within feet of the beaches themselves.

Chris tells me that his parents coined the term *bure* for the bungalows at their resort. Previously, the word had referred to a large communal building in a Fijian village that housed the men of a clan. In a 2008 article in the *New Zealand Herald*, Bill Clark is said to have decided on *bure* because he figured the more literal word, *vale-vakaviti*, would be too much for visitors to get their tongues around. Today the word is used all over Fiji to refer to guest bungalows at resorts. In both name and essence, the traditional Fijian home was remade for the Western tourist.

The concrete building here joined the bures in the late sixties, as resorts were beginning to make more efforts to maximize capacity. By the 1970s, the resort could accommodate 400 guests at a time. Paradise Point, the hollowed-out resort next door where the caretaker we met now lives, also opened in the 1960s as a more economical option.

Today the bures of the Korolevu Beach Hotel are long gone—the resort closed in 1983. Chris's parents are buried on a bluff at the far end of the bay. But under the thick brush, traces remain. Just a few months ago, when he was walking down the beach, he decided on a whim to turn into the considerable tropical brush. He surprised himself by coming directly upon the concrete steps that had once led up to his home. I ask Chris if he enjoyed his childhood, at least the part before he turned eleven and shipped off to boarding school in Sydney. "It was heaven on earth," he says, as we come upon a platform that once served as the floor of a bure, the square footprints of the tiles still visible. This would have been a prime bure, close to the ocean and facing it directly.

AS FIJI'S TOURISM INDUSTRY GREW, THE COUNTRY CONTINUED TO LOOK to Hawaii as a beacon. Because its leaders had the benefit of building on lessons that Hawaii learned the hard way, and often the hard-to-reverse way, by the 1960s Fiji recognized both that beach tourism was its future and that there might be a wrong way to do it. In an article in the *Honolulu Advertiser* of July 10, 1964, with the headline "Fiji's Tourism: A Bright Hope for Beautiful Island Chain," a commission studying the Fijian economy is quoted as reporting: "It is held that 'Fiji must not become another Hawaii,' where an entirely synthetic version of local culture has been developed to divert the tourist."

That they weren't entirely successful becomes evident upon arrival to Denarau Island, a mostly artificial piece of land just off the west coast of Viti Levu, where I am staying at the Westin and where tourism in Fiji is currently anchored. Most tourists spend at least a night on Denarau before dispersing along the coasts or to islands farther afield. In doing so, they can choose from, in addition to the Westin, a Sofitel, a Sheraton, a Hilton, a Radisson Blu, or a Wyndham. Upon my arrival to Denarau, I receive a shell necklace. At night I watch four indigenous Fijians perform a variation on their traditional dance, their costumes made of synthetic materials.

Denarau Island became Fiji's national tourism hub despite a notable lack of both natural and cultural assets. It's built upon swampy, mangrovey land. Not only does most of the shore here have no beach, but it also sits near the mouth of the Nadi River, which keeps the seawater consistently muddy. Only one road leads in from the main island, and at the entrance, a guarded gatehouse keeps Fiji out. This is the exclusive domain of foreigners. No one who works on the island lives on it.

Just before my trip to Fiji, I spoke to Andrew Thomson, who knows exactly how Denarau Island happened, because he was there for it. Today he lives in Portugal, but he hails from Fiji, where in the late sixties he worked as an assistant manager at Castaway Island, one of the early resorts in the Mamanuca Islands. One afternoon his boss instructed him to take a guest named Charlie Pietsch to the mainland, from where he would travel back home to Hawaii to take care of some urgent business. Pietsch happened to be a hotel developer interested in expanding to Fiji, and Andrew showed him some islands along their journey that might make good settings for a resort. Only by coincidence did they go by Denarau. Thomson didn't see any value in the place, but Pietsch took one look at it and said he wanted to build his resort here. When Thomson asked why, Pietsch said one word: location. It was close to the airport in Nadi and to the city's labor supply.

Pietsch built his resort and opened it in 1975 as a 300-room Regent, a brand eventually absorbed into the Four Seasons—it's the present-day Westin. By this time, Thomson was working first in the Caribbean and then Hawaii, but, in the late seventies, Pietsch convinced him to come on as general manager of the Regent. By the late eighties, another resort, the Sheraton, had joined the Regent.

With the Fiji military coup in 1987, tourism in the country shut down, at which point a Japanese investor named Harunori Takahashi bought all of Denarau, including the two resorts, and began a mighty expansion of its footprint, which Thomson came in to oversee. They hauled in 88 million cubic feet of earth from a nearby mountain to fill in mangrove swamps and raise the elevation of the island, and built a geotextile barrier around it to protect from storm surges—a protective measure far ahead of its time. "I was very keen to do it, and the Japanese at that time had so much bloody money that it didn't matter to them," Thomson says.

On the new island, they developed an eighteen-hole golf course, a port and marina with a shopping area, five additional hotels, and hundreds of condos and individual villas. Today almost all tourist boats to the outer islands leave from Denarau.

I'd been told a couple of times that Denarau Island is the Waikiki of Fiji, but that analogy doesn't quite fit. Overrun as it is, Waikiki feels like a place that grew organically, and could have used a little more central planning, in fact. In spirit, Denarau is more closely aligned with a planned community in the exurbs of Las Vegas, empty desert one day and a manufactured neighborhood the next, with its ring of interchangeable hotel brands surrounding a golf course and water park, a neighborhood of private homes and the marina off to the side. There's no main street, or shopping at all outside the marina. Denarau epitomizes an inevitable outcropping of far-flung beach tourism, in which travelers leave their comfort zone at home only to ensconce themselves in another version of it at their destination. A place like Denarau lets them be far from home while never having left.

Thomson told me to take a look at the property line between the Westin and Sofitel next door. I do so, and find a steep bank rising at least four feet to the Sofitel property, in a straight line perpendicular to the shore. The Westin's land sits well below the rest of the island simply because it was already there when they raised it. This embankment shows just how much earth was hauled in to create the whole of Denarau Island.

I meet Chris Clark at the Westin's restaurant for lunch one afternoon and am surprised to find that he likes the place, because I don't. Then again, for him this outing is quotidian, in no way remarkable the way it is for me. Having traveled to the other end of the world for my tofu and tomato salad, my hopes for the cuisine are higher. We sit at a table fronting a patch of sand that has clearly been deposited from elsewhere, the telltale sign being the loose rock seawall holding it in place. After we finish eating, Chris brings out a trove of documents, old articles, letters, and photos, and we start to pore through the history of the Korolevu Beach Hotel.

As we look at a photo of one of the old bures, our Fijian waitress happens to see it as she refills our waters.

Ahh, she says, gesturing at the photo.

Do you still have those in your village? Chris asks her.

No. In my mother's village there is one. In mine, no more.

Any staff member at any resort in Fiji today will tell you that her home is made of concrete, and certainly doesn't have a thatched roof. Resorts, in fact, are the only places left in the country to still construct traditional Fijian houses. This is a running theme around the world—that beach resorts tend to use the traditional architecture of the localities in which they're based, while the localities themselves no longer do. It's one example of the practice of "reifying and aestheticizing regional differences" defined in an oft-cited paper about Caribbean culture and tourism by David Bennett and Sophie Gephardt. It is the "synthetic version of local culture" warned of in the report on Fiji tourism from the sixties.

THE BEACH RESORTS HERE HAVE REDEFINED FIJI EVEN FOR THOSE WHO live here. I'm reminded of a moment back at the Korolevu site, when we turned off the beach to get onto the old road into the property. I was taking photos, and I asked the caretaker's daughter if she wanted to take some. I was expecting to teach her how to use an iPhone, but she grabbed it from me and got right into the camera app. She took some photos of a creek and handed the phone back to me, over it.

As we continued walking, I made some small talk with her, mostly about school, but also about the Korolevu. We walked single file along one of the paths on the property that I figured her father keeps clear, and as we neared the beach again, she said to me, her tone suggesting she was trying something out that she once heard someone else say, "I live in paradise."

VATUOLALAI AND THE NAVITI RESORT

We immerse ourselves in a more recent iteration of Fijian paradise just down the road from the Korolevu. Here, Scott and I have booked into a bure at the Naviti Resort, situated on thirty-eight acres of oceanfront land and adhering to the now-standard Fiji resort format—a stand-alone thatched-roof building with an open-air lobby, freestanding bures sprinkled along the grassy lawn closest to the ocean, multistory structures farther back housing more economical accommodations, and a large, central pool that attracts far more swimmers than the bay itself. Near the road there's a golf course. In total there are 220 guest rooms.

We chose the Naviti not because of word-of-mouth recommendations or glowing reviews on Tripadvisor. In fact, we'd been warned away from the hordes of Australian children that were likely to have taken over the place at this time of year, the week before Christmas. We're staying here because soon after landing in Fiji, I met Apisalome Movono, a researcher at the University of the South Pacific, in the capital city of Suva, who has spent a significant chunk of his career studying the Naviti Resort and the adjacent village of Vatuolalai, members of which own the land on which the resort sits. The relationship now goes back half a century, to when developers set their sights on this beachfront in the early 1970s. I want to see how it plays out in the flesh, and to see for myself what happens to a place after fifty years of beach tourism.

The extra expenditure required to stay in a freestanding bure is worth it. On our little wooden porch, we gaze out past a red-flowering tree, past the grassy lawn and to the ocean itself. A bird takes an entertaining dip in one of the two birdbaths flanking our entrance. We make a cocktail with some juice bought at the resort's general store and a bottle of Absolut purchased at the duty-free a week ago. It's a pleasant, restful reprieve after a hectic few days of traveling. A hundred yards to our right, a purple wooden shack on stilts marks the point where the resort property ends and the village begins. A hundred yards to our left, the hordes of Australian children have in fact materialized by the pool. But right here, sitting on our porch, it almost feels like we are somewhere off the beaten path.

IN 1970 THE VILLAGE OF VATUOLALAI WAS ABUZZ WITH THE THRUM OF the everyday. Built up on a stretch of land overlooking a Pacific Ocean bay where the waves broke gently, its one hundred or so residents lived in homes built using wood beams and thatched roofs sourced from the local trees, bound together with coconut fiber ropes that precluded the need for nails and provided beautiful architectural detail, using a technique known as *magimagi*.

Vatuolalai was composed of two clans that coexisted as equals; one owned the land directly on the oceanfront, the other owned the land directly inland from it. Just offshore, there was a thriving reef. The villagers used the waterfront for fishing and as a source of other food, like land crabs. They used the landlocked property for farming taro and coconut, among other crops. Behind the village, hills and streams and rivers provided other sustenance. Directly to the east of the village lay its ancestral beach, central to its identity, a spot of both spirituality and leisure, and host to a thriving ecosystem. Some of the flora and fauna here were so important to the village that they became its totems. In Fijian culture, totems serve as a unique symbol of the village, a fingerprint of sorts. Village elders saw their ancestral beach as their "classroom" because, as Movono would later write, "it was where villagers would learn about the trees, birds, shrubs and natural resources that they depended on for daily consumption and specific traditional events."

The beach was a well-known turtle nesting ground. Large seabirds also used it for nesting and protection during storms. It was populated with smaller birds, too—the Peale's pigeon, the Fiji wattled honeyeater, the Fiji goshawk, and Vatuolalai's totem bird, the golden plover, which were numerous here thanks to the abundance of the fiddler crabs it fed on. The village's totem fish, the giant trevally, a silvery creature that can grow to be as big as 175 pounds, flourished just offshore, feeding on the smaller fish that, in turn, fed on the magnificent coral reef in the bay.

SINCE ANYONE COULD REMEMBER, THE TWO CLANS OF VATUOLALAI HAD collectively used their land and the water to provide for all of life's needs. They lived under the Fijian concept of *solesolevaki*, a term that, as Movono explains, refers to "the direct opposite of individualism." It dictates that everyone in a community is obliged to work together toward common ends. If a new home needed to be built, everyone pitched in. Those with construction skills put the building up, erecting wood poles or binding them together using *magimagi*. Others gathered and prepared construction materials, or cooked food for the workers. With *solesolevaki*, there was no basis for individual prosperity, because every person's well-being was bound exactly to the next person's.

On many days, the women of the village headed to the nearby rivers—fresh water was the females' domain—where they harvested their totem prawns, plus fish and eels, and gathered ferns and wild yams that grew near the river's edge. They also took advantage of their distance from the village and its men to talk freely. It was a female bonding extravaganza. When they weren't up at the river, they made oil and traps and wove mats in the village, specialized skills that had been passed down from one generation to the next.

The land and the skills and the sense of togetherness made Vatuolalai a self-sustaining community, insulated from the risks and fluctuations of the wider world. Villagers preserved many of the land crabs they caught, stored yams, and smoked fish, so that when a cyclone hit, which it inevitably would, they'd have food stores to get through it. When there was a wedding to celebrate, villagers came together to weave mats for the ceremony, source food from their land, and spend days transforming it into a feast. They made elaborate wedding costumes out of mulberry bark, decorating them with paint made from local trees.

AS LIFE PROCEEDED IN THIS MANNER, AN OPPORTUNITY PRESENTED ITSELF to the villagers. Developers wanted to build a beach resort on the village's land. The villagers were well aware of the Korolevu Beach Hotel three or so miles down the shore, currently in its heyday, attracting rich Americans and Australians to its thatched-roof bures. The lifestyles there were intriguing, the spending power they brought with them even more so.

Unlike other countries that became British colonies, in Fiji the indigenous people had their rights to land ownership enshrined early on. Since 1940, the iTaukei Land Trust Board (formerly the Native Land Trust Board) has protected and negotiated on behalf of Fijian landowners. Somewhere between 80 percent and 90 percent of the country's land is owned collectively by clans within indigenous Fijian villages. (The Korolevu was the rare Fijian resort to reside on freehold land owned by the Clark family.) Originally, land negotiations almost always involved leases for agriculture, especially sugar, but that was about to change.

Developers signed a ninety-nine-year lease with the clan that owned the waterfront land, and members began receiving periodic rental payments. For the first time, they had the purchasing power to acquire goods produced outside their immediate surroundings. Villagers in the clan not receiving the payments experienced new feelings that ran counter to *solesolevaki*, of wanting for themselves what someone else in their village had. Still, as part of the land-lease agreement, villagers from both clans would receive preferential employment at the new resort, meaning there would be opportunity all around.

As construction on the resort got under way, workers cleared the Polynesian chestnuts—the village's totem tree—until there were none left. In their place, coconut palm trees were brought in to dot the grounds and communicate the concept of paradise to tourists. One village matriarch, now in her seventies, likens that experience to having her limbs removed. A seawall was built along the length of the beach. Grass was planted to create sprawling lawns. Gradually the property stopped looking like a unique place in the world and started looking like a beach resort.

The Naviti Resort opened in 1973 and, just like that, turtle nesting became rarer on this beach. The fiddler crabs that attracted the village's totem golden plover bird disappeared, and in due course so did the golden plovers. Changes to the land caused silt to build up at the mouth of the Nahala River, which ran through the village's property, blocking its totem trevally fish from swimming upstream, where they typically laid their eggs. During heavy rains, the silt washed out into the bay, smothering the coral reef by blocking the sunlight it required to survive and grow.

Thanks to the seawall, the beach's sand began to creep away. This usually happens when such a wall gets built, which among scientists was common knowledge by the early 1970s. The sand relocated, re-assembling as two sandbars a few hundred feet offshore. Eventually the two sandbars grew into islands. At some point the resort built a wall around one of those, too, along with a wall *between* the two islands that seemed intended to serve as a breakwater. They planted grass and palm trees on them, which made them look like permanent fixtures of the landscape.

WE'RE READY FOR A SWIM AND COULD HEAD TO THE BEACH, BUT THE ONE here at the Naviti is no one's idea of fabulous. All the loungers are up on the grass, behind the seawall, because sand is in such short supply. I wonder why families from Australia, where there is no lack of

The seawall behind the beach that went in during construction of the
Naviti Resort contributed to a cascade of ecological changes.

gorgeous beaches at their disposal, choose to come here. It can't be for
the cost savings, because Fiji is by no measure a bargain.

Instead of the beach, we decide to brave the crowds at the pool.
Bula, says every Fijian who passes by us on the path. *Bula*, I say in
return. Like *aloha* in Hawaii, it's a catch-all term that would be hard
to use incorrectly.

We order cocktails at the "swim-up" bar, where we are standing,
actually, in three feet of water. The staff members running the bar
don't have any patience for small talk or niceties, although like most
other Fijians working at the resort, they also strike me as dedicated
to their work. Order placed, we sit off to the side and wait for our
drinks, conversation rendered pointless by the cacophony of sound
trapped under the dome covering this section. All of the adults are
drinking booze of one sort or another. Most of the kids are drinking
mocktails. As far as I can tell, we are the only guests from America.

Cocktails in hand, we head to the far end of the pool, where things are a little calmer. We set our drinks on the concrete edge and rest our elbows there, too. To our right, the "spa"—a hot tub that's not hot, a common amenity in these parts—is filled to overflowing with pukish green water. A sign helpfully points out that it's OUT OF ORDER. In every other direction, vacation is revved up to full throttle.

IN VATUOLALAI, THE FINANCIAL INFLUX FROM THE RESORT TRANSFORMED daily life, although as Movono will tell me when I meet him, "What we've discovered is, there's a blessing and a curse in these landowning rights." The blessing was obvious in the improved socioeconomic fortunes of the village. The curse was more complicated.

As another matriarch of the village put it, "The impact of tourism was almost immediate; one moment we were working together for the betterment of the community and the next we were working for our interests and that of our families—turning more individualistic. . . . One day we are fishing together with the catch shared equally and the next it was every fisher for herself."

Women started working at the resort when it opened, and almost immediately they lost their valued social time up at the rivers. Not too long after, they also lost their collective knowledge of how to use the river's resources to their advantage. Eventually the women of Vatuolalai no longer knew how to make oil or traps or weave mats. If they wanted oil or a mat now, they bought it. On the other hand, they now had their own purchasing power, which produced a sense of independence.

At first the village supplied lobster and other seafood to the resort. But by the 1990s, the fishing had dried up and villagers were no longer able to provide this resource. Runoff from the resort and its golf course had served as a fertilizer to an ocean algae whose increasing presence killed off some of the coral reef, in turn diminishing the availability of seafood even further. Most of the village's totems were severely curtailed, often to the point of vanishing completely.

Of the totems, one villager said, "Our totems are almost becoming legends; stories that we only tell our grandchildren."

By the late 1980s, an entire generation in the village had grown up with the resort next door, raised in an environment that prioritized individual interest over the community. The new generation didn't feel the loss of the totem animals and trees in the acute way that the older generations did, and its members barely engaged in the village's traditional activities. Villagers that continued farming focused not on a resilient variety of crops, but on those, such as cassava and sweet potato, that could be easily sold.

In the first days of 1993, Cyclone Kina hit the Coral Coast, devastating infrastructure, drowning livestock and crops, and forcing the Naviti to close for repairs. The foods the village historically relied on in the wake of a cyclone had not been prepared this time, and the villagers had no choice but to look to government handouts for survival.

In 1996 the resort built a concrete walkway out to one of the new islands. This further inhibited the natural tidal flows, damaging the remaining reef and driving the lingering fish populations still farther out to sea. Before long, the village's traditional fishing techniques, using handheld spears and casting nets, were no longer viable. Fewer people were fishing anyway, but those who did now used modern techniques. Eventually, eight in ten village households concluded that it was easier to purchase fish than it was to fish for themselves.

In 1998 villagers didn't know that they were watching the last turtle nesting that would ever occur on this beach. It was really no surprise, considering that there was hardly a beach to speak of anymore. At some point they noticed that they didn't see the Peale's pigeon or Fiji wattled honeyeater or Fiji goshawk anymore, either, along with their totem golden plover. A dam built to supply water for the resort led to the near disappearance of once-abundant freshwater prawns.

The younger villagers stopped learning the traditional dance of their village. At the resort, they performed dances from other parts of Fiji or even other Pacific nations that proved more popular with the tourists. These are the dances that now get passed down.

Today, 92 percent of the more than two hundred village residents are involved in the tourism industry, either through direct employment at the resort or an ancillary tourism business. The U.S.-based company Warwick Hotels owns the lease on the property, and in the landowning clan, each person receives up to the equivalent of about $2,000 US every year from it, doled out in incremental payments every three months. It's a nice sum in a country where the minimum wage is currently $2.68 Fijian dollars per hour, or about $1.29 US. One twentysomething man in the village explains: "My people have little to worry about; every three months there's money in the bank. If we want to work, it's there waiting for us . . . so we can afford to live the dream here." During my two weeks in Fiji, more than one person mentions that you can always tell when the land lease payments have come through because all the bars are packed. Employees of the hotel itself bring home an average of about $90 US per week, well above the minimum wage.

The new spending power has led to lifestyle changes, especially in villagers' diets. The rates of diabetes, high blood pressure, and heart problems in the village have skyrocketed. A retired hotel employee who is now diabetic notes the shift he made in his eating habits when he started working at the Naviti. "We were earning money, which allowed us to live a good life," he says, "which to us meant having the freedom and the means to eat 'good' food. . . . However, only now do I realize that the better food was what our forefathers ate." Movono says that almost two-thirds of the village households have at least one diabetic. The silver lining here is that villagers now have access to fairly advanced health care and can afford to travel to the urban centers for it.

AT BREAKFAST DURING OUR STAY, IT'S EASY TO FIND THE "GOOD" FOOD. We drink sugary juice, scarf down a pain au chocolat, and order from the omelet station. The fruit is the freshest thing on offer, though if we wanted, we could have our fill of hash browns and cereal and breakfast meats, too. It's all prepared to cater to the most common of Western palates. The eight- and nine-year-olds' eyes widen with possibility at the sheer amount of food to choose from.

For dinner we head to the adults-only restaurant, where the offerings are more refined, but still indulgent. I dine on some vague fusion of French and Italian food while listening to live music performed by a local guy with one of the most exquisite voices I can remember having heard. As a sign of its luxury, I assume, this restaurant sits overlooking the golf course, far from the children, who are not allowed.

In the morning, I stroll the grounds along the shore, thinking that I'll take a walk across the footbridge to the islands created by the seawall all those years ago. I get to the bridge only to find it in a state of disrepair so extreme that crossing it has been forbidden. On my walk back, a woman who works at the resort is clearing used dishes and other breakfast detritus from a picnic table. As all of the female employees do, she wears a red hibiscus flower tucked behind an ear. In this case, it's her left ear, which means she's taken, romantically speaking. Two Australian teenagers sit near her with their coffee cups. The woman and the teens don't seem to notice each other. They seem in fact to exist on separate planes.

When I walk around the village, I take in the church and community center, solidly built and well-maintained structures of a scale that would be unfamiliar to many Fijians. I wonder what the adoption of Christianity has done to the village's traditional ways, on top of everything else. All the homes in the village are made of concrete, with tin roofs. There are none built using traditional techniques. However picturesque those thatched-roof houses looked as part of a landscape, they typically had no windows and only a small door. Women cooked inside them over fires; they were perpetually smoky, and terrible for one's long-term health. No traditional Fijian house had a covered front porch. As a tourist, there's no way you'd want to stay in one.

I notice nice cars parked in front of a few of the homes. Some of these houses rise two stories and have fresh coats of paint. Fifteen of them were constructed by the resort. Others show more wear. Every home now has a flush toilet, and most have televisions, gas stoves, and refrigerators. The resort provides the village's water free of charge.

In the buffer zone between the resort and the village, I check out the independent businesses owned by members of both clans; they offer tours of the area, handicrafts for sale, spa services like massage and mani-pedis, and even hair braiding and henna tattoos, two ubiquitous services at beach resorts around the world, with no cultural connection to native Fijians. Most are housed in shacks built with wood and corrugated metal and painted all colors of the rainbow. Women own eleven of the fourteen. (They also make up a majority of the hotel staff.) In addition to these, I'll learn that eight of the seventeen households in the landowning clan hold exclusive contracts to provide transportation, entertainment, and on-site retail handicrafts to the Naviti Resort, ensuring more steady streams of income.

Many villagers now send their children to the better schools in the capital city, Suva. The landownership situation has resulted in an unexpected outcome—six villagers from the non-landowning clan have been motivated, perhaps through the payment imbalance between the clans, to graduate from university. One has become a lawyer. At the same time, not a single member of the landowning clan has completed his or her higher education.

When a cyclone hits, or when political instability keeps tourists away, as it did during the military coups of 1987, 2000, and 2006, the villagers find themselves out of work. Of the 2000 coup, one villager recalls that despite a 25 percent drop in tourism to Fiji and many layoffs at the resort, "We were not too discouraged because we knew we have our land and fishing grounds to fall back on. However, when we returned to the village, we realized that we didn't even have any tools such as forks, spades, knives, and fishing gear." If the resort were ever to close permanently—or be off-limits to international travelers for an entire year due to, say, a global pandemic—the village would have no fallback plan.

The villagers have lost their self-sufficiency in smaller ways, too. Today, when there's a wedding to celebrate in the village, for example, someone has to come up with something in the vicinity of 7,500 Fijian dollars, or $3,500 US, to pay for the woven mats and coconut oil and food that no one knows how to make anymore.

AS IT HAPPENS, I NEVER SWIM IN THE OCEAN AT THE NAVITI RESORT. THE beach isn't really inviting, and at high tide, a portion of the resort's ocean frontage has no beach at all. It's nothing like the beach over at Korolevu, left alone for all these years. At one time, probably a little before 1972, the two were almost identical.

We reserve a paddleboard and head out to the sandbar islands. They don't seem much used, even though there are palm trees dotting them and the brush has been semi-cleared. We climb onto one and really the only thing to do is take in the panoramic view of the resort and village. It's easy to tell where one ends and the other begins—at the border of the resort, the series of tall palm trees ends abruptly. Looking away from shore, I swear I see the nascent makings of yet another sandbar.

When we return the paddleboard, I ask the young woman manning the water activity desk about the islands. She's from Votua, the village at the end of the resort opposite Vatuolalai. She grew up looking out at this bay. Does she know when the islands emerged? I ask. She doesn't know what I'm talking about, has no idea that the two islands haven't been there forever. *We are the same*, she says, indicating with a gesture of the hand herself and then me. Meaning that neither of us knows what it was like here before the resort.

FIVE

NEW FRONTIERS, PRECARIOUS BUSINESS
Nicaragua and Senegal

NICARAGUA

Nicaragua is Costa Rica ten years ago. In the waning days of 2016, I heard this from myriad surfers and venturesome travelers ahead of a New Year's trip Scott and I had planned there. The two countries shared a Pacific Ocean seaboard, but while Costa Rica had already grown too popular for its own good, the thinking went, Nicaragua was the under-the-radar treasure. Same coastline, none of the condos. Now was the time to go.

The fortunes of the two Central American nations had long diverged for reasons rooted entirely in politics. Costa Rica upheld a successful democracy throughout the last half of the twentieth century, with tourism beginning to develop en masse in the 1980s, overtaking coffee to become the nation's top export in 1993, then eventually its biggest overall industry. Nicaragua, meanwhile, had only recently achieved the measure of political stability that generally serves as a prerequisite for tourism development. Like Costa Rica, it boasted endless beaches, ideal year-round swell for the surfers, great food, and a bikini-friendly climate. Unlike Costa Rica, a dollar could still go a long way here.

Matt Dickinson was all in. In early 2010, after a stint working in commercial real estate back home in Toronto, the twenty-seven-year-old had given himself four months to explore opportunities else-where. With the windswept tan and bleached locks of a longtime surfer, plus a perpetual smile, Dickinson—Dickie to everyone who knows him—is the kind of guy who collects friends. His enthusiasm would be cheesy if it weren't so genuine. He's just the person you'd want to go into business with, and he wanted to develop a hotel. Dickie had in fact originally planned to head to Costa Rica, but after a conversation with a friend who'd grown up there, he realized that Costa Rica's beaches had already seen enough development. *It's great there, but it's done*, his friend told him. *You missed that boat*. Dickie shifted his gaze just a bit north on the map.

By the time Dickie showed up, Nicaragua seemed like a country on the make. It enjoyed a low crime rate that, given its poverty and geographic proximity to key points in the cocaine trade, baffled even the experts. The government and the locals seemed eager to cultivate tourism. It was already the country's second-biggest industry, and it was growing. By 2013 the country would welcome over 1 million international tourists. People in New York and Los Angeles spoke of it as a place to get to before it was too late.

Nicaragua is Costa Rica ten years ago. It was becoming the unofficial tagline of Nicaraguan tourism.

After flying into Managua, Dickie made his way south to San Juan del Sur. In the 1990s, the former fishing village became one of the country's first tourist centers, as surfers were beginning to fan out along the nearby shoreline. Unlike most other countries, Nicaragua allows private ownership of beaches. It also prohibits construction within fifty meters of the high-tide line. These two restrictions meant that the best surf beaches didn't feature many accommodations. Most visitors stayed in San Juan, which is tucked into a bay with a beach but few surfable waves, then headed out to the surf spots each day in shuttle buses. One of the best of these spots was Playa Maderas.

"I remember the first day I surfed Maderas," Dickie says. "I stuck around, missed the first bus out, and so sat on the beach and watched the sun set while waiting for the next bus, and it was just beautiful. All the tourists had left and it was just like, five or six people left on the beach watching the sunset." Juxtaposed with the surf schools and sunbathers and surfeit of hotels in Costa Rican hotspots like Tamarindo and Dominical, here was that most appealing of amenities—empty coastline. He was hooked.

By the time of my own visit to the shores of Nicaragua, Dickie and two partners had opened one of the seminal resorts of the new Nicaragua travel scene. Maderas Village would play a key role in the country's emergence as a preferred destination among an influential set of international travelers, riding on what seemed like a perfect storm of newfound political stability and buzz. Like Costa Rica ten years ago.

FOR MOST OF THE TWENTIETH CENTURY, NICARAGUA SUFFERED UNDER A dictatorial dynasty—first at the hands of Anastasio Somoza García, who rigged the presidential election of 1937 in his favor, and after his assassination, by a series of family members and an associate. The dictatorship would last more than forty years, until the socialist Sandinista National Liberation Front (SNLF) seized power in 1979 from the second Anastasio Somoza. Within a couple of years, the SNLF's Daniel Ortega emerged as the country's leader, by which point many Nicaraguans of means had fled to either the United States or Costa Rica, leaving behind a population with few economic resources. Over the following decade, former members of the Somoza army organized into guerrilla groups known as the Contras, who were infamously backed by the U.S. government. The result, in effect, was civil war.

Despite the ongoing conflict, the Sandinistas set about appropriating about 40 percent of the country's arable farmland—half of which belonged to members of the former regime—along with businesses, homes, and other property. This was done in the name of wealth redistribution, but curious outcomes included Ortega seizing and occupying a 6,800-square-foot house, with grounds taking up a whole Managua city block, for himself.

Also among those properties confiscated was Montelimar, a beachfront former sugar plantation, which the Somozas had in turn confiscated from a German landowner in the 1940s, with World War II as its rationalization. Anastasio Somoza had turned the plantation into his personal estate and even built an airstrip on it for easier access—and easier escape, as it would turn out. He took off from here en route to Miami when he fled Nicaragua after the Sandinistas took over.

The Sandinistas moved right in and—with a $10 million loan from Italian investors—turned Montelimar into Nicaragua's first beach resort, an hour and change by car from Managua, looking onto a white sandy beach almost two miles long. The project echoed similar initiatives in Cuba, another country that was using high-end tourism, and especially beach tourism, to support the communist policies it forced on its citizens. In the beginning, Montelimar accepted only American dollars.

In a shock to everyone, Ortega lost reelection in 1990. With his exit, so went the civil war between the Sandinistas and Contras. That was the good news. The bad news: Nicaragua's economy was in ruins. Half of its citizens lived in poverty. In all of the Americas, only Haiti was poorer. International tourism hardly existed, with just 106,000 international arrivals that year. But now international aid money began to trickle in and, after that, foreign investment. When the price of coffee—Nicaragua's most important crop—crashed after the deregulation of the international market, the country made a deliberate turn toward tourism. In 1997, Nicaragua's minister of tourism told the *New York Times*, "We are on the brink of an awakening to tourism. We want to make tourism the main product of Nicaragua."

But the country had major reputational hurdles to overcome with travelers who associated the very name of Nicaragua with violence and lawlessness. At the country's single resort, international guests proved difficult to lure. The same year the minister of tourism spoke to the *Times*, the general manager of Montelimar spoke to the *Christian Science Monitor*, complaining that "when someone says they're thinking about vacationing in Nicaragua, people still become a little shaky."

A FEW WEEKS AFTER ARRIVING IN SAN JUAN DEL SUR, DICKIE GOT INvolved with running a modest hostel called the Dreamcatcher, up in the jungle near Playa Maderas. Then he met Dave Grossman, a New York City lawyer who'd just abandoned a bike trip through Central America, and who was eager to escape the city grind. They hit it off, and Dickie, Dave, and another partner ultimately took over the Dreamcatcher property. They acquired three more acres around it and set about turning it into what would become Maderas Village. They bought two of the three acres from a former Sandinista general who'd been given a large swath of seized land, and the other from a German stem cell doctor who'd moved to Nicaragua after being banned from practicing in Germany in the 1990s. They accepted guests in the existing main house throughout construction of the cabanas that would dot the property. Meanwhile, they navigated the Nicaraguan court system, among other reasons to sue for secure road access to the land the German doctor had sold them. Outside of court, they had to fend off a local family demanding moblike protection payments.

Grossman took on the task of sourcing wood for the construction, heading out on what he describes as "crazy, cowboy, wild-west trips" to the remote northern region of the country, which all the guide-books generally warn travelers to steer clear of. They got their wood, but the process was a nightmare. Property challenges and wood sourcing aside, the construction of Maderas Village was a relative breeze. "We were building everything in a way that was ideal for the Nicaraguan government," Dickie says. "We were like a case study of what they wanted to see more of, because we were building with sustainable materials, we were using all hurricane wood or plantation-sourced wood, using the palm leaves that regenerated so quickly. We put in the eco-septic system. And we were bringing the right crowd in. It wasn't a hostel crowd. It was people who were actually coming in and paying real money. We were hiring a lot of staff. It was a pretty ideal development for the Nicaraguan government." The engi-neering and planning were far beyond what the government required, so permitting was no problem. Maderas Village officially opened on Christmas Day 2011.

It joined Morgan's Rock, a fifteen-bungalow eco-lodge opened in 2004, and the Buena Vista Surf Club, running since 2006, as the new wave of Nicaraguan tourism, which picked up speed from there. In 2013, the ultra-luxury Mukul Resort opened fifteen or so miles up the coast, with its collection of thirty-five freestanding huts and villas on a private beach. In 2015, the Japanese-inspired Hulakai opened near Maderas Village. In 2016, a couple from the Hamptons opened Verdad Nicaragua Beach Hotel in the surf-yoga mold of Maderas Village. Montelimar remained the country's only large-scale resort, with 293 rooms and three pools, but small hotels were proliferating. In San Juan del Sur, the influx approached saturation.

Mukul was draped in more obvious luxury, but the coolest kids went to Maderas Village. Its scenic yoga studio attracted urbanites looking to reset. Its communal vibe attracted creative types look-ing to blend their artistic pursuits into their vacations. In 2015, the resort added a recording studio that would be used by members of

MGMT and Broken Social Scene. It was part hipster vacation scene, part groovier WeWork, and word was getting out.

WE TOUCHED DOWN IN NICARAGUA DURING THE LAME-DUCK PERIOD OF Obama's presidency, a time when the march of progress I'd never doubted suddenly seemed rickety. The worst might be yet to come, it turned out, and I took with me to Nicaragua the early stages of a new and more jaded perspective. Scott and I first spent a few days on Little Corn Island, off the Caribbean coast of Nicaragua. It was a difficult journey—seasickness was involved. Little Corn operates outside the primary Nicaraguan tourism industry, more Caribbean than Nicaraguan in feel and less publicized generally. Interestingly, the Corn Islands are more touristed offshoots of Nicaragua's mainland Caribbean coast, which operates as a semiautonomous zone, where English is more common than Spanish, and where tourism infrastructure is nearly nonexistent.

On New Year's Eve, we flew back to Managua and rode in a hired car the couple of hours to San Juan del Sur. The town itself exuded an expat vibe. That night we bought beers from a street vendor—the beers in Nicaragua are served gloriously cold, always—and rang in 2017 as we wandered the town's main drag, fireworks exploding in all directions. We ended up on the stairs down to the beach a bit after midnight, watching locals playing soccer on the sand.

This was my first trip to Nicaragua, but Scott had been here twice before; both times, he'd stayed at Maderas Village. For this trip, we decided after a couple of nights in San Juan del Sur to try the beachfront outside of town, which remains a tricky proposition in Nicaragua. We ended up at Playa Hermosa, with its rare shorefront hotel, an eight-room place that labeled itself an eco-lodge and would prove by turns enchanting and stifling. There were delights, to be sure: a white cow ambling down the beach during breakfast, then breaking into a jog; the perfect sand dollars emerging in the sand every time a wave rolled out; the passionfruit juice at breakfast that tasted like sunshine itself. After the sun moved behind the building in the late afternoons, the porch just off our room did a great magic hour.

But there were frustrations, as well. The advertised ceiling fan in our room turned out to be a small oscillating fan attached to the wall *near* the ceiling. At the restaurant by the hotel, they regularly ran out of tortillas, which were key to their menu, yet they forbade guests from bringing food onto the property. My bathing suits, even when I hung them out to dry, ended up smelling of mildew. The wind died down in the dead of night, just when I needed it most.

I mentioned all this to Dickie. "That's pretty par for the course," he said of Nicaragua's evolving approach to customer service. "The general attitude is almost more of this almost confrontational approach towards clientele. . . . You have to pay me for this and I'm gonna deliver this, but these are the rules. It just creates frustration."

Maderas Village managed to minimize those frustrations, and in doing so helped advance the country's appeal for travelers. Dickie believes this factored significantly in Maderas's immediate popularity.

From the start, Maderas paid above-market-rate wages to its 150 staff, a move that not only seemed fair but also cultivated trust in the owners and a broader understanding of beach tourism for the employees. The hotel paid well, "but we also demanded a lot," Dickie told me. "If people were out drinking in the garden until one thirty or two, we expected servers to stay working. If someone wanted breakfast at four p.m., they could have breakfast at four p.m. If someone wanted a cocktail at nine a.m., they could have a cocktail at nine a.m."

The country was still learning, but optimism was in the air. My visit to Nicaragua coincided with a time of speculation in beach tourism here. Everywhere, someone was looking to get in on it. At the restaurant on the Playa Hermosa, we chatted with a guy who was born in Atlanta but calls himself Nicaraguan. His family currently owned a hotel on a beach farther north. The hotel is safe, he told us, because "everybody is scared of" a friend of his family. That, apparently, was the pitch. He encouraged us to think about investing in Nicaragua. I listened to his spiel and ate my guacamole. The year following this conversation, new investment would boost the tourism industry to 12.7 percent of Nicaragua's economy. This would be the peak of beach tourism in Nicaragua.

JUST AS IT ALL CAME TOGETHER, IT FELL APART AGAIN, FOR REASONS THAT had been simmering under the surface of the nascent prosperity. Ortega had regained the presidency in 2006 in a democratic election. In the ensuing years, he increasingly showed authoritarian tendencies, which the population tolerated so long as his generous social programs continued and the economy grew, which it did, at a clip of 5 percent annually between 2013 and 2017, though it's important to note the economy was propped up in part by aid from oil-booming Venezuela.

As Venezuela got caught up in a national meltdown of its own, aid to Nicaragua began declining, from a high of $559 million US in 2014 (equivalent to almost 5 percent of its GDP) to just $30 million US in 2017. The Venezuelan money had been making Nicaragua's social programs possible. With its resources dwindling, in early 2018 the government announced pension reform that would cut benefits and raise taxes. Students came out to protest in Managua in solidarity with the senior citizens most affected by the changes. Ortega had his government respond with deadly force, cracking down on the protests and killing hundreds.

By the time I sat down with Dickie in April 2019, we weren't at Maderas Village itself, or some beachfront spot nearby. We were at a café overlooking his favorite park square in Lisbon, Portugal. Maderas had closed the previous June. Dickie and his partners thought they'd have to remain shut for July and August but expected the worst to be over by the fall. But Nicaragua now found itself a year into a new era of political upheaval. "It's a frustrating standoff right now, where it's not getting better," he told me. "The population is suffering, the economy is being strangled, it's a bad situation for everyone. All the businesses there have just been devastated."

In 2019, real GDP in Nicaragua contracted more than 5 percent, and it was expected to contract further in 2020. In the year following the uprising, tourism revenues dropped by more than 77 percent. The high-end tourists have evaporated, while the few remaining tourists are of the backpacker type that no one seems to want anymore. An estimated seventy thousand employees in the Nicaraguan tourism industry lost their jobs in the months immediately after the protests erupted. The industry to which the country had hitched its wagon had all but disappeared.

A YEAR AFTER WE MEET IN LISBON, I GET IN TOUCH WITH DICKIE AND DAVE Grossman to see if there's any news about Maderas Village. By now we're all locked down at home, thanks to COVID-19. Maderas Village is still closed, but they have hope for reopening. Between Christmas 2019 and New Year's, Grossman hosted a private gathering on the property, "just to get the wheels back on the bus a little bit," as he puts it. He estimates that before coronavirus hit, half the hotels in San Juan del Sur were reopening for business. They'd just rented the entire property to a circus school that planned to use it periodically and had arrived for the month of March. The aspiring circus performers got stuck there as the pandemic revved up and borders closed down. Someday when it's all over, "I'm going to leave a stern review about the believability of this part of the storyline," Dickie writes to me in an email.

Trapped circus school aside, even if Nicaragua solves its political problems, critical damage has been done. "We spent eight years communicating to the world that Nicaragua was a safe place to come," Dickie says. "They had made so much progress, and the people on the ground are so lovely and work so hard to earn the freedom that they were starting to appreciate. To see that be taken away from them is just devastating. The tragic characters in this aren't any of the business owners, aren't any of the foreigners like us that lost a bunch of money in the deal. . . . It's the Nicaraguan people that can't go anywhere else."

Their situation has only been exacerbated by the Ortega government's handling of the coronavirus pandemic. As it took hold in March, the president disappeared from public view for five weeks, offering no guidance or regulation. The country never implemented a lockdown, allowed large gatherings and sporting events to continue, and vastly underreported its cases and deaths, insisting it had the virus under control when clearly it did not.

Well before COVID became the prevailing topic of our time, Nicaragua experienced how uniquely vulnerable tourism can be when things get hairy in a country. It's one of the few industries that require their consumers to show up in person to the place of manufacture. If things look bad, those consumers have any number of other countries to choose as an alternative, and they show little loyalty even to places they love once they feel their personal safety is at risk. After a series of terrorist attacks in 2015, including one at a five-star beach resort along the country's Mediterranean coast, Tunisia saw its tourist numbers plummet. The Dominican Republic suffered a similar fate after tourists began coming down with a mysterious—and often deadly—sickness at resorts in 2019. Even tourism stalwarts like Mexico and Greece suffered industry declines in the face of cartel violence and debt crises, respectively.

Potentially even worse for low-income countries like Nicaragua, where tourism is just gaining a foothold, instability scares off investment. "They've made it impossible to invest in the country," says Grossman. "That's the biggest problem." There's no indication yet that Nicaragua will be able to regain the hard-won confidence of foreigners and wealthy citizens who might open their wallets. For Grossman, none of that detracts from Nicaragua's allure. "Nicaragua will forever be my number one," he says. But even he has moved on to Panama.

SENEGAL

The flight time of my trip from New York City to Dakar runs a little over seven hours, direct on Delta, and I mention this before anything else because no one I've talked to in the States can believe it's this easy, this straightforward, to go to Senegal. Assuming you live within striking distance of JFK airport, getting to the Senegalese capital is just about as complicated, and takes almost exactly the same amount of time, as getting to Paris, which people in New York have been known to do for a long weekend. *Surely you have to transfer through Europe*, they've said of this westernmost country on the African continent. *Surely it will take you at least a day to get there*, they've said. Several times, I've zoomed out on the world in Google Maps to show someone that going through Europe would make no sense, geographically speaking. I admit that before I booked the flight myself, I didn't know it was this simple, either.

The flight to Senegal isn't really the point, of course. Nor are the beaches along the country's 330 miles of Atlantic coastline, which no one back home knows about, either, nor the five-star resort at one of them that I'm booked to stay in for the first few days of the trip. The point is that for the evolving beach tourism economy that Senegal hopes to see thrive, none of this matters if no vacationer knows she can access them.

The vacationer, in this case, is one and the same as those who have often lamented to me that there are no empty beaches left in the world, that they've all already been lined with hotels or villas or ruined by industry or cities. These laments stick with me, especially later in the trip, when we'll drive up to the Maison d'Hôtes Niokobokk, a tiny resort half an hour south of the city of Saint-Louis, in the north of Senegal. The land here is so empty and so flat that the proprietor will see us coming from a kilometer away; he'll be standing out front to welcome us and inquire what we're doing here, since we haven't booked a room. We'll ask if we can buy a drink and see the beach, and he'll welcome us through to the pool in back. We'll walk down to the ocean and watch a couple of fishing boats from Saint-Louis float by. The beach is wide, windswept, completely empty of people, and featuring just enough plastic detritus to show that it isn't regularly kept up.

It's not like this only around Niokobokk. The beaches are plentiful in Senegal. Many of them are beautiful, others have great surfing, and the country has been eager to fill them with vacationers. The obvious question, then, is, Why hasn't it happened?

Countries like Nicaragua have shown that the first prerequisite for a stable tourism industry is a stable political environment. Senegal is stable, remarkably so, as the only country in continental West Africa never to have experienced a coup since it gained independence from France in 1960. Journalists often note with something like surprise that its elections lead to actual transfers of power. But beaches and a stable government do not an industry make, unless that government gets behind the infrastructure and communications necessary to make it so. The government of Senegal has talked a lot about prioritizing tourism development, but has followed through only in fits and starts.

ONE AFTERNOON WHILE EXPLORING THE SHORELINES AROUND DAKAR, I set out to see the site of the former Club Med at the tip of the Cape Verde Peninsula, on which Dakar sits. When it opened in the seventies, the Club Med lay miles outside of Dakar on untrammeled land fronting an empty nook of a beach. By the time the brand exited the property in 2009 or so, the sprawl of Dakar had subsumed it. The grounds no longer boasted a remote location, but instead presented as an urban resort. Business travelers often stayed there when they had meetings in Dakar. After Club Med departed, new management renamed the property Hotel Almadies, and quickly garnered a collection of some of the most brutal Tripadvisor reviews I've ever read. It's been slated to be renovated as a Sheraton since at least 2015.

On my way, I drive past the King Fahd Hotel, once a Meridien and now well past its prime. I drive by the American embassy, the shiniest building I've seen so far in this country, and then through a new neighborhood of contemporary mansions and slick apartment buildings still being built. Finally, I pull up to the gatehouse at the entrance of the Club Med. The guard won't let me through, but he tells me about an access point to the beach through a local market adjacent to the property. When I do gain access, I find the beach still as attractive as ever, but with the resort's wood and canvas umbrellas disintegrating in the sun. In the brush, a curved brick and concrete staircase, disembodied from the building it once serviced, has fallen on its side. The Club Med's pool is still there, empty and dusty. It's nowhere near Sheraton status. Still, I am standing at a symbolic starting point of beach tourism in Senegal, part of the first wave of development that came in the early 1970s. After independence, Senegal began looking to diversify an economy that at the time was overly reliant on its annual peanut harvests. High-end hotels began proliferating in Dakar right around the time the prime minister was making a speech at the Plaza hotel in New York City promising new incentives for tourism investment.

During this initial phase, the Hotel Teranga—now a Pullman—brought luxury accommodations to the shore near downtown, while the Hotel Diarama joined the Hotel Ngor, which hulked over the bay and its Ngor Beach. It was also near one of the first great surf waves discovered in Africa, just off Ngor Island, a quarter mile into the water. (The Hotel Ngor housed the guys in the seminal surf film *Endless Summer* during the first stop of their journey.) These were soon joined by the Club Med. Some of the most promising beachfront resort action was simultaneously developing in Casamance, the lush south-ernmost region of Senegal, which is geographically divided from the rest of the country by another country, the Gambia. Another Club Med opened there, in Cap Skirring, along with a number of other resorts that brought in French-speaking holidaygoers, especially, who were attracted by the common language and a general familiarity with Senegal as a former colony. By the early 1980s, tourist arrivals to Senegal ranked second only to Kenya in all of sub-Saharan Africa. The young industry was booming.

This would turn out to be the peak. Madji Sock, a partner in the Dakar office of Dalberg, a development consulting firm, explained to me that when a separatist movement in Casamance erupted into conflict in 1982, tourists began avoiding the region. To compensate, the area around Saly, just south of Dakar, was quickly designated as a beach vacation alternative. Saly became—and remains today—the primary beach tourism zone in the country. However, even with that successful transition, the tourism sector began to stagnate, mostly due to neglect from the government in the face of its many-pronged challenges as a young country trying to find its footing.

The neglect became more intentional when Abdoulaye Wade became Senegal's president in 2000—a position he would hold for twelve years—and openly rejected the idea of tourism as a tool for his country's prosperity. The lack of centralized support, planning, and regulation from his administration trickled down; beaches suffered and hotel properties declined, while new investment was not encouraged. Onetime luxury properties such as the Club Med and Hotel Diarama became worn out. Over the first decade of the twenty-first century, total nights spent at hotels in Senegal declined steadily.

ARRIVING IN SENEGAL, I LANDED AT THE STATE-OF-THE-ART BLAISE DIAGNE International Airport, opened in 2017 to replace the outdated and musty airport around which Dakar's urban sprawl had long encroached. This is the kind of new airport that not only eases the anxieties of tentative travelers, but also can serve as a reliable regional hub. It also happens to unload passengers safely south of Dakar, meaning that the drive to my resort in Saly, Le Lamantin, took just forty-five minutes, avoiding completely the traffic clog of the big city.

At Le Lamantin, there was fresh paint on every wall, squeaky-clean floor tiles, meticulous landscaping, excellent food (even if little of it is Senegalese), a beach raked fresh every morning, and an immaculate pool, where as I lounged a man replaced the thatched roof on a small building next to reception, the golden new stuff covering the old, which had faded to gray in the sun. Signs like these indicate a resort that is succeeding, and that has the cash flow to maintain itself.

When I left the grounds, I found that for the moment at least, other resorts along the Saly coast haven't fared as well of late. Scott and I walked along the beach, finding properties showing varying degrees of wear and tear. Their palettes seemed always drained of color, even when the pool was a bright shade of blue, or especially then. The loungers were perpetually missing their cushions, while the poolside cafés never seemed to be open.

But for the first time in a long time, certain conditions have come together that may alter the trajectory of this coastline. The key takeaway of our beach stroll is that there is once again a beach to stroll along.

By the time Macky Sall took office as president of Senegal in 2012 and promptly reprioritized tourism development, the beaches of Saly had largely disappeared. A World Bank study in 2014 estimated that 30 percent of Saly's waterfront hotels no longer had usable beaches. One of the area's popular resorts, the Hotel Espadon, would close in 2015 after the beach in front of it disappeared completely and waves began destroying its protective walls. Other oceanfront resorts struggled to survive. In addition, fishermen could no longer store their boats on the sand. Without a place to keep their boats safe, they could no longer fish. The area's entire economy didn't work without its beaches.

In 2014, the Senegalese government released its Plan for an Emerging Senegal, a strategy for economic development meant to thrust the country into the reaches of middle-income status by 2035. Of the four industries targeted in the plan, tourism was seen as the one perhaps most capable of creating jobs for the 60 percent of the population—both men and women—under the age of twenty-five. During his first term, Sall began implementing policies to make the industry more attractive to both investors and visitors. Flight taxes were cut in half in a bid to make getting to Senegal more competitively priced, and visas on arrival for tourists replaced a formerly complicated visa application system.

In 2017, the World Bank approved a $74 million loan to Senegal for a project "to create conditions necessary to increase private investment in tourism in the 'Saly' area." As a major part of the project, a Dutch firm was contracted to build breakwaters and replenish the

New breakwaters in the Saly area have helped bring robust beaches back to Senegal's most popular resort destination.

beaches with sand. The project began in late 2018 and ended in early 2021, and brought 2.8 miles of Saly coastline back from the brink—it once again has a robust sandy coastline. (It's estimated that in five to ten years, a small beach replenishment will be necessary.) The Hotel Espadon has yet to reopen, but assuming the property eventually gets back into shape, there will now be a wide beach in front of it. The breakwaters make the view toward the horizon slightly less appealing, but they have benefits in addition to keeping the sand in place. Swimmers are now protected from the full force of the ocean, and fishermen don't even need to pull their boats onto the sand anymore, as anchoring them behind the breakwaters provides protection enough.

The Saly coastline restoration project represents exactly the kind of government involvement that has been lacking for Senegal's tourism industry for much of its history, and the kind that's necessary for its survival. The result is undeniably promising, but Senegal has a long way to go in fostering its beach tourism on a number of other fronts. In April 2020, Senegal's Ministry of Tourism released its "Strategic and Operational Plan for the Development of Tourism and Air Transport" for the next five years, in which it acknowledged its shortcomings, pointing out that within the country's beach tourism industry, "the appeal of yesteryear has gradually faded," in part due to the failure to keep Saly competitive by international standards. The plan came on the heels of the country ranking 106th out of 140 countries in the World Economic Forum's 2019 Travel & Tourism Competitiveness Index. For comparison, Nicaragua ranks 91st, even accounting for its recent political problems. Of the many factors used to compile the index, Senegal ranked relatively high on Natural Resources and efforts at Environmental Sustainability. It ranked lowest on Human Resources and Labor Market, and Prioritization of Travel and Tourism.

In line with the global trend, Senegal hopes to ease reliance on the mass tourism of midrange beach resorts in favor of a tourism sector catering to high-end cultural and eco-tourism, and the expe-riential tourism that's come into vogue in the past decade. In this conception, beach resorts are meant to become one part of a more holistic whole.

To make it happen, Senegal needs to develop a training infra-structure for tourism jobs in order to harness the potential of a pop-ulation that has exploded since independence. In the early seventies, Senegal had a population of just 4 million. Today it has surpassed 17 million. Senegal has a large labor force to draw upon, one that needs to see job creation. But few within it currently have the skills in language, customer service, and technology necessary for employ-ment in the kind of high-end tourism the country is looking to create.

In my initial notes taken during this trip, I wrote: *Marketing and branding needs to . . . exist.* Senegal hasn't galvanized resources to market itself abroad as a worthy destination. That's why no one in New York knows how easy it is to get there, or that the beaches are so good and plentiful. It will take a targeted publicity campaign to change those perceptions. The 2020 plan acknowledges the need for vastly improved marketing of Senegal as an international destination, and lists its agency of tourism promotion, created in 2014 to replace a previous one that had been shut down, as a key actor in executing those goals. This agency needs to become more active, and its efforts more visible and clearly communicated, especially in English, which for better or worse remains the lingua franca of international tourism.

Senegal's tourism plan also calls for digitizing everything from hotel booking to payment options to restaurant and museum reser-vations to marketing. Outside of the biggest hotels and the most ex-pensive restaurants, credit card payment hardly exists in Senegal, and many vacations are still handled by traditional travel agents, not on-line booking systems. Scott and I were able to book our lovely room in a historic guesthouse in Saint-Louis online, but had to pay for it in cash at the end of our stay. We also had to pay in cash for our stay at a small surf camp in Dakar, for which there was no online booking system. Uber and many other app-based services for travelers have yet to launch in the country.

Senegal also needs to address the high cost of travel within the country, which hinders its competitiveness with other developing regions of the world, such as Southeast Asia, which draws tourists at least partly on the strength of its being a bargain. The little things add up quickly, such as the cheese we ordered one night in Dakar at a waterfront restaurant called Cop21 (named after a major climate change conference that took place in 2015, a strange choice considering the erosion of the shoreline directly below the terrace). We reminisce about that cheese to this day, it was so good. But like most food that tourists consume in Senegal, it was imported, and certainly cost far more here than it would have in France.

On a larger scale, poor public transportation options also often mean that hiring a car and driver is the only way to get around in comfort, further adding to the expense. Hotel rates tend to be high in Senegal because of high costs of constructing the hotel itself to international standards in a country where again, most materials need to be imported, and because debt financing costs more here than in other parts of the world that are perceived as more stable investments. Nearly every source I consulted, from Dalberg to the World Bank, noted the lack of thorough data on tourism in African countries from both their governments and outside institutions, another factor increasing the perceived risk for foreign investment—anyone relying on due diligence needs to see data, and when data is lacking, it serves as a barrier to entry.

While the New York City–to–Dakar flight is convenient, it also tends to cost as much as double a similar flight to Paris. There are several reasons for this. Countries in Africa often favor their own airlines at the expense of welcoming more flights from competitors, and they charge high taxes and fees to airlines that do serve their airports. The total price of my flight to Dakar included $139 in taxes and fees charged by the Senegalese government for things like "Infrastructure Development" and an "Immigration User Fee"—this even after the government lowered them a few years back. The taxes levied by France on a similar flight to Paris, by contrast, are just $67.50. In addition, with fewer airlines serving any given route, there is little incentive to keep prices low.

In Senegal today, there's one flight per week from Dakar to the Casamance region, and none to Saint-Louis—what exists is both expensive and inconvenient. By contrast, Southeast Asian countries began liberalizing their air control policies in the 1990s, which played no small part in the tourism boom there. Sub-Saharan Africa would benefit from an "open skies" agreement that works. A study by the International Air Transport Association found that aviation policy liberalization would lead to a decrease in fares to African countries of 25–30 percent, at the same time that traffic would increase by over 80 percent, leading to more overall revenue.

I'M SITTING AT A SMALL CAFÉ ON THE BEACH IN YOFF, A FORMER INDEPEN-dent village that has long since been absorbed into Dakar. The café is part of the Malika Surf Camp, a surf school and guesthouse owned by Marta Imarisio and Aziz Kane, an Italian-Senegalese couple who met in Aziz's home village, eleven miles up the coast, via their shared love of surfing. Marta has just made a smoothie for me and now sits down to chat for a few minutes—a rare break for her.

Marta and Aziz opened Malika in 2010. For Marta, it was a crash course in navigating a government that wasn't necessarily eager to foster her business. Her experience highlights both the challenges and the potential of beach tourism in Senegal.

"The problem is, [in Senegal] nobody's gonna tell you exactly what you have to do," she says. "And they're always going to tell you to come tomorrow. So for me, as a European, if you tell me to come tomorrow, I'm gonna come tomorrow. And if you tell me for one week to come tomorrow, I'm gonna come tomorrow every day. I didn't realize that 'come tomorrow' means you're gonna pay. Aziz would always say to me, if you pay once, they know that they can always ask you for money, so it's better to smile and wait. And this is what I did."

What could have taken one month with bribes paid took six months. Marta's business papers did eventually come through, but her experience reflects that of many people getting businesses off the ground in Senegal, who complain of, as one U.S. government document put it, "excessive and inconsistently applied bureaucratic processes, nontransparent judicial processes, and an opaque decision-making process for public tenders and contracts."

Marta has also had to learn to deal with differing views toward a woman running a business than what she was used to back in Italy. "My character was really strong and I have to learn how to talk to [locals], learn how to react, because if it's a man, and a man is maybe a little more direct, they can accept it, but not from a woman." She says that there were times when men were only willing to talk to Aziz, not to her.

When I ask her what she would like to see change in Senegal tourism, Marta says, "I would like a little more responsibility from the government," especially in creating awareness about environmental issues around the beach and ocean.

She also notes the difficulty she's had in finding surf instructors who are right for the job. "[Tourists] want surf lessons in English, and in good English, or in good French," she says. "Not everybody can speak English or French." (Despite being Senegal's official language, only about a quarter of the population can read and write in French, with Wolof being far more widely spoken. English is rarely understood.)

The Malika Surf Camp provides a great example of how even one small business can impact an area. "The surf school and surf camp bring a lot of tourists and a lot of expats that normally didn't come to Yoff," Marta says. "So there was a little bit more money into this area. At the beginning there was only one lady with a couple of tables selling fish and rice [on the beach], and now you have at least four or five ladies with like twenty tables selling fish and rice, and you have another restaurant here, another surf school here." When Malika opened, there was no electricity on the beach; now there is. In addition, this one business has created nine local jobs: Malika Surf Camp employs four surf instructors, two cooks and cleaners, one boat driver, one gardener, and one surf equipment attendant (plus a Belgian who helps out with bookings and the beach café), in addition to providing a career for Marta and Aziz.

ON SOME FRONTS, THE OPPORTUNITY FOR BEACH TOURISM HAS BEEN ALready squandered. Especially around Dakar, a city surrounded on three sides by the Atlantic Ocean, unwise and overdevelopment has caused extreme erosion. But even in Dakar, opportunity remains. There's the old Club Med that may or may not become a Sheraton. There are the surf spots that can thrive even without a sandy beach. There's Ngor Island, a charming, beachy respite from the chaos of the city proper. There's the Terrou-Bi Hotel, a five-star place with a private beach where we spend our last couple of nights in Dakar. The beach is private because the resort built it for its guests from scratch. On the terrace of the lobby bar here, a multicultural mix of men and the very occasional woman do business. I decide a number of them must be commodities traders. Honestly, it's the most interesting people-watching I've encountered at any resort in the world. Instead of surrounding myself with the standard beach vacationer, here I'm witnessing a subsection of international dealmaking that I don't typically have access to. Also, of course, there's the northern side of the peninsula, where Marta and Aziz run their business on a robust beach that still lines the shore.

Dakar is a cosmopolitan, fashionable city. Provided that it can preserve the beaches that remain, one can imagine the shores becoming something akin to the scene in Miami—a sophisticated, culturally interesting, and festive environment for a beach vacation.

Both north and south of Dakar, opportunities abound for beach tourism, thanks to endless beaches and the strides the Senegalese government has made in fostering tourism development. Good things are happening. In 2016, Senegal launched a new airline, Air Senegal, that started a nonstop flight between Dakar and New York City in 2021—competition for the Delta flight. Air Senegal's home airport so far is a success. Roads in the country have been improving.

Club Med reopened its resort in Casamance in 2010 after tensions in the regions eased. And in 2016, France lifted its advisory against travel to Casamance. More recently, Club Med has begun construction on a new resort in Nianing, nine miles south of Saly. If completed as planned, it will become the largest resort in the country. The Spanish hotel company RIU has progressed on a plan to build hundreds of new hotel rooms on Pointe Sarène, just south of Saly. The arrival of new large resorts must be met with a commitment to doing it right—ensuring responsible development that protects shorelines and making sure the resorts benefit local communities. Again, a centralized government approach will be necessary to ensure positive results.

But there's activity on the ground and optimism in the air. What remains to be seen is whether the fits and starts that have defined beach tourism in Senegal since the 1970s can, with recent renewed focus, become something more permanent.

PARADISE LOST
(TO OVERDEVELOPMENT)
Tulum, Ibiza, and Cancún

TULUM

Along the shore road in Tulum, the boutiquey beachfront du jour on Mexico's Riviera Maya, there's a haphazard sense to the buildings, like they were put up in a day and could be taken down just as quickly. Their bamboo walls and thatched roofs give them the rickety charm of an old piece of driftwood. You can't see the ocean from here, although you can sense it. The buildings instead blend into the jungle, completely al fresco affairs erected in slapdash clearings. In keeping with this shipwrecked aesthetic, which you may have already guessed to be less spontaneous than it appears, they do not accept credit cards. They give you a crappy exchange rate if you want to pay in U.S. dollars, while all the ATMs dispense only U.S. dollars. This fact rates as average in the list of things in Tulum that make no sense.

Higher on this list lies the willingness of a normally high-maintenance set of people, the types who would not hesitate to send back a hundred-dollar bottle of wine, to forgo access to hair dryers or plumbing that can handle toilet paper. Higher still: the amount of money they are willing to shell out to do so.

There is of course good reason to want to be here. The beach is a stunner, with fine white sand and water of a color that writers have long strained to describe fittingly. It drew a trickle of intrepid travelers starting in the 1980s, which famously grew into a flood over the following couple of decades. Still today, considering the overcrowded beaches to the north in Playa del Carmen and Cancún, those in Tulum can seem blissfully unpeopled. And for those besotted by wellness trends, there's yoga and vegan food and no shortage of shamans to show the way.

But if you like gluten and unaffectedness and not getting ripped off, as I do, you may spend your time in present-day Tulum in a state of prickly bemusement. Tulum has become a study in paradoxes, where "eco-resorts" run on bungalow-size diesel generators, their waste seeping through the delicate limestone ground into the vast underground river system that provides the Yucatan's main source of fresh water. Where $500 a night does not guarantee you'll have air-conditioning in your room; where in my $300 room, the water is brackish and no matter how vigorously I shampoo my hair, it never feels clean. Where the special inclusive beautiful vibe that everyone talks about only seems to function properly for attractive people.

To go to Tulum today means immersion in a Western subculture that has become widespread but that no one has yet given a proper name to, composed of some combination of hippie and hipster and yogi and foodie and burner, people eager to spend perverse amounts of money in the pursuit of low-key cool. I sit on the deck of my resort, order a mojito, and watch a parade of them, a guy strolling down the beach with both snorkel gear and a pair of Rollerblades, another wearing taut swim trunks and green cowboy boots. The drunkest guy at my hotel's beachfront bar wears a T-shirt that reads, simply, "People." A subset of women here spends a decent amount of time posing for photos. Another forgoes bikini tops. This afternoon, one woman is wearing a one-piece bathing suit pulled only halfway on.

I think of the taxi driver who brought me to Tulum. As we drew near, he described the area to me as *mucho gringo*. Looking out the window, I didn't see what he meant at first, but as soon as we turned off the main highway onto the road that goes to the beach, the vibe changed. BFFs in sundresses cycled down the bike path side by side. A couple lingered at an artfully rendered taco stand. The *mucho gringo* intensified as we reached the beach road. The taxi driver didn't linger after dropping me off.

The pageantry is a recent phenomenon here. I have a friend, Tyler Gore, who went to Tulum twenty-five years ago. Back then, he tells me, "it was just grass huts" for ten dollars a night, hammock included for sleeping, plus some cheap beer and food and "lots of semi-naked German hippies beating drums far into the night." From the beach at night, he saw more stars than he knew could be visible from Earth. He enjoyed sleeping in a hammock.

After talking to Tyler, I tracked down a *Let's Go* guide to Mexico from 1992. It mentions the busloads of day-trippers coming to look at the Tulum ruins, the remains of a great Mayan city on the shore just north of the current beachgoing epicenter. But just as Tyler remembers it, the beaches themselves featured only embryonic indications of the coming resorts, enabling travelers to "escape the conventional tourism just a short distance away." Also barely mentioned is the town of Tulum itself, some way inland. The guidebook lists five options for accommodation on the beach, all of them best for those who "don't mind minimalist conditions." If I have to guess, I'd say Tyler got his beers and food at Don Armando (on the site of present-day Hotel Zazil Kin), owned by the guy of the same name.

I have another friend, Leah Flax, who visited Tulum in 2011, staying for a week at the Amansala Resort, home of "Bikini Boot Camp." She went with her boyfriend at the time, who was the only guy there. They ate a strictly healthy diet and woke up every morning to the sound of a gong, after which they headed to the beach for a scheduled walk. Of the beach Leah says, "It was just pristine, gorgeous. The water was great. It definitely felt like paradise." Of the crowd at Amansala she says, "They were kind of basic. Wealthier, but basic."

I have yet another friend, Lionel Beehner, who headed to Tulum more recently, looking for a few days off from the New York grind. His experience? "Try spending under fifty dollars for a few nachos and guacamole."

THE OVERDEVELOPMENT CYCLE

The cycle of tourism development seen in Tulum was codified in 1980, when R. W. Butler, a geographer at the University of Ontario, published "The Concept of a Tourist Area Cycle Evolution: Implications for Management of Resources." In it, Butler defines the phases a tourist destination inevitably passes through. First comes the Exploration Stage: A small number of visitors come to an area for its natural beauty or cultural interest. There are no tourist facilities, and transportation can be arduous. Rather than locals catering to the tourists, the tourists must assimilate to a certain extent into the local culture.

With the early tourists having cultivated a known means of transportation to a place and engaged in some early word of mouth, a location enters the Involvement Stage, in which locals begin to offer services and accommodations specifically to travelers. A rudimentary "tourist area" emerges, with locals and visitors interacting heavily.

A tourism market thus established, the location enters the Development Stage. Marketing and advertising become commonplace, while "local involvement and control of development will decline rapidly. Some locally provided facilities will have disappeared, being superseded by larger, more elaborate, and more up-to-date facilities furnished by external organizations, particularly for visitor accommodation." In other words, the Hilton will now be happy to welcome you. The tourist changes during this stage as well, skewing toward honeymooners and families—those with more disposable income but less time off work than your average backpacker.

When the number of tourists comes to rival that of the local population, the location enters the Consolidation Stage, in which tourism has become a major driver of the area's economy. Stirrings of local disillusionment become evident. Older hotels come to be considered undesirable. You'll hear repeat visitors reminiscing about how much better the place used to be.

And then, Stagnation. Peak tourist numbers have been reached. Related environmental, social, and economic problems are now present. As Butler writes, "The area will have a well-established image but it will no longer be in fashion." Think the Costa Brava in Spain. Think Goa. Think Daytona Beach. Think, of course, Cancún, just up the road from Tulum.

Inevitably, the area now enters the Decline Stage. It struggles to compete with newer areas. Some tourist facilities start catering to locals (particularly hotels converted into condos or retirement homes). Locals once again participate directly in what's left of the industry. Tourists no longer think of the area as a true destination, but instead use it for short, easy trips.

At this point, some areas—but only some—enter a Rejuvenation Stage. Success requires a major pivot, as when former spa towns in the European Alps reoriented toward skiers, or when Britain revived its faded seaside resorts by shifting the focus to museums (Margate) or the tech industry (Bournemouth) or the gay community (Brighton).

The life cycle, according to Butler, is remarkably consistent across geographies and types of attractions for tourists. "The rates of growth and change may vary widely," he wrote, "but the final result will be the same in almost all cases."

I FIND MYSELF ANALYZING EVERY RESORT I COME ACROSS VIA BUTLER'S life-cycle stages. I read in William Finnegan's surfing memoir, *Barbarian Days*, about his exploring the South Pacific in the 1970s in search of a perfect wave. He and his friend find it, just off the uninhabited Fijian island of Tavarua. They pay local fishermen from the main island of Viti Levu—home of the Korolevu and Naviti resorts—to drop them off there and pick them back up a week later. There is no sign of human life on the island, save for a seldom-used fish-drying rack that Finnegan decides to use as a bed. This is what the Exploration Stage looks like. (Today the wave is well known as one of the world's best surfing waves, and has been named Restaurants, after the foreign-owned resort restaurant it breaks squarely in front of.)

I go to San Juan del Sur in Nicaragua, where international brands are starting to come in: Development Stage. I visit Nias, an island in Indonesia with another world-class surf break, which has a number of basic guesthouses owned by locals but no high-end comforts: Involvement Stage. I land on another Indonesian island, Bali, with too many hotels and way too much traffic. People still go there, but they complain about it: Stagnation Stage. No one really makes a special vacation out of Panama City anymore: Decline. Atlantic City, not for the first time, is making a play at a comeback: Rejuvenation.

Tulum today is textbook Consolidation Stage. Already in the 1990s, when my friend Tyler visited, it had entered the Involvement Stage. That's why a cabana and a hammock were available for him to rent on the beach. Had he brought a *Frommer's* with him instead of low-budget *Let's Go*, he might have discovered that a few kilometers south of his cabana, a spot called Osho Oasis had already been offering yoga retreats for the better part of a decade. (At some point renamed Maya Tulum, it's still going strong today.) Farther south still, a Mexican couple named Jose and Ana had opened their eponymous hotel in the 1980s, offering guests an early whiff of luxury along this stretch of the Yucatan coast.

In 1994, Zamas Hotel opened, providing another anchor and a nighttime scene in what would eventually become the "Tulum Hotel Zone" along the beach. By the turn of the millennium, the freeway down to Tulum from Cancún had been expanded to four lanes and word was starting to spread. A Portuguese transplant soon opened Uno Astrolodge, upping the hippie-chic luxury quotient. In 2002, along came the Amansala Resort and Bikini Boot Camp, attracting—in addition to my friend Leah—celebrities with easygoing demeanors that were belied by their ripped abs. It would also begin to accumulate a litany of complaints on Tripadvisor, with grumblings of paying $300 or $500 a night for a room with few comforts.

Coquí Coquí opened in 2003, its Argentinian-model owner providing a direct line from the New York fashion industry to Tulum, a development that would define the area in the following years. This could be considered a turning point. In 2004, there were twenty hotels on the Tulum beachfront, give or take. Then, in 2006, the road from the freeway and town to the beach hotel zone got paved and things really took off. Today there are well over one hundred hotels on the beach, mostly owned by foreigners.

Among those hundred-plus hotels, you won't find Coquí Coquí or Uno Astrolodge. Both were seized in 2016, along with fifteen other properties, by government-backed parties claiming ownership of the beachfront land on which the hotels sat. It wasn't the first time this had happened—the first such incident occurred all the way back in 2002—but this was the most sensational.

In Tulum, no one thought to challenge land ownership until the land started to be worth something. But with values skyrocketing, a number of parties might now be making claims on a single plot of land. Such claims along Tulum's beachfront zone can come from several directions. In 1973, Mexico created a system of collective farming in an effort to make use of the country's underpopulated regions. Over the years, members of the collectives sold off plots of land, sometimes once, sometimes multiple times to different parties, all of whom now believe it's rightfully theirs. Other Mexicans are claiming ownership that dates back to before the farming collectives were formed. The winners of these disputes tend to be those with the best connections to the Mexican government.

Because legal battles over property have proven so dicey, the big chains have so far kept their hands out of Tulum. A majority of the considerable profits from the resorts along the beach go to the expats who built them. It's the Consolidation Stage, yes, but so far, the shaky land ownership situation is holding off a more overtly corporate form of overdevelopment.

THANKS TO THE INFLUX OF NEW RESIDENTS ARRIVING TO WORK IN THE tourism industry, Tulum became one of the fastest-growing cities in all of Mexico. In 2000, its population stood at 6,700. By 2020, that number had nearly quintupled, to more than 33,000. Infrastructure along the beach is mostly nonexistent, while the main town has hardly kept up with the pace of new residents. As a result, the place whose marketability rests largely on its perceived eco-friendliness is in reality a budding eco-disaster. The resorts along the beach are not hooked up to the power grid—there is no power grid beyond the town. Most beach hotels run at least partially on diesel generators, an energy source better than coal, but far worse than natural gas, not to mention truly "eco" options like wind or solar power.

All those thousands of tourists also produce a lot of waste, which is where the situation really goes downhill. Tulum's landfill reached capacity a few years ago, and a new one proved inadequate. Often, trash is dumped wherever it's least likely to be noticed, deep in the jungle.

The Tulum beach resorts aren't hooked up to a sewer system, either. Patricia Beddows, an earth scientist specializing in caves and karst, and director of the Environmental Sciences Program at Northwestern University, has been researching on the Riviera Maya since the 1990s, and has seen firsthand how wastewater is handled. Beddows says that some hotels along the beach use clandestine soak-away pits, or wells that gradually let water soak back into the underground system. Other resorts have septic tanks that they pay to have emptied into tanker trunks, but don't know where the waste ends up from there. Beddows has followed trucks as they illegally dump in the jungle—a risky business on her part. "These guys are dangerous. They know what they're doing is wrong," she says. Other hotels have with the best of intentions built creative wetlands—which use a carefully calibrated biological system to treat wastewater. The problem here, Beddows says, is a complete lack of scalability. A creative wetland requires meticulous care to remain effective, and even when maintained properly the ones in Tulum don't have enough capacity to handle peak tourism seasons.

While a sewage treatment plant went in for the town of Tulum a few years back, Beddows says that across the peninsula, "some of the [sewage] plants in the Yucatan are just like large food blenders, and then they pump it down. Deep well disposal. Even if it's been fully treated and chlorinated, it doesn't matter, you are injecting massive amounts of nutrients into this groundwater system."

So a lot, if not most, of Tulum's wastewater ends up in the Yucatan Peninsula's underground water system as it weaves through vast karst caves. Beddows tells me that because the system is interconnected by rivers, it has a unique ability to spread contaminants over large distances. Over time, the nutrients introduced will wreak havoc on the system, including the region's drinking water.

"It's just absolute sadness," says Beddows, "because they are reproducing all of the 1950s technology and all the 1950s development approaches, and have not learned from history." In a nutshell, old waste

Since 2015, sargassum seaweed has often overwhelmed the beaches of the Riviera Maya. Removing it has become a never-ending project.

disposal technology involves "dilute and distribute," which typically means that minimally treated wastewater eventually gets dumped in the ocean or other bodies of water—like an underground river system. New technologies, on the other hand, employ "concentrate and contain." Done right, waste can be turned into sellable commodities, including energy. Of course, Beddows points out, the United States is hardly leading the way in adopting sustainable practices, so expecting a country with fewer resources to do so can be a bit hypocritical.

The wastewater also serves as a fertilizer for sargassum, a seaweed that has exploded along the Riviera Maya and sabotaged many a vacation. Sargassum's list of transgressions includes blocking the sun that coral reefs need to survive (as does sunscreen, unless it's the reef-safe kind), blocking newly hatched turtles from making their way from the sand to the ocean, making swimming a murky proposition, and smelling like a rotten mountain of eggs. The seaweed first showed up on the Riviera Maya in 2015 and has ebbed and flowed since then. The wastewater in Tulum actually causes the sargassum to grow after it continues on its journey, making a mess for coastal towns in the Gulf of Mexico. The stuff washing up in Tulum itself was likely fertilized first by the phosphorous- and iron-rich sand of the Sahara Desert—which is growing larger thanks to climate change—then by agricultural runoff in the Amazon Basin off the coast of Brazil once it crossed the Atlantic. The global system at work.

When we rise with the sun in Tulum one morning, workers are out there already raking it into piles. Sargassum is often removed with heavy machinery on wheels here, a practice that over time compacts the sand until it is more or less one huge block. When a big storm inevitably hits, the sand, instead of washing away gradually, breaks away in one big chunk. Sea turtles also can no longer dig nests in the dense sand. If the turtles disappear, we lose a key controller of unwanted creatures like jellyfish and sea urchins, Beddows says.

I TAKE A LONG WALK DOWN THE BEACH ONE MORNING BECAUSE I READ somewhere that a place called the Real Coconut, inside the Sanará Tulum resort, has a coconut yogurt breakfast dish that I'd be a fool to miss out on. Twenty-five minutes later I find it. I sit inside because at this late morning hour there's no escape from the sun in the outdoor seats. The coconut yogurt is fine. It comes with not enough fruit nor "supersprinkles," the restaurant's name for its homemade granola. But it's beautifully presented, and I confirm that it Instagrams well. I also order an iced latte. I leave the restaurant twenty dollars poorer.

I decide to walk back along the road, full as it is of boutiques, coffee shops, matcha tea shops, restaurants, and bars. In front of the hotel, I pass a sandwich board advertising sound healing on Friday nights, a gong bath on Saturdays. When I look it up later, the resort's website says the latter will open up your chakras and release blocked energies. Who needs a functioning sewer system in Tulum when you have access to a gong bath, I guess.

In the first shop I enter, I seek out the price tag on one of the smaller straw purses, just to gauge the scene. It's the equivalent of $280 US. I check out a couple more shops and they are all the same. The famous restaurant Hartwood isn't open, but its wood-fire oven is already going at the back of a pretty simple gravel lot with far fewer tables than I would have expected.

This roadside culinary and cocktail scene dominates the social aspect of Tulum, despite that great beach just yards away. Pedestrians like me vie with bikers, cars, and commercial trucks for their claim to the narrow, perpetually packed two-lane expanse of asphalt. There are no sidewalks and only nominally a shoulder. I feign calm and keep walking, ducking under overgrown foliage and away from the occasional motorbike.

Scott joins me partway through the trip, and at night we dip into Gitano, the cocktail bar that ushered in Tulum 2.0 when it opened in 2013. It's another outdoor space backed by the lush jungle, with the same soundtrack of mellow techno that we hear everywhere in Tulum. After cocktails, we have dinner at a restaurant called Safari. To get to it, we walk in the dark along the perilous beach road, which of course also has no streetlamps, because what would power them. The restaurant serves good Mexican fare that ends up costing us $65 US, including one cocktail each. The Tulum Beach Zone has become thoroughly removed from the greater Mexican economy—drive the few miles inland to Tulum town and a restaurant meal costs roughly a quarter as much.

Back in New York, I tell Tyler about the takeover of Tulum by the *mucho gringo* crowds, and about multipronged challenges to his vacation destination of a quarter century ago. I ask if he's surprised to learn what's become of Tulum. "I'm a little sad," he says, "but it was already . . . the fact that I was there and that German hippies were there. It was a place like that." What he means is that he recognizes that he wouldn't have been there himself twenty-five years ago if the cycle hadn't been under way already before his arrival, and if his friend Alice back in New York hadn't recommended he check it out based on her own vacation. And I wouldn't be talking to him about my own recent trip there if the development hadn't continued apace.

WRISTBANDS AND CLUBLANDS

A trip to the north of Tulum shoots us a few stages forward in the tourism development cycle. Thirty years ago, Playa del Carmen was a speck of a fishing village, nearly unpopulated, as was this entire coast before the highway running down it opened in the late 1960s. The *Let's Go* from 1992 describes it as having "little to offer the excitement hungry tourist." Today the city rises up from the sea, anchoring a coastline that welcomes nearly 5 million vacationers per year. A wall of resorts lines the beach. I spend one afternoon here during my trip and find that actually, I don't hate the place. It reminds me of Nice. The beaches, though, are struggling. Workers perpetually endeavor to clear the sargassum even as more of it lulls onto shore. At the first stretch of water I come upon, sandbags appear to be keeping the beach in place, in full view of nearby sunbathing hotel guests. To swim, one would have to climb over them. A major beach replenishment here in 2010 hasn't lasted the decade. I feel like I'm looking at an "after" photo, the "before" being Tulum's as-yet-unruined beaches.

North of Playa del Carmen, of course, lies Cancún, where I've reserved a one-night stay at an all-inclusive resort. Before the trip, I scrolled through the many resorts' online photo galleries, as well as their Tripadvisor reviews. To a one, the pictures of the rooms underwhelmed. Every so often, I came across a review that hailed a resort as a respite within the cacophony that is the "Hotel Zone," the barrier island just off the mainland where all the big resorts reside. No vacationers seemed to like Cancún but some seemed to have discovered a spot within it that can make them forget this fact. I could have picked an adults-only resort to soften the blow, but decided that if I'm going to do this, I may as well go for it, screaming kids in the pool and all. I suspect I won't be the first guest of a beachfront all-inclusive to wonder how it came to this.

IN 1936, AN AMUSEMENT PARK OPERATOR NAMED BILLY BUTLIN, A WELL-FED man with a round face and a huckster's grin, opened a "holiday camp" fit to host a thousand people on the shore of Skegness, an unfortunately named town on England's east coast, about a three-hour drive from London. The British middle classes were just warming up to the concept of the summer holiday, and Butlin thought he could harness their newfound interest. He took Henry Ford's approach to carmaking and applied it to leisure, with standardized offerings, employees focused on a single task within the operation, and a strategy of high volume making up for low margins. Those standardized offerings encompassed meals, activities, and amenities, all included in the weekly rate, the first time resort pricing had been structured in this way.

Butlin's holiday camp was a success, so much so that for its second summer in 1937, he expanded it to accommodate two thousand holidaymakers. He'd open another camp in Clacton before World War II got under way. Then troops took over his properties for the duration of the war. It's perhaps fitting that, in photos of the early Butlin camps, they often resemble barracks. The buildings skewed utilitarian, and, despite proximity to the water, ocean views were often nowhere to be found. As soon as peacetime reigned again, Butlin got back to work, reopening his original two camps and eventually running ten total, mostly in England.

Fast-forward to the summer of 1950, when a thirty-eight-year-old Belgian yoga aficionado named Gérard Blitz opened a tent village in the town of Alcúdia, on the Mediterranean island of Mallorca. He had some utopian ideas for which he wanted to provide the right atmosphere, centered on the idea that life is meant to be happy. Blitz set up two hundred army surplus tents and made them available to vacationers, who would share a communal bathroom and eat meals at square tables for eight that were designed to cultivate new acquaintances. It was a low-budget setup, but old-fashioned luxury wasn't the point.

That summer, about 2,500 people, mostly French, stayed at this, the proto Club Med. Their food and drink and on-property activities were included in the rate. In addition, Blitz hired staff to socialize with the guests, eat meals with them, party with them, and participate in all of the included activities with them. This echoed Butlin's "redcoats," staff whose primary job was to get guests involved in the activities of his camp.

The concept proved so immediately successful that Blitz partnered with Gilbert Trigano, whose company had supplied the tents, to open the first official Club Med in Salerno, Italy, in 1954. Here, as in the original incarnation, the supposedly authentic experience didn't include interactions with the communities or cultures directly abutting the Club. In fact, the "villages," as the resorts were called, appropriated cultural elements from farther afield. Grass huts replaced the tents, borrowing from the Polynesian village aesthetic introduced in Fiji and elsewhere, marking the first time these structures were implemented in Europe. In addition, staff and guests alike were encouraged to wear the Polynesian pareos available in the on-site gift store, while enjoying a vacation insulated from a less tidy exoticism just outside the property.

The 1950s were a more formal time, a fact of culture that extended to how people vacationed. Club Med sought to upend that, cultivating a reputation, as the *New York Times* would put it in 1974, as "a haven of informality and escape, a refuge for the young at heart fed up with the paunchy tie-and-jacket crowd that populates too many of Fodor's favorites." Wear your bikini to lunch? Why not. Cavort with a staff member, or "gentil organisateur," as they're called at

Club Med? The #metoo era was still decades away. The young and attractive swarmed the place, happily sleeping in tents with no electricity, no TVs, and no running water, in exchange for what they saw as a more genuine experience.

Trigano, by this time the head of Club Med, rationalized the approach to the *New York Times* in 1976, telling the reporter, "No matter how far you go, you find yourself in the same place. Proust wrote about that definitively. But after all, if the club allows each of us to know ourselves a little better, it will still be doing a big service."

Not everyone found the insularity charming. During the historic student uprisings in Paris in the summer of 1968, the Situationists, the avant-garde group that found much to disdain in the trappings of late capitalism, expressed the emerging reaction to it. They incorporated Club Med into their protest graffiti: "Club Med: A cheap holiday in other people's misery." The phrase reverberated and later made its way into the Sex Pistols' 1977 song "Holidays in the Sun."

By 1972, sixty-four Club Meds dotted the globe, alternately located on beaches and ski slopes. Blitz had long since decamped from the company's daily operations. The brand had distanced itself from the youthful anything-goes atmosphere of its early years, pivoting toward the family-friendly holidays that would become nearly synonymous with the idea of the all-inclusive resort.

The all-inclusive resort became a beach tourism staple, but its reputation didn't fare well as it evolved. Free association with the word today might bring up visions of bad buffets, rickety rooms, and color-coded wristbands to be worn for the duration of a stay. Parents of young kids, desperate for the path of least resistance and a good bargain, often seemed to be the only thing keeping them afloat. Yet stay afloat they did. One survey conducted in 1992 found that 23 percent of warm-weather vacation bookings went to all-inclusives (with 30 percent going to cruises, and the rest to traditional hotels and resorts). More recently, major hotel companies have come around to the concept, hoping to take advantage of a segment that grew 20 percent between 2014 and 2019. Hyatt launched two all-inclusive brands in 2013, and in 2019 Marriott announced plans to open its first two major all-inclusives in Mexico and the Dominican Republic at a cost of $800 million. In 2021, the company brought nineteen Blue Diamond Resorts all-inclusives into its Autograph Collection offerings.

EIGHTY MILES SOUTHEAST OF MALLORCA IN THE MEDITERRANEAN, THE ATmosphere cultivated at the proto–Club Med there has found a new outlet, as another type of beach vacationer spends her trip navigating velvet ropes and forty-dollar cover charges and the blooming crescendo of an EDM track. Given these points of interest, the beach itself isn't necessarily the destination in Ibiza; more often, it serves as the hangover recovery zone during the daytime hours, before the action shifts back indoors all over again as night descends. At the world's party beach resorts, no one is looking for paradise—more like ecstasy, in one form or another. Nowhere embodies the ethos of the beach-as-nightclub better than this once sparsely populated island, where I've just had three after-dinner drinks in my hotel room in preparation for a night out. My destination is Es Paradis, one of the seminal nightclubs on the island and the one that tonight is throwing a "paint party"—at which humans will pay a cover to get doused with paint by staff wielding enormous plastic guns.

This is the kind of innovation that Ibiza has been bringing to the nightclub space since the drug ecstasy and electronic dance music met here in the eighties, each leaning on the other to make it interesting, and together creating the island's world-famous rave culture. The first Ibiza nightclubs had opened in the early seventies, providing an alternative to the Club Med vacation just as the brand was beginning its family-friendly pivot, and celebrity-soaked Pike's Hotel came along in 1980, a few miles from shore in an early display of the secondary role the beach would come to play in the scene. These spots set a precedent of debauchery, but the next wave of clubs and DJs and drugs invented a new genre of nightlife altogether. The paint party is a twist on the foam parties that Ibiza made famous in the early 1990s, with dance floors covered in several feet of suds.

Es Paradis opens at midnight, so I aim for a 1 a.m. arrival, unfashionably early in the try-hard-to-not-care logic of nightlife, but late enough to pass, I'm hoping. I walk along the buzzing concrete beach walk in the town of San Antonio, situated in a deep bay with a man-made beach, and the town currently most responsible for Ibiza's hard-partying reputation. Along the way, I take in muscles that can't have been achieved naturally, hair extensions, and the kinds of fake eyelashes that might work on reality television but look ridiculous in person.

I'd always envisioned Ibiza as a place that exudes cool. Before landing here, I expected to be reminded of Tulum, with its carefully fashioned mellowness, or South Beach, with its overt pretension. Ibiza's reputation doesn't reflect the place on the ground today. By the nineties, hard-drinking tourists, often young and unruly and conventional, had arrived and taken over the southern half of the island, with San Antonio as their epicenter. I'm not prepared for what this town has become, which can best be described as a northern British town relocated to someplace sunny. The waitresses are English. The pubs are definitely English. All signage is in English. I'll never encounter another American during my four days on Ibiza. The tourists, I conclude, didn't actually want to leave home in England; they just wanted it to be warmer out. The restaurant and bar staff around town are noticeably more attractive than the clientele they serve, which gives the impression of a performance being put on for the tourists.

When I arrive at the club, a Subway sandwich shop's sign across from its entrance helpfully lights the street. I'm anticipating a line at the door, and am vaguely worried about how a bouncer might respond to a forty-two-year-old with flat sandals and no friends. But there is no bouncer. Instead, an English-speaking woman tells me to pay, without telling me how much to pay. The amount, I wrest from her, is 30 euros—not too bad for Ibiza, from what I understand. I pay with my card, but then the machine is out of paper. By the time we're done with the transaction, a line has indeed formed behind me.

Inside the club, several distinct seating sections and small dance areas surround a central dance floor. Multiple bars throughout the space guarantee a short wait for a drink. As mega-clubs go, this one is fairly pleasant, and as you'd expect, a world unto itself.

At a little after two, staff emerge armed with giant paint guns, which they unleash on the dance floor. I linger around the edges and avoid a direct hit, preoccupied with how the clubbers will get this stuff out of their clothes, and also how the club itself will get it off of the dance floor. The paint glows under the black lights. It seems to infuse the crowd with an extra layer of energy for dancing. Even I'm dancing now, and at some point, I realize that I'm having fun at Es Paradis. Paradise, just missing a letter; Paradise slightly askew.

YOU'LL RECALL THAT IN NINETEENTH-CENTURY MONTE CARLO, THE "BATH-ing establishment" existed merely to give cover to the drinking and the gambling. That tradition continues in Ibiza. The crowds in San Antonio aren't coming to the beach for the beach—a point driven home by the general unsightliness of the beaches around town. During a daytime wander along the waterfront, I see people sunbathing on a strip of sand at the edge of a parking lot and others doing so on top of a seawall—very Martin Parr. The beautiful beaches are outside of town, and while I see some of the prettiest turquoise seawater of my life at one of them, the effort required to get to it via bus from my hotel is only sort of worth it.

The Ibiza model eventually emerged in other locations, like Goa, the former Portuguese state in India, and in Thailand, where the full-moon party originated. These places took an early hippie scene and contorted it into a more standardized strain of hedonism. Here the party is central and the beach incidental, and in an exhibit of just how true this is, consider that the Ibiza clubs are losing business to-day not to a new, shinier beach location, but to Las Vegas, a land-locked city in the desert.

As Ibiza was perfecting the rave in Europe, over in the States college students were cultivating another form of beach party. What started out as an annual collegiate swim meet in Fort Lauderdale, Florida, by the late 1950s had evolved—or devolved, depending—into raucous weeklong parties as the first-ever generation of middle-class teenagers with disposable income came of age. The spring break tradition was here. In the early sixties, more than fifty thousand college students descended on Fort Lauderdale. By the eighties, Daytona, where indulgence was taken to new heights, became the epicenter of this new collegiate ritual, buoyed by MTV, the recently launched cable station that broadcast the mayhem to living rooms nationwide.

My own participation in spring break brought me to South Padre Island, Texas, during the spring of my sophomore year, when I was nineteen years old. By this time, in the late 1990s, spring break had taken over southern U.S. coastlines and begun migrating to Mexico—notably Cancún—and the Caribbean, where the legal drinking age tended to be more agreeable to college students.

I try to recall the appeal now, but can only remember that the beach was the vehicle for a party. I remember drinking all day and, after an early evening breather, drinking all night. I remember doing my first and only beer bong. Given this and the couple of decades that have since passed, it's perhaps not surprising that I don't remember much else. I certainly don't remember appreciating the beach.

But I was then, as I am now in Ibiza, participating in a distinct subgenre of beach vacation. The beach in this case exists to provide a communal space in which to practice a certain kind of behavior—"A modern alternative to everyday life," as Dean MacCannell puts it in his book *The Tourist: A New Theory of the Leisure Class*. MacCannell also writes, "Presumably sightseeing, along with religious fervor and patriotism, can be important for the development of a certain kind of mind." Ibiza and college spring breaks everywhere remind me that beach tourism behaves differently from other types of tourism. It's not about the development of a certain kind of mind at all. Instead it's about escape from the things that plague the mind back home.

IN EVERY SENSE OF THE WORD, CANCÚN IS A PLANNED RESORT AREA—ON the land it inhabits, nothing existed before 1970, aside from a coconut plantation. Few people had ever laid eyes on the barrier island. A 1963 *New York Times* article about the imminent building of the coastal highway makes no mention of Cancún, because in 1963 there was no Cancún.

Cancún was not a town that grew into a resort, but an empty island that the Mexican government willed into a resort town, chosen by a computer's algorithm for its ideal climate, lack of unwelcome wildlife, relative infrequency of hurricanes, and nearby labor supply. Of twenty-five finalists in the running to become the next great Mexican resort destination, preference was given to poor areas that could use the economic lift. The Yucatan Peninsula certainly fit this bill. The first resorts were built at the same time as a town on the mainland for ten thousand workers, hospital and schools included. Like Atlantic City, the city was laid out in anticipation of a beach resort well before a beach resort existed. In a move with echoes of the rail lines built for places like Monte Carlo and Atlantic City, the planners of Cancún built a new major airport to lure visitors.

Cancún's official date of birth was January 23, 1970, when the Playa Blanca resort opened. They planned for 2.5 million visitors per year. Fifty years later, the predetermined resort welcomes well more than twice that number, and is a large part of the reason that Mexico now absorbs 45 million foreign visitors per year. The city for 10,000 workers has ballooned into one of 800,000, its inhabitants lured here largely by the promise of reliable employment.

Unlike other beachy locales that have lost their original charm, there's no traveler who came to Cancún in any decade past and experienced anything but what is on offer today. In the case of Cancún, there was no Exploration or Involvement Stage. They zeroed in straight on overdevelopment.

I'LL BE STAYING IN ONE OF MORE THAN 35,000 HOTEL ROOMS IN THE beachfront Cancún Hotel Zone, at one of the forty-six all-inclusive resorts listed on Expedia. Scattered among them are a number of mega-nightclubs. The bloodline of both Club Med and Ibiza culminates here.

I get to take in the whole of the Hotel Zone on the drive from the airport. It does not tidily sync up with my expectations, which were: an anxiety-inducing concentration of people and development. I expected a "strip." I didn't expect this orderly four-lane road that leads from one sprawling resort to another, each set far back from the traffic in an arrangement that in some way resembles an English estate.

At the northern end of the island, as the van is approaching my own resort, the anticipated strip of retail and drinking establishments does materialize, although it's not the complete brain-basher it might have been. More like a mall in California.

My arrival at the Dreams Sands Cancun Resort & Spa coincides almost exactly with that of an angry, soot-colored storm coming in off the ocean. When I walk in, the lobby is a flurry of flip-flops and sun-kissed limbs. A staff member finds me, relieves me of my suitcase, and escorts me to the Club Floor, which I have apparently booked. I get checked in, head down the hall, and find my room flooded thanks to some poorly sealed windows. Back to the lounge, where the guy who checked me in goes about finding an alternate room.

While I wait, I devour a heap of buffet-style penne with cheesy tomato sauce. It's good in the way pasta is no matter where in the world you get it. Then I head for the bartender, whose margarita-making skills have just been praised by a woman who appears not to be on her first one of the day. I follow her lead and order one. It tastes like Spring Break 1997. I overcome the compulsion to have several and only drink the one, even after working through the strange logic of their being free. The logic of the all-inclusive.

It hardly seems possible that this experience is what people choose to spend $220 on—the amount of my room, all inclusive—multiplied by however many nights they end up sleeping here. But the proof is in the sheer number of guests milling about.

In my personal orbit, those most enthusiastic for Cancún have been new parents and twenty-year-olds, for entirely different reasons, one involving on-site child care and the other a legal drinking age of eighteen. Both factions seem to appreciate a good swim-up bar. At the Dreams Sands, as expected, families dominate. I imagine staying in this room, with its two double beds and general lack of privacy, as a family of four, and I could cry. This is what the Stagnation Stage does to me.

BECAUSE IT'S STORMY IN CANCÚN—LOOKING OUT THE WINDOW OF MY hotel room feels like watching a newscast during a hurricane—the lobby bar is packed, mostly with older people. All the families are recovering from the day up in their rooms, I guess. I don't even think to try Spanish first with the bartender when I ask what wines they have by the glass, and he offers white or red. We go further into it and he specifies a Cabernet or a Sauvignon Blanc. I order the latter, which is a totally decent glass of wine served in a scratched-up plastic glass.

I walk around for a while and then head back to my room. In the elevator, a neon-colored meringuey dessert has been spilled down the wall just under the floor buttons. Cleaning it would have required holding the elevator, and the elevators are too few and too small in this place to begin with. I might have left it, too.

At dinnertime, of the eight on-site restaurants, I choose the Mexican one. It almost feels like an act of defiance. As I wait for the hostess to deal with me, more people come in behind me and I feel feverish over being a party of one in this, a place where a solo traveler fits in about as well as she would at a key party. The hostess takes it in stride and leads me to a table by the window, where I can watch this storm stubbornly refuse to move on.

David Foster Wallace said the following about luxury cruise ships, but it applies here, too: the product offered is "not a service or a set of services but more like a feeling: a blend of relaxation and stim- ulation, stressless indulgence and frantic tourism . . ." That's Cancún, although the product here is less high-end than what Wallace got on his cruise. I certainly wouldn't call the food "beyond belief," as he did of his experience. It's okay in the way a nondescript Mexican restaurant that you wander into in any American city is most often okay. My tortilla soup makes me reminisce about the really great one I had in Mexico City a few years ago. I drink a Dos Equis with it.

The resort has recommended that guests stay indoors until the storm passes, so after dinner, I poke into Desires, the on-site night- club. At a little after 9 p.m., its prevailing clientele is made up of fourteen-year-olds who can't believe they're in a nightclub.

AROUND 8 A.M. THE NEXT DAY I AM STANDING IN LINE AT THE RESORT'S coffee shop. The sun is out and the air is radiating a post-storm crisp- ness. A middle-aged guy stands behind me wearing a T-shirt reading "Save Water. Drink Beer." He orders a coffee.

A little later, I take a walk down the beach and am surprised to see that two doors down from my resort, the high-rises give way to smaller condo buildings and even single-family homes. Down the beach in the other direction, Cancún's 35,000 hotel rooms stand in formation. Seawalls and walls to hold in swimming pools and walls that I can't discern the purpose of have thoroughly messed up the beach. I take a photo of a couple sunbathing on loungers in front of the Hotel Riu, a charmless white wall to their right, a seven-foot-tall stack of loungers their backdrop as they lay claim to a strip of sand that at high tide can generously be called five feet wide.

All along my walk, sargassum clogs the sand. It's currently the hardest-to-ignore repercussion of climate change on Mexico's Caribbean coast, but other, less visible problems are no less urgent. The visitor can easily achieve willful ignorance of the dying Mesoamerican Reef just offshore, the second largest in the world after the Great Barrier Reef, off Australia's coast. If she is lucky, she will also avoid firsthand experience of the storms that now hit this coast. When the algorithm chose Cancún, Category 5 hurricanes were a relative rarity along Mexico's Caribbean coast. That is no longer true. Wilma arrived in 2005, relieving Cancún of virtually its entire eight miles of beach. A $70 million beach replenishment project was required to restore the island. Still, like in Waikiki, the rampant construction of high-rise buildings and seawalls is causing severe sand erosion even when the weather is good.

At 11:58, I stand in line near the pool, waiting for the lunch buffet to open. When it does, I eat three small slices of formerly warm margherita pizza while watching staff members perform a lightly choreographed dance routine to pounding music at the edge of the pool. They try to get the swimmers in on it, with varying degrees of success. Both those participating and those avoiding it seem slightly embarrassed by the whole thing. Beyond the pool, there are no available loungers on the sand. Stake your claim to one by 10 a.m. or forget about it. The frantic stressless tourism indulgence can be a competitive realm.

SEVEN

A GLOBAL JUGGERNAUT

Vietnam and Portugal

DA NANG, VIETNAM

I arrive at night to a whirl of motorbikes and neon lights, in the fast-growing coastal city of Da Nang, in Central Vietnam. The neighborhood where I'm staying, the oceanfront My An, has gone up seemingly overnight, people will tell me. The simple, tidy room I've booked just a couple of minutes' walk from the ocean didn't exist five years ago. Before that, My An was a sleepy, sparsely populated quarter, and before that even, it served as a major hub for U.S. forces during the Vietnam War, known here as the American War. The young woman managing this little hotel tells me that the fast and furious development surrounding us caters to foreigners. The daily construction is constant—it's the first thing I notice when I arrive. Every third or so lot contains a functioning building, while all the others are pre- or mid-construction. A digital nomad scene is being cultivated here amid palm trees and surfboards, as developers hope to lure the kinds of travelers who can do their jobs from laptops anywhere in the world with strong Wi-Fi, space to concentrate, and occasional access to a printer. The idea is that they'll settle into a place like My An for weeks or months at a time. Coworking-by-the-Sea.

My An lies at the northern end of a beach that runs more or less uninterrupted for the eighteen miles between here and the World Heritage–designated town of Hoi An to the south. Until the past decade or two, the coastline was largely empty, save for the occasional fishing village or backpacker spot. Take the six-lane coastal road today and you'll see one resort after another in various stages of construction, hulking concrete masses being assembled Tetris-like into a vertical grid of hotel rooms. Each of the resorts, both present and future, has delineated its property with a perimeter wall as unfriendly as it is unsightly. Riding by one afternoon on my way to Hoi An, I notice one in particular surrounding a property in development by Indochina Capital, a major Vietnamese real estate firm. Its slogans (in English) whizz past: *A lifestyle combining natural beauty, culture, and history.* Whizz: *An emerging leisure destination in Asia.* Whizz: *Central Coast, Land of Heritage.* The vision for the Da Nang coast is being defined before my eyes.

On this coastline, arguably the epicenter of tourism development in Vietnam, the majority of foreigners come not from America or Europe, but from new centers of the global middle class. Among the high-end resorts, a sampling reveals the new Shilla Monogram catering predominantly to South Koreans, while the Crowne Plaza and its adjoining casino welcome mostly Chinese guests. The Da Nang coast in this way provides a microcosm of global beach tourism's future. Westerners invented the beach resort and spread the concept to all corners of the globe; then citizens from all corners of the globe decided to get in on the fun.

AS RECENTLY AS 1990, CHINA HAD NO MIDDLE CLASS TO SPEAK OF, AND barely a trickle of its citizens traveled beyond its borders. Since then, the transformation of Chinese society has been nothing short of "one of the most fascinating human dramas of our time," as the Brookings Institution's Cheng Li describes it. Those in the Chinese middle class or above now number more than 700 million people who bring with them a robust inquisitiveness about the world outside their borders. A people who thirty years ago had close to zero familiarity with the concept of the international vacation might have now become its biggest collective force.

Of course, that inquisitiveness would have been stifled several decades ago. Only as Chinese citizens accrued disposable income did the Chinese government gradually—if reluctantly—loosen restrictions on their access to the world. They gained the right to travel abroad in tightly controlled tour groups only in 1997. In 2000, many members of the nascent middle class received paid time off on certain national holidays such as the Chinese New Year and National Day, and a modest 10.5 million people traveled beyond China's border. In 2009, finally, the Chinese government dropped its tightest restrictions on overseas travel. At the same time, a courtship began on the receiving end, as other countries began to ease visa requirements for Chinese tourists in an effort to lure them and their new spending power. Chinese international travel grew accordingly. In 2018, 150 million Chinese people traveled abroad.

This growth has generated a windfall for the industry. In 2000, Chinese travelers spent $10 billion overseas, according to the World Tourism Organization. By 2019, that number shot up to $255 billion. By contrast, that same year U.S. citizens spent $135 billion on overseas travel, no longer the dominators of the market. The Chinese will only increase their share of the global tourism market, from 22 percent in 2017 to a projected 30 percent by 2028. This kind of national middle-class growth has happened before—in Japan in the 1960s and in South Korea in the 1990s, for example. But the sheer scale generated by China's 1.4 billion–strong population endows it with the power to remake the global tourism industry entirely.

While China has been leading the way, it is part of a phenomenon occurring around the world. India's middle class is hot on the
heels of China's, and across the Middle East, Africa, and Central and
South America, middle-class populations are popping up in longtime bastions of extreme economic inequality. Every year across the
globe, in fact, 160 million people are joining a middle class that to-
taled a whopping 3.2 billion in 2016. Another way to put this is to
say that as of 2016, 3.2 billion humans now had disposable income
with which they might choose to travel. Sometime during the last
few years, maybe while longtime travelers stood in line at an airport,
maybe while they sat in a lounger facing a white sand beach, the
scales tipped, and now there are more humans in the middle class
than outside of it.

The middle class isn't expected to expand exponentially forever—
by 2030, in fact, the growth will likely have peaked. During this time,
the mature middle classes of North America and Europe will hardly
grow at all and will come to represent less than a quarter of the entire
middle class. At the same time, India's middle class will likely grow
faster than China's. While Indian citizens are often still subjected to
strict requirements for tourist visas from other countries, including
providing tax returns and even letters from employers, these restrictions will loosen just as they have for the Chinese and help propel the
industry ever further into the forefront of the global economy.

There's no authoritative data on how much beach travel specifically contributes to the $9 trillion tourism industry, which only
emphasizes how overlooked it has been. Within the tourism industry, there are now more than 7,000 beachfront resorts, according to
STR, a data and analytics firm specializing in hospitality sectors—
not including small hotels with fewer than ten rooms and hotels that
are not directly on the beach. STR says that beachfront resorts today
average 129 rooms, significantly more than the 92 average rooms in
all hotels worldwide, which means they also employ more workers
than the average hotel, and have larger carbon footprints.

The online travel agencies (OTAs) likely have a good idea of the total number of hotels that serve beaches, but the Expedias and Booking.coms keep their databases tightly guarded. Still, a search on Booking.com for beachfront hotels and resorts in the entire state of Florida returned 419 results for beachfront properties and 712 for those with access to a beach. The same search for the country of Spain returned 285 beachfront spots and 596 with access to a beach. For Thailand, 778 beachfront hotels and resorts and 1,254 with access to a beach. That's over 2,500 beach-oriented hotels in just three destinations. In the Da Nang area, there are already 322 hotels and resorts by the beach—more, it's worth pointing out, than in Miami Beach.

MY FIRST NIGHT IN DA NANG, I TAKE A WALK AROUND MY AN TO FIND SOME dinner. A couple of blocks over, I spot a place trumpeting the familiar markers of a backpacker scene—surfboards as décor, a chalkboard menu, American indie rock. I walk in and order a veggie burger. When it arrives, I see that it is simply a burger without the meat, just a bun with some fixings, and a side of fat fries. Weirdly, it's not the worst.

First thing the next morning I head to the beach, walking the few minutes east until I hit the big road running along the coast. Even before crossing, I can see the ocean, and it feels close, but navigating all these lanes will take a couple more minutes. And then I'm on an urban, mostly empty stretch of sand. This is China Beach, where American servicemen stationed in the country during the Vietnam War would famously repair for a bout of R&R. Rather, it *was* the famous China Beach. The Vietnamese know it as My Khe, and they'd appreciate it if you'd follow their lead. Back in the war days, young soldiers would fan out from a beachfront snack bar and, fingers crossed, figure out how to chat up one of the sunbathing army nurses. Tom Yarborough, an Air Force combat pilot in Vietnam and author of the memoir *Da Nang Diary*, recalls the hedonistic atmosphere that could take hold there. Instead of the official reason of R&R, they headed to China Beach for "I&I"—Intercourse and Intoxication.

My Khe is a good beach, but nothing distinguishes it from certain other good beaches, like those long, straight, unbroken ones you find on the Jersey Shore or in Florida. The American GIs probably felt right at home here, like they could squint into the sun and forget this wasn't a good old American summer vacation. Today, just behind the beach and back across that many-laned road, a wall of new high-rises presents a united front. Most are hotels bearing names unfamiliar to the American traveler—the Rosamia, the Serene. On the former China Beach, Chinese and domestic tourists take their holidays.

From here, I take a long walk south on the beach. Occasionally I see a few of the round bamboo "basket boats" that the Vietnamese use for fishing. Less occasionally, I run into off-season vacationers in front of their resorts. Mostly I have the beach to myself. On the way back up, almost back to Da Nang, I stop at a place called Sunrise Cafe, where I order a watermelon juice that the guy makes from a

Hotels along the shorefront in Da Nang cater
mostly to Chinese and domestic tourists.

whole watermelon right in front of me. This seems like a hostel, and I'm glad I'm not staying in it. White twentysomethings sit around on the big porch overlooking the water from mismatched furniture, most of them on their phones. Next to me, surfers talk about surfing; the waves aren't good but sometimes surfers want to surf bad enough that they don't care. This is a remnant of an earlier iteration of Da Nang beachfront tourism, before the well-financed developers came to town.

BACK IN DA NANG, I'M SITTING ON THE SECOND-FLOOR TERRACE OF A REAL estate office that caters to the new influx of foreign buyers in the area. Across from me sits Peter Frieske, the firm's owner, who is in a unique position to understand what's happening on the Central Vietnamese coast. A Polish citizen married to an American woman, he came here in 2010 for an adventure. "After a year, we decided we were gonna stay two more," he tells me. A few years later still, here we are, chatting in an afternoon heat that will soon become too much for both of us. Luckily, his office is well air-conditioned.

Frieske's timing was great. Vietnam has been eagerly positioning itself to take advantage of the new global market for tourism for at least a couple of decades. In the decade following the Vietnam War the country struggled to reestablish a functioning economy. Left with an obliterated infrastructure and millions of young people killed, frozen out of both international aid and trade, with a poverty rate of 70 percent, and having suffered significant brain drain during the war and directly after, Vietnam was among the poorest nations on earth. The government slowly recognized that the situation was untenable and in 1986 implemented a program, called Doi Moi, aimed at transitioning to a market economy and liberalizing international trade. Among other initiatives, Doi Moi enabled private ownership of independent businesses.

The reforms took several years to become legally enshrined, but by the mid-1990s, poverty was decreasing. In 1994, the United States lifted its trade embargo with Vietnam. The economic progress continued and led to the beginnings of a tourism market. The first beach resort catering to foreigners opened in 1995. By 2008, more than 4 million foreigners were visiting Vietnam every year.

Then, in 2015, this country of nearly 100 million people relaxed its laws around foreign ownership of property, allowing noncitizens not only to purchase property but to purchase it with the intent to use it as a vacation rental. This final step has sent Vietnam's tourism industry off to the races. Only one country in the world—Togo—saw its tourism industry grow faster between 2015 and 2017 than Vietnam. Arrivals grew by 29 percent here in 2017 alone, to almost 13 million. In 2019, tourism accounted for nearly 9 percent of Vietnam's GDP.

Today more Chinese travelers come to Vietnam than citizens of any other country. In 2017, about 4 million Chinese traveled to Vietnam, making it their fourth-most-visited destination, after Thailand, Japan, and South Korea (with the United States in fifth place). Nowhere in Vietnam is the growing presence of Chinese tourists more visible than around Da Nang. "Central coastal Vietnam is the closest nice beach from Mainland China. So with that geographical and cultural proximity, it's a natural destination for the growing middle class," Frieske tells me. "It's been growing very quickly. I mean you see a new resort opening every three months or six months." This is despite a turbulent relationship between the two countries going back centuries, and continuing disputes over islands in the South China Sea today.

Many of the new resorts would fit right in in Cancún or Waikiki, with most of the high-end places—the Four Seasons, the InterContinental—still catering to Westerners. Others seem set on expanding our accepted notions of scale. Coco Bay, a project originally pegged for 12,000 hotel rooms over 77 acres halfway between Da Nang and Hoi An, has since been scaled down thanks in part to legal troubles with its "condo-hotel" model. Twelve thousand hotel rooms would have been an enormous amount—remember that all of Oahu, with its entrenched, mature beach tourism industry, has 27,000 hotel rooms. As the Coco Bay project evolved, it became clear to its owners that the target market would need to shift as well, from European and American tourists to those from South Korea, Japan, and China.

Farther south along the coast, past Hoi An, a $4 billion project called Hoiana is well under way—developed as a joint venture between Vietnamese firm VinaCapital, Hong Kong firm Gold Yield Enterprises, and Macau's casino player Suncity Group. They will unveil Hoiana in seven phases over thirteen years—the scale of the project brings to mind an entire metropolitan area created from the ground up. It will cover 2,400 acres and span two and a half miles of beachfront. On the grounds, visitors will find a luxury Rosewood Hotel, a major golf course, a swimming pool seemingly the size of the Central Park reservoir, if the renderings are accurate, timeshares, a condo-hotel, villas, and major shopping and conference facilities. (The opening of Hoiana's first phase was pushed from 2020 to 2021 due to the COVID-19 pandemic.) Frieske says that with the exception of the luxury Rosewood, most of Hoiana will be marketed toward mainland Chinese travelers as well.

But can the surge of development last? It's all happening on beaches with an uncertain future thanks to both climate change and the damaging by-products of the construction itself. The Vietnamese government has been slow to enact measures that might mitigate the threats to its two thousand miles of coastline, and developers have subsequently proceeded with their own short-term interests in mind. I see what the whole coastline could be in for when I visit Cua Dai Beach near Hoi An, the first in the area to be developed for resort tourism. Sandbags sit where beaches once hugged the coast. Part of a concrete walkway has snapped off into the ocean after the sand beneath it washed away. Seawalls have gone up in a haphazard manner that belies a lack of central planning. None of it is attractive, or a place where you'd want to throw down your beach towel for the afternoon.

Three factors have caused this calamity. The construction of damns on the Thu Bon River, which flows into the ocean directly next to the beach, has prevented sand deposits that normally replenish the beach from reaching it. Illegal sand mining just offshore has done the same with another natural source of sand, and additionally caused both increased flooding and erosion. Those two challenges are compounded by increasingly intense typhoons—at least four of which typically strike Vietnam every year between June and November. One particularly intense storm hit in 2014 and washed away the majority of Cua Dai Beach; despite piecemeal efforts at repair, it has struggled to hold sand ever since. Recently, prices at the resorts on this stretch have been consistently lower than at comparable resorts up the shore where the beach remains intact. At least one major resort has closed, even as others open nearby. So far, such cautionary tales have had little impact on plans for shoreline development, in Central Vietnam or elsewhere around the globe.

ONE AFTERNOON, I PULL UP IN A GRAB—SOUTHEAST ASIA'S UBER—TO THE seminal luxury beach resort on the Central Vietnamese coast, the Four Seasons Resort Hoi An, also known as the Nam Hai. As we approach, I notice that its perimeter wall is one of the more forbidding along this road. The driver pulls up to the property's gates, where I explain that I have an appointment. *An inspection?* the guard asks. Yes, exactly, sure. He lets us pass. I suspect my being white helped me gain easy entry. Inside the wall, somehow the wall seems not to exist. The grounds are lush and landscaped strategically to give the impression of going on indefinitely.

I'm here to meet Thao Nguyen, the resort's sales manager, who will be showing me the property and joining me for lunch. She takes me first to check out the beach, which goes on as far as the eye can see in either direction, with a boisterous ocean breaking against it. The most notable thing about it is the absolute emptiness, also as far as the eye can see. Aside from myself, Thao, and a groundskeeper, we are alone. We leave the beach to see the main pool, just up a flight of stairs. Here it would be hard to snag a lounge chair were I on the hunt for one, all these visitors having flown all this way from Australia and Europe and the States to get to a beachfront resort to jostle for a spot at the man-made body of water. Thao confirms that most guests prefer the pool to the beach. To be fair, it's a spectacular pool. But also to be fair, it derives none of its dazzle from being located in Vietnam.

Opened in 2006 as the Nam Hai, the property was developed by Indochina Capital, the same firm with the zingy slogans on the wall up the road. At the outset, Indochina hired Singapore-based General Hotel Management Ltd. to manage the resort. This is a common arrangement in developing countries, to bring in a foreign management company with experience attracting guests from the richest countries. Indochina Capital later sold the Nam Hai to co-buyers HPL, also based in Singapore, and ASB Development Limited, run by a major Dubai investment group. Since 2016, it's been operated as a Four Seasons, a brand essentially co-owned by Bill Gates and Saudi Arabian prince Al Waleed (the brand's founder retains a 5 percent stake). This is a resort made for Americans, built by the Vietnamese, currently owned by entities in Singapore and Dubai, and run by a company owned by an American billionaire and a Saudi prince. In the world of high-end beach resorts, it is fairly typical in this regard.

Peter Frieske tells me that for now, the majority of developers along the beach in Da Nang are domestic, but that foreign investment is growing. Right now, Vietnamese companies like Indochina Capital and Empire Group are largely dictating the direction of the Da Nang beach tourism market. However, profits from a place like the Nam Hai stream back to the elite in the urban centers of the country, bypassing the local community around the resort itself. As the industry skews toward foreign entities, more money will leave the country entirely—a phenomenon known as "leakage." In Vietnam, leakage already amounts to about 27 cents out of every dollar spent on tourism—a number that's actually far better than the average in Southeast Asia of 47 cents of every dollar, according to research by the World Bank. Still, this means that more than a quarter of tourism revenues, including those of beach resorts, leaves the country.

Much of that is taken by the international management companies. Until the past six or seven years, Frieske says, even the management companies at Da Nang's resorts tended to be local. But now, as the area enters the expansion stage, he's seeing the international brands come in. The Four Seasons and InterContinental are now joined by Pullman (an upscale brand operated by the French company Accor), the Hyatt, the Hyatt Regency, and Wyndham.

These management companies extract steep fees for their services. Let's say a Marriott opens in Vietnam, with the resort itself owned by a Vietnamese company. Marriott both operates and puts its name on the property, and in return earns an industry-standard management fee of between 2 percent and 4 percent of the property's gross revenues as a base. This is a percentage of revenues, not profit, and requires that the owner cover expenses like payroll and utility bills. Under this agreement, Marriott makes a profit from the property even if the resort itself is not profitable, a guaranteed chunk of change leaving Vietnam for Maryland, where the company is headquartered. Management agreements also often include incentive fees, which pay a percentage of revenues after a certain level of profit has been reached. Marriott is a publicly traded company, but if this scenario featured the Four Seasons instead, the management fee would ultimately be split between the fourth-richest person in the world and a Saudi prince.

Not surprisingly, Chinese businesses are becoming a presence in the hotel industry. Huazhu Group, founded in Shanghai in the mid-2000s and operating properties under brands like Joya, Orange, and

Hanting, has so far amassed a portfolio of more than 5,000 hotels on its way to becoming the fifth-biggest hotel management company in the world. Huazhu Group started by focusing on hotels within China but has been expanding internationally and going more upscale. By comparison, the world's biggest hotel management company, Marriott, operates just north of 6,500 hotels.

Since 2015, the Chinese company Fosun International has owned Club Med, that most French of resort brands. While France still comprises Club Med's biggest market, the picture is morphing. China is now Club Med's second-largest market, with six resorts there and more in the pipeline. Current Club Meds in China feature karaoke rooms and mahjong tables, two diversions popular with their growing Chinese customer base.

For the Vietnamese living around Da Nang, getting a stake in their own local beach tourism industry can be challenging in the face of so many well-funded interests. Locals here don't have strong land ownership rights. As Tuong Vu, director of the Asian Studies Program at the University of Oregon and author of *Paths to Development in Asia: South Korea, Vietnam, China, and Indonesia*, explained it to me, "The law allows the government to requisition land for various purposes, including 'development in the public interest,' but in practice, developers often make deals with local governments to acquire land at cheap prices from which they privately benefit." Because the existing land users are often cut out of the deal, on beachfronts and elsewhere, land protests have grown more common over the past few decades as Vietnam develops its economy.

This system has derailed the livelihoods of some locals who long ago started their own independent tourism businesses, like Hoa Nguyen, who opened his beloved backpacker's hostel, Hoa's Place, in 1994 on the beach south of Da Nang. When the government started moving to evict many longtime entrepreneurs in his immediate area a decade or so back, Hoa put up a fight even as other businesses accepted their fate and left their properties. In the end, he too had to leave, but in exchange for giving up his land and business, was given a plot of land nearby that measured 16 feet by 100 feet, much smaller than the footprint of his original business. On it, he had to rebuild from scratch on a reduced scale. Today at the old Hoa's Place, you'll find the four-star, 264-room Melia Danang resort, run since its 2015 opening by a Spanish company.

For other locals, things have gone differently. Thao Nguyen, the sales manager at the Four Seasons, was born and raised in Hoi An before it gained UNESCO World Heritage Site status in 1999 and became a tourist magnet. She tells me that a generation ago, someone like her would have lived by necessity with extended family into adulthood, including marriage and children. Thanks to her career with the resort, she and her husband own their own home, with individual bedrooms and modern appliances. Her pride in the resort is not affectation, and she shows not a hint of distress over the fishing village that got cleared away to make way for the Nam Hai. The job has changed the trajectory of her life. Her career at the Nam Hai started at the reception desk and ten years later, here she is, in a position I'd honestly been anticipating would be filled by a foreigner.

Thao isn't a stakeholder in the resort, but she has materially benefited from it. Hoa Nguyen, who established beachfront accommodations years before anyone else was interested in doing so, didn't fare as well, cast aside when the big companies from outside wanted to come in.

THAO TAKES ME AROUND THE FOUR SEASONS' SPRAWLING GROUNDS IN A golf cart, which she drives with a confidence that borders on recklessness. I hold on tight and feign nonchalance. We end up first at a building housing a kitchen used for cooking classes, where one is just wrapping up, the four participating hotel guests getting ready to taste their work. The kitchen is state of the art, but more Greenwich, Connecticut, than Hoi An, Vietnam.

Next she shows me a couple of the resort's villas, which are inspired by traditional Vietnamese homes, with a raised platform bed, and lower down, a lounge area. The beds are one-hundred-percent Western. I know this because a couple of days before this, I visited a traditional Vietnamese house with a bed and family shrine in the front room. A typical Vietnamese bed is indeed a platform, but one that can serve other functions during the day, with a woven bamboo mat laid over it for sleeping at night. The kinds of mattresses Westerners sleep on make no sense to the Vietnamese, who prefer the air circulation provided by the woven mat. When I saw the bed in the Vietnamese house, I expressed skepticism. The Vietnamese man showing me the place said that the Vietnamese feel the same about Western beds.

Every hotel I've stayed in, from Los Angeles to Singapore to Zanzibar, has accommodated me with a Western mattress. But a diversifying middle class also means diversifying tastes in creature comforts. Millions of Chinese travelers will expect to have their own preferences catered to. Feifei Yang, a singer and musician in New York originally from the city of Panjin, in China's Liaoning Province, conducted an informal survey for me of people she knows back home in China, to see how they approach their beach vacations. The first thing I learned is that although the Chinese, too, traditionally sleep on much harder beds than Westerners, they don't mind softer mattresses in their hotel rooms. In other ways, their expectations differ.

Answers from Feifei's friends show that the international Chinese traveler prioritizes cleanliness and luxury more so than her Western counterpart. Of the luxury, Feifei says, "Everybody's chasing that because even the middle class, or even lower than that, they always want to improve their lives' quality. That's one way to show their friends and family and show the world that they are in that [higher] class. The Chinese always take photos . . . just to show, oh, my life is beautiful, I'm fancy." When she says this, my mind shoots back to an early afternoon on the terrace at Le Sirenuse, Positano's most celebrated hotel and one where my cocktail cost 25 euros. I was joined by a Chinese couple at the next table. The guy inhabited the role of the classic Instagram boyfriend. The gal wore a strappy floral dress and a crystal-encrusted Chanel logo hair clip. They soon rose from the table and she posed at the terrace's railing holding her cocktail, Positano and the Mediterranean behind her. The photos had nothing to do with the Amalfi Coast and everything to do with the mind-bending view *as a backdrop* for a photo meant to showcase the woman.

Feifei's personal observations are confirmed by McKinsey's periodic surveys of Chinese consumers, which have found that "spending patterns of Chinese tourists overseas . . . consistently indicate a desire among Chinese shoppers for higher-quality products and services." Chinese travelers are eager, as a related McKinsey report put it, to "trade up."

Of cleanliness and orderliness, a friend of Feifei's described how preferences manifest. A musician and frequent traveler in her early thirties living in Fuxin City, in Liaoning Province in northeast China, she dislikes Bali—a common destination for the Chinese—because she finds it crowded and dirty, and prefers Phuket, Thailand, thanks to its cleanly presented upscale restaurants and varied nightlife. These preferences have little to do with the beaches themselves. Her perception may also be influenced by Thailand's moves to accommodate Chinese tourists. In 2018, for example, the country opened Chinese-only immigration lanes at its major airports, including the one on Phuket. These efforts have helped make Thailand the most popular international destination for Chinese tourists.

Feifei has noticed that the habits of younger Chinese travelers are starting to look more like their Western counterparts. "They will tend to go to somewhere not that expensive, not so commercialized, but still very beautiful," she says. And they travel more independently. Americans see Chinese tourists traveling in groups and tend to assume that they prefer it this way. But this practice is in part left over from the early days of Chinese overseas tourism, when the government only allowed tightly controlled group trips. In addition, a Chinese tourist may find comfort in a group because she speaks neither the local language nor English, the lingua franca of global travel. As the percentage of Chinese travelers that speak English grows and more locales begin to cater specifically to Mandarin speakers, group travel is losing its appeal for the Chinese. Their growing sense of independence is helped by the emergence of China's own online travel agencies, like Ctrip.com, which have empowered Mandarin speakers to plan their own vacations without the help of a traditional travel agent or tour company.

Western hotel companies are now stepping up to cater to Chinese cultural preferences. "When I first went to Hawaii, it was my first stop in America," Feifei tells me. "I was a little bit shocked because they didn't have slippers [in the room]." Today these companies likely know better. In the past few years, Hyatt, Hilton, and InterContinental Hotel Group have all launched programs to accommodate Chinese guests with—in addition to slippers in their rooms—Mandarin television stations, Mandarin speakers on staff, perpetual access to hot water for tea, payment options Chinese visitors use back home like Union Pay credit cards (the Visa or MasterCard of that country) and mobile payment apps WeChat Pay and Alipay, and areas in the hotel for groups to continue socializing when not in the restaurant—the Chinese do not share Americans' proclivity for disappearing into one's hotel room for some solitude after meals.

Feifei notes one major challenge of beach tourism for Chinese tourists. "Asian girls always try to stay pale. They don't want their skin to get dark. We hate tans," she says. You're unlikely to find a Chinese beach traveler sprawled on a lounger, soaking up the sun. In fact, a Chinese traveler will probably place amplified importance on amenities like umbrellas. The scene of Sara Murphy on the French Riviera with a string of pearls down her suntanned back would arouse no envy in this new international jet set.

ESTORIL, PORTUGAL

Scott and I have booked our second stay at the Villa Laura in Estoril, Portugal, for the first week of April 2020. In an alternate version of that year, the trip happens and we make it to the oceanfront hotel on the coast near Lisbon, one of the few we've ever loved enough to seek out again. But in this, the real version, the week of March 9 arrives in New York City to see Broadway go dark and the St. Patrick's Day Parade canceled, along with all large gatherings. Major American sports leagues shut down around the same time that Donald Trump declares a national emergency. Then schools and restaurants close. Before long, we are sheltering in place. We are thinking we'll have to postpone the trip until May. But things only get weirder, and on March 17, Europe bans most travel from the United States to European Union countries, including Portugal. Airlines cancel our flights; the Villa Laura refunds our money. It's becoming clear that we won't be going anywhere near Portugal for the foreseeable future. With the spread of a virus that didn't even have a name two months ago, the free flow of people and currency that makes the beach resort business possible has come to a screeching, astonishing halt.

For the many countries that have made international beach tourism into the central engine of their economies, the ramifications of the COVID pandemic could hardly be more grim. According to the World Travel & Tourism Council, before the pandemic, tourism contributed over half of the Maldives' total GDP. In Aruba, that number was nearly three-quarters. In Fiji, it was 34 percent. Some larger mainland countries also relied heavily on the value locked up in their shorelines. In Mexico, tourism accounted for 15 percent of GDP; in Uruguay, over 16 percent. Even in European countries with advanced economies and mature tourism industries, such as France, governments had been reimagining their tourism offerings in order to remain competitive on a global scale. Some smaller European economies, like that of Portugal, a country of just over 10 million people with more than five hundred miles of Atlantic coastline, relied even more heavily on their coastlines. Tourism there has recently accounted for 17 percent of GDP, with more than 90 percent of international tourists coming to the coasts.

Villa Laura likely wouldn't be a successful business without the arrival of international travelers. On a wider scale, the Portuguese economy doesn't work without the constant influx of sunseekers from other countries. In hindsight, the precariousness of this overreliance can seem obvious, but Portugal was simply cashing in on the same resource that had long provided its greatest economic successes. In the sixteenth and seventeenth centuries, Portugal was the richest nation on earth thanks to a vast colonial empire accrued via its maritime prowess—the coastline enabled it to sow the seeds of a globalized world. But the country never used that imperial wealth to establish economic drivers back home, and by the mid-1800s it had lost most of its influence and was the poorest country in Western Europe. In 1926 Portugal came under an isolationist dictatorship that would last almost fifty years. The economy continued to suffer, and when the Carnation Revolution toppled the regime in 1974, Portugal had the lowest per capita income in Western Europe.

Over the course of the dictatorship, a small tourism industry hummed along here without any outsize economic sway. In Estoril, a casino opened in the 1910s—another Monte Carlo imitator—establishing the town as the first seaside resort in the country, along with the neighboring town of Cascais. During World War II, European royals found refuge in Estoril, where they were cosseted by Portugal's neutrality, and lent the area a regal aura that would endure. Villa Laura sits along this coast, a onetime private retreat for a wealthy family. The first—and so far only—time we stayed in the hundred-year-old clifftop spot near the casino, it had just opened as a hotel and we were in love with it, enchanted by our room with its panoramic windows framing the blue of the Atlantic in a way that hit us as artistic, by the long table on the lawn at the top of the cliff where we had our breakfast, by the nonchalant virtuosity of its décor. It's the kind of boutique hotel that can signal a new status for a beach location. At the foot of the cliff, reached by a long and sinister stairway, we found a beachy cove. From here one could walk all the way to Cascais along the water, which I did one blustery afternoon to find that kind of ancient, pristinely preserved European town that has long given its central streets over to tourism entirely.

Villa Laura and its surroundings are a remnant of a different era of Portugal's tourism, when it was exclusively the domain of the rich. Mass beach tourism got its start here only in the 1960s, when the government encouraged development of the Algarve coast, at the southern end of the country, after seeing similar efforts succeed in neighboring Spain. Tourism grew modestly for the next several decades, until the 2008 financial crisis consumed the globe, hitting Portugal especially hard. Along with other southern European countries and Ireland, Portugal suffered a major debt crisis, and in 2011 accepted a 78 billion-euro bailout from the EU and International Monetary Fund.

With this opportunity to reset, the government resisted austerity measures and looked to tourism. It began courting low-cost airlines, with Ryanair and easyJet soon establishing routes to the country's tourist destinations. As of 2017, nearly half of international flights landing in Portugal were run by low-cost carriers, up from just 5 percent in 2002. The country also recruited foreign investment and launched marketing campaigns overseas. All this happened to coincide with the discovery of a monster surf break offshore from the town of Nazare, an anchor for the exploding popularity of surfing in Portugal, another beach tourism market where one didn't previously exist. And of course, the country had its eye on the Chinese middle class. In 2019, a direct flight launched between Beijing and Lisbon, while Portuguese officials stated a goal of attracting a million Chinese tourists per year.

As of 2019, one out of every five jobs in the country came from the tourism sector. Portugal was a new darling of international travelers. Brits were flocking to the Algarve for their beach breaks. Europeans, Brazilians, and Americans were heading to Lisbon, Porto, and its nearby beaches. With their new oil-derived riches, the monied elite from the former Portuguese colony of Angola were parking substantial amounts of wealth on the Cascais and Estoril coast. The momentum seemed fated, and unstoppable.

THEN CAME 2020. THANKS TO THE PANDEMIC, INTERNATIONAL TRAVEL WAS down 72 percent globally in the first ten months of the year. In June it was down a staggering 93 percent from the same month in 2019. Unlike some global industries that have managed to thrive in the age of COVID, tourism at its most basic level requires the movement of bodies, and bodies were in lockdown. The coronavirus pandemic has given us a visceral understanding of what happens to a tourism-dependent country when the tourism goes away.

While Portugal fared relatively well during the spring of 2020 in terms of the number of cases within its population, its tourism revenues came in only slightly better than the global average, nosediving 65 percent between January and September. After its successful containment during the first wave, Portugal reopened to many international travelers in the summer of 2020, then by the fall was on its way to becoming a virus epicenter. In January 2021, the country went into a national lockdown for the second time. Similar to many economies that are highly reliant on tourism, Portugal's GDP contracted by 7.6 percent overall in 2020. When the third wave hit in the early spring, Portugal once again closed its borders even to other EU nations. Flights from the United States, United Kingdom, and Brazil were mostly banned.

Surveying the damage, government officials have begun calling for Portugal to diversify its economy going forward to safeguard against future disruptions to the global system. For Portugal, this would mean not only moving beyond tourism, but creating more varied offerings within the tourism industry itself, a strategy that was under way before COVID but took on increased urgency after—less emphasis on beach breaks, and more on natural and cultural sights inland; steering visitors away from airports and toward destinations reachable by train; spreading tourists out so they aren't overwhelming the ecology or culture of a single place. In these ways, Portugal is looking to join the many countries that see the pandemic as an opportunity to pivot their tourism industries toward more responsible, sustainable practices.

In the summer of 2020, the pivot also meant promoting travel among its own citizens. Portugal joined any number of other countries, Vietnam included, in promoting domestic tourism as a stopgap measure. But in these less prosperous countries, there's no easy replacement for the wealth that foreigners bring with them. Considering that in 2017, Vietnam's 13 million foreign tourists collectively outspent its 73 million domestic tourists, it's clear that this plan is a Band-Aid on a bullet wound.

COVID CAME ALONG AS A SHOCK TO THE GLOBAL SYSTEM, CHANGING EVerything we thought we knew about travel in the space of a few weeks, and making the dependability of the industry's services suddenly seem slippery. It's a once-in-a-lifetime crisis, but the COVID-19 pandemic could be a sneak preview of the challenges in store for beach tourism as a result of climate change. In the case of Portugal, the country is heating up much faster than the world average, with droughts and wet periods also becoming more extreme. This is in addition to rising seas. Some researchers expect to see Portugal's summer tourist season split into two separate seasons, one in the spring and one in the early fall, as July and August become too hot for comfort. The famed golf courses in the Algarve will become less popular, in addition to the beaches. The economist Richard Tol has even suggested that those interested in Portugal real estate look to the north of the country, as the Algarve will by the end of this century become too hot for too much of the year to make sense for vacationers. In this light, the Villa Laura farther north has situated itself well. But overall, the country will have no choice but to shift its tourism offerings.

Climate change will have cascading effects that disturb the global system beyond the weather and disappearing beaches. As the changing world has begun to force many people to flee their homes for more livable lands, nationalist political movements have begun to percolate, with citizens of many countries perceiving a surge of migrants as an external threat to be squashed. Abrahm Lustgarten gave one compelling example of the domino effect wrought by climate change in a feature for the *New York Times Magazine*:

> Drought helped push many Syrians into cities before the war, worsening tensions and leading to rising discontent; crop losses led to unemployment that stoked Arab Spring uprisings in Egypt and Libya; Brexit, even, was arguably a ripple effect of the influx of migrants brought to Europe by the wars that followed. And all those effects were bound up with the movement of just two million people.

As climate change renders many highly populated areas uninhabitable, the number of climate refugees could reach into the hundreds of millions, with untold political implications. Meanwhile, in less drastic scenarios, a country's citizens may be eager to travel to Vietnam or Portugal when their own currency is strong on the global market, but if the currency weakens, they'll stay closer to home. Or travelers may lose their appetites for long-haul flights as their impact on the environment becomes harder to ignore. Or a changing political system may make travelers hesitant to implicitly condone a country's policies by traveling to it, as happened in the United States when international arrivals dropped some 4 percent in the months after Donald Trump became president. Or anti-Asian sentiment that cropped up in the wake of COVID could make those coveted Chinese tourists reluctant to head overseas.

In its most recent national election, Portugal showed signs of rising extreme right-wing populism, while Brexit has had a cascading effect on the country—the United Kingdom ranks as Portugal's largest source of tourists outside of nearby Spain, and no one knows if they'll keep coming in such large numbers as the dust on the country's exit from the European Union settles.

Which is all to say that globalism can be finicky and a tricky hook on which to peg an economy. After a record 1.5 billion international arrivals in 2019, global travel fell by a full billion arrivals in 2020 at a loss of $1.3 *trillion*, according to the UN World Travel Organization. The COVID pandemic showed the vulnerability of the industry in the starkest terms, making beach tourism an impossibility for places like Portugal and Vietnam—possibly in a foreshadowing of more permanent challenges to come as climate change accelerates.

In March 2021, I try to book a room at Villa Laura for the following autumn, but find nothing available. I try for May 2021, then March 2022. It seems they aren't accepting reservations at present. I send an email to my contact at the hotel from our previous stay, hoping for news on a planned reopening date. I receive no answer, and a couple of weeks later send a follow-up email. As of this writing, I'm still waiting for a response.

EIGHT

THE LONG HAUL
TO THE HIGH END

Sumba (Indonesia)

A counterintuitive truism of contemporary beach travel dictates that the most coveted shorelines are the hardest to reach. This holds true on the regional level. The Hamptons, of all the beaches accessible from New York City via land, take the longest to get to—those that can afford it bypass the inevitable traffic jams by taking helicopters from Manhattan. And along the French Riviera, St. Tropez is the beach you can't get to on a train. On a global level, a place that requires a final leg involving an extra boat, small plane, or multihour drive can signal the height of exclusivity. When I visited the Caribbean island of Anguilla and its coveted beaches, for example, I flew first into the crowded tourist magnet of St. Martin (called Sint Maarten on its Dutch side), and from there had arranged to take a boat for the final leg (on my return, I'd take a small plane). During my four days spent enjoying the sparse crowds on Anguilla, I met no vacationer who wasn't either working in finance, related to someone working in finance, or newly married—the hedge funders and honeymooners crowd. The inconvenience of getting there has become a form of conspicuous consumption.

This is something I consider as I WhatsApp with my butler, Simson, at the Nihi Sumba Resort, on Sumba, a remote island of 750,000 people in the Lesser Sundas of Indonesia. The resort regularly makes magazines' lists of the best hotels in the world. Two years in a row *Travel & Leisure* readers voted it their favorite on earth. A Nihi Sumba guest will want for nothing. She will sip masterful cocktails and drink thoughtfully vetted French wine. She will take in shoreline views from a mellow hilltop and walk along sand where hers are the first footprints, at least on this day. She will wash her hair with what could be the world's best shampoo—made exclusively by and for the resort to showcase the scents of the island. The Wi-Fi in her villa will never fail. She will have copious amounts of outdoor living space and indoor living space all to herself.

In Bali, with its millions of tourists and 500-plus starred hotels, a budget beach vacation can easily be found. But staying at Nihi Sumba for a week in one of Indonesia's poorest regions can cost roughly the amount I made in my first year out of college. At a place like Nihi Sumba, accessed via Bali, all but the unreasonably rich have been weeded out by the extra steps required to get there, never mind the nightly rate once they've arrived.

If this happens to be you, fair warning that you are on your own to get to the Bali airport, a far nicer place than, say, LaGuardia Airport in New York. Once on the ground, your search for the VIP lounge will be the last time you have to navigate the world by yourself for the length of your stay, because it is here, some 350 miles away from Nihi Sumba, that the resort takes you into its gentle fold. You find a good seat in the lounge, you get your cappuccino and your plate full of nasi goreng (a fried rice dish common in the region), and just as you settle in, a young Indonesian man with perfect English walks up and asks if you are Sarah. When you say yes, he seems so genuinely relieved to have found you in the terrifying tangle of this world-class airport that you almost start to believe that you wouldn't have been able to make it out alive without him.

He produces the forms required to check in to your villa, so that when you arrive at Nihi Sumba your time won't be squandered by the minutiae of paperwork and credit card holds. When you're finished checking in, the nice man tells you to relax and not worry about anything, he'll come get you when it's time to board the plane. He does, and escorts you to the gate, where as a Nihi Sumba guest you skip the line.

When the plane lands, another young Indonesian man with perfect English is waiting for you next to the baggage claim. The resort has sent two vehicles to the airport: one to whisk you away immediately, another to wait for your luggage so you don't have to. Inside your car, a chilled coconut and freshly baked bread provide much-needed sustenance, because obviously you haven't eaten since the airport lounge an hour and a half ago.

You will sip from the coconut and nibble on the bread as you ride through the town of Tambolaka, which quickly gives way to the countryside. During the ninety-minute drive, you will take things in as they whiz by: a girl balancing a bucket of water on her head, a boy rolling a tire with a stick, other little boys playing soccer. Water buffalo, dogs, one gray pig. Some small rice terraces, fields of corn. A kid washing his hair at a well. Another with a goat on a leash. The occasional ATM, and a stone carver at work. Some rather nice houses that wouldn't be out of place in a modest American suburb. A guy carrying a few enormous shoots of bamboo. A prison. A family eating dinner on its front porch. A quarry.

Children recognize the Nihi Sumba jeep and run toward the road waving furiously when they see you. You of course wave back, even though you do not know if their enthusiasm for you is genuine or pre-arranged. You've already checked in to the hotel, after all; the experience has begun. You pass a couple of horses tied up with two ropes, one on each side of their heads, to keep them from moving much or bending down to eat grass, and this will cause that momentary pang of sadness that you've learned to ignore when you see unpleasant things while traveling.

BACK TO MY BUTLER. I MUST HAVE MENTIONED TO SOMEONE ALREADY that I'm dying to see a turtle release, because the minute I step out of the vehicle, I'm introduced to Simson, who tells me I'm just in time, it's about to happen, and leads me straight down to the beach. Good thing I didn't have to check in on arrival, or worry about getting my luggage to my room, right? Nihi Sumba specializes in what has come to be known as barefoot luxury—it's laid-back here, with no overt signs of elitism—so they don't call Simson my butler, they call him my guest captain. But really, he is my butler.

I get to the beach and, after a minute spent cursing the kids for hogging the turtle release show, I swoon with delight, watching these little black hatchlings flap toward the water, then get torpedoed by an incoming wave, only to keep going. Fewer than one in one thousand will survive into adulthood, but the release nonetheless strikes me as an event of bottomless optimism.

When it's over, Simson walks me to my accommodation, gives me a tour of the place, then leaves me to settle in and freshen up before dinner. I'm staying in the cheap seats, a two-story hillside villa that during high season goes for about $2,200 per night (tax and meals included, but not drinks or extra activities). Villas closer to the beach and/or with more square footage are pricier. On the first floor, I have an outdoor living room with sofas, dining table, and minibar, an indoor air-conditioned TV room, and a half bath. There's also an achingly landscaped yard, two swish lounge chairs facing the expansive view, and a plunge pool. Upstairs, the bedroom opens onto a deck with more lounge chairs and a deep copper bathtub. The bed itself is the most dramatic one I've ever slept in, surrounded entirely by

At Nihi Sumba, one of the world's most revered beach resorts,
the villas have two levels, private pools, and multiple bathrooms.

a curtain-like mosquito net draped from the upper bars of a canopy,
twelve or so feet above the floor. Just off the bedroom, the bathroom
is entirely outdoors, entirely private, and entirely wonderful.

A little later, Simson wants to know via WhatsApp if I would
like him to get a tuk-tuk for me tomorrow when it's time to head to
the stables for my sunset horseback ride. By this time, I'm relaxing
on my second-floor deck and have lit the candles arranged around
the lounge chairs and copper bathtub. I look out to the ocean and
consider his question. A quarter moon looks back at me.

This kind of travel, if it is the norm for you, can quickly distort
your understanding of your relationship with the physical world you
inhabit. Buffered by luxury, you may come to regard the world as a
place without challenges. You may come to understand it as friction-
less. You may never experience the humbling that accompanies not
speaking the local language. You may never have the slightest idea of
what the locals really think of you. You may never develop the where-

withal to care. As long as you continue to pay good money, the locals you interact with won't mind in the slightest, or they'll pretend not to.

I take a sip of my beer and watch the last of the day disappear over the ocean and I know that I do want Simson to get me a tuk-tuk, yes. Simson always makes sure I get where I need to be, and the next day he'll let me know when it's time to go meet the tuk-tuk. When I am a couple of minutes late, he scolds me gently. Do the very rich always require such hand-holding?

MY FIRST NIGHT AT THE RESORT, I GO TO DINNER IN THE MAIN RESTAURANT, where the sand floor reminds everyone again that this is not a place to worry about things like high heels. This is the kind of place where, when people get married, the bride goes barefoot under the hem of a deceptively simple $10,000 dress. I order the cauliflower risotto, which is delicious and also, you'll notice, a contemporary twist on an Italian dish with no connection to Indonesian cuisine. I watch the young couple at the table across from me. She's English and gorgeous and he's American and strikes me as a guy who grew up reliant on but also unnerved by his own wealth. They might be on some kind of exaggerated date, but it's clear they are not in love. I'll encounter them throughout my stay, but won't ever figure out how two kids in their twenties who don't seem to know each other very well got here. She laughs often and at a decibel level that suggests a history of getting away with most behavior. He calls every male *bro*. In some ways they are emblematic of the guests here, who come from around the globe, but only sort of. I'll meet people from New York and San Francisco and Hong Kong and Perth and Melbourne and Boston, but no one from, say, Erie, or Sioux City. I'm told that guests come from Europe, too, but they're absent during my stay.

For lunch the next day, I meet Julien Laracine, Nihi Sumba's managing director, and while waiting for him I pass the time eavesdropping on a conversation at the next table involving "a micro-financing scandal" and a "stay at the Four Seasons." When Julien arrives, my objective is to figure out some details of how a resort this meticulous runs on an island with so few resources. I zero in on the cauliflower risotto. The cauliflower came from Bali. "We receive daily cargo shipments [from Bali]," he tells me. "We are running a high-end resort. Our guests are pretty easy to deal with, but fair enough, they have high expectations." Between the 70 or 80 guests at the resort at any given time, and the 380 employees, the kitchen here produces more than 1,000 meals per day. The resort is now able to source some food locally, some of the time: grains, tomatoes, fruit, chicken, eggs, and fish. But Nihi Sumba doesn't work without Bali as a resource.

Still, Nihi Sumba has made strides toward sustainability. James McBride, co-owner of the resort, dislikes the very concept of the eco-resort. "It's a gimmick," he says, "a chance to give you a shitty shower." He believes there are better ways to run sustainably without turning it into a marketing scheme.

The resort recently opened its own water-bottling plant, which desalinates water drawn from the ground on the property. According to McBride, the plant now produces four liters of potable water per second. Before the plant opened, the resort provided drinking water to guests via plastic bottles imported again from Bali. Now it provides it in reusable glass bottles—a vast improvement in terms of reducing both single-use plastic and the fuel burned to fly it over every day.

A few years ago, Nihi Sumba got hooked up to the island's power grid, and where previously it got its electricity entirely from privately owned generators, today the generators only kick in during the peak early evening hours, and account for just 20 percent of its total electric supply. The Wi-Fi at Nihi Sumba is strong and consistent, and it turns out that the Indonesian government laid fiber optic cable on the island a couple of years back, so the resort no longer has to pay for satellite internet, which was costing north of $10,000 per month.

In this way Nihi Sumba went from the least green internet source to the most.

Despite these improvements, and the resulting lowered carbon footprint, a central element of the resort's model remains stubbornly problematic: Two-thirds of Nihi Sumba's guests come from the United States, more from the West Coast than the East Coast. The long-haul flight to Bali encapsulates the biggest unaddressed problem with faraway beach tourism, and also arguably the biggest threat to it in the longer term: Long-haul flights cause more environmental damage than anything resorts are doing on the ground. For most resorts, business depends on them.

At the 2019 Asia-Pacific Sustainable Tourism Conference in Chiang Mai, Thailand, I jumped to attention when one of the panelists, Jeff Smith, vice president of sustainability for Six Senses Resorts, called air travel "an elephant in the room . . . for sustainable tourism." He didn't stop there: "If we're traveling, there are definitely carbon emissions related to that travel, and for us really to address climate as an industry, we need sustainable modes of transportation."

This fact can't be overstated. In its current manifestation, air travel negates sustainability at beach resorts. This point was driven home by a travel agency called Responsible Travel, when it released a study breaking down the carbon footprint of vacations on offer from its partners. One of them measured a trip from the United Kingdom to the Croatian island of Vis, with its ancient town and mesmeric alcove beaches. Assuming a traveler flies to Croatia en route to a seven-day holiday, his carbon imprint from the travel to get to the holiday will be more than 4.5 times that of the food and accommodation consumed while there. And that's just flying across Europe.

In the case of Nihi Sumba, the round-trip flight in coach from Los Angeles to Sumba via Bali, for example, emits somewhere around 5 metric tons of CO_2 per passenger. Compare this to the 16.5 total metric tons of CO_2 emitted by the average American per year. Or the Indonesian per capita average of just 2.2 metric tons. Consider these numbers and it won't be surprising that transport to vacation destinations accounts for roughly three-fourths of tourism's total carbon emissions.

When I speak with Smith on the phone a few weeks after the conference, I mention what he said. "I dropped that bombshell, didn't I," he says, and we have a laugh over it. Because it's true, no one in the hotel industry wants to talk about it. When I ask him to elaborate, Smith tells me that Six Senses encourages guests to offset their flights' carbon emissions, but beyond this acknowledges that solving the transportation problem doesn't fall under the company's purview. "I feel that it's legitimate that this is externalized and it's up to the airlines," he says.

Airlines of course have a responsibility to pursue innovations that will make their business less damaging. While air travel has grown more efficient on a per-flight basis, overall emissions are up sharply over the past few years thanks to an increase in global travel. More fuel-efficient planes are now being produced, and within ten years the first electric-fuel hybrid planes will likely go into commercial use. Airlines are dipping their toes into running on biofuels, the best of which might reduce emission by as much as 80 percent. United Airlines uses biofuel to at least partially power its flights out of Los Angeles. In 2020, JetBlue, Alaska Airlines, and American Airlines began using biofuels in flights out of San Francisco, and Delta announced a $1 billion effort to become carbon neutral over the course of the decade. Scandinavian Airlines plans to use biofuel in all domestic flights by 2030. The type of biofuels used matters here—those produced from palm oil, for example, are far worse than those produced from municipal waste—but for all of these airlines, the moves are a step in the right direction.

Still, air travel is decades away from true sustainability, and it doesn't fall entirely to the airlines to solve the problem of transportation's carbon footprint. Self-branded eco-resorts in Indonesia, the Maldives, Fiji, and elsewhere are marketing heavily in ways that encourage long-haul flights. Six Senses isn't exactly steering potential guests to book the resort closest to home. I can imagine a day when the damaging nature of the flights to get to Nihi Sumba represents the biggest threat to the resort's continuing success, regardless of the good work the resort does on the ground.

WITHOUT THE SERVICES PROVIDED BY NIHI SUMBA AND WITHOUT THE easy flights to the island, one might find it nearly impossible to reach this southern coast of Sumba. One might, in fact, experience echoes of what Claude and Petra Graves did when they arrived for the first time in 1988. He was a surfer, she wasn't, and they wanted to find a place to build a resort where they would both be happy. They'd identified their nonnegotiable criteria: an island too big to be circumnavigated by foot in an afternoon, with good sand quality, a natural channel for boats coming in and out, a nearby surf break, good fishing, and good diving; they needed it to be sparsely populated, but with an interesting local culture, a landscape with hills and contours, a beach contained by headlands on either side, and a location within four hundred miles of a major airport—in Indonesia, this likely meant four hundred miles from Bali. They needed a place where, taking all its characteristics together, guests would want to stay for a couple of weeks. Claude and Petra identified five places around the world that might fit the bill, and with his life savings (and eventually, some additional investment from his family), they set out to explore them. Sumba was their first stop.

I sit with Claude Graves at Nihi Sumba's bar one night while he tells me the whole story. After making it to the island, they hiked eighty miles of the shoreline looking for a perfect spot. In these pre–Google Maps days, "I was working off an 1880 Dutch chart, which was actually quite accurate," Claude says. The three local tribes along this coast were on hostile terms, so a man from one tribe wouldn't step onto the land of another, for fear of reprisal. For Claude and

Petra this meant securing a new local crew at each change of territory. They were able to hire one man who had good relations with all three tribes. When they'd reach a new territory, the current crew would return home while the intermediary would go ahead to the next tribe to round up some new guides.

They discovered one empty beach after another. The locals were, according to Claude, "scared shitless of the water. They're not a fishing culture, which is surprising for an island." They in fact mostly steered clear of the beaches altogether, leaving them pristine. "When we got here, it was like the spitting image of what we had in our minds," says Claude. They found one beach on this southern coast of the island facing the Indian Ocean, with soft sand, a killer surf break, protective headlands on either side, and a backdrop of hills.

They never scouted out the remaining four destinations on their itinerary. They went back to Seattle, where they'd been living, put everything in storage, and got all the gear they'd need to live on the beach in Sumba while they plotted their resort—gas lanterns and fishing poles and cases of wine and a Zodiac boat. They were ready to do their own stitches if someone got cut up. They also had their back molars removed, which made chewing certain foods difficult, but prevented potential urgent medical situations: "No hospitals. There was nothing here. If shit went wrong you were fucked up," says Claude.

It took two and a half days to get back to their chosen beach from Bali. Once there, Claude and Petra would stay on for the first year and a half living in a shelter they'd build with a grass roof and no walls, just behind the present-day main restaurant. They had no nails, but built tables by lashing bamboo stalks together. They got water from a nearby creek and fed it through filters they'd brought along. The wine ran out after the first couple of months. A year in, they got a kerosene refrigerator, and could suddenly save the fish they caught and drink a cold beer during the hot evenings. Three or so times a year, someone would come visit from Bali, but mostly it was just Claude and Petra, fishing first thing in the morning and again at sunset, taking extra catch up to one of the villages, which helped them ingratiate themselves. Claude usually got a few surfing sessions in. "Life was sunrise to an hour after sunset," he says. They lived on the shore here for years, gradually piecing together some modern conveniences.

They were trying to secure some of the oceanfront land, but the locals didn't understand the beach resort concept. "So I took some of the more senior guys [in the nearby tribes] to Bali for a few days so they could come back and see what we were talking about," says Claude. In this part of Sumba, water buffalo, not cash, was currency. "We had to swap buffalo for land," he says, "so we had to go get buffalo and figure out the value." It took them four years to secure the land they needed. During that time, they lost count of how many times they got malaria.

They built a road into the property—the first in the area. They started clearing the land and rehabilitating it after the slash-and-burn farming that had been going on for ages. They hired locals to work on the project. "Trying to create a work ethic was probably the hardest thing," Claude says. "Nobody had watches, nobody had any concept of working for money. Or a proper eight-hour day—what was that?"

The resort's opening—it was called Nihiwatu in the early years—was thwarted by the Asian financial crisis of 1997 and then an earthquake that destroyed most of what they'd built. They rebuilt and opened, finally, in 2000, right around the time the island's airport opened. But then came 9/11, and then the bombing in Bali in 2002. "It really wasn't until 2005 that we had our first full season," Claude says—seventeen years after they first arrived on Sumba in 1988.

As Claude and I chat, someone arrives in a flurry and sits to my right. I register him only peripherally until I notice that his leg is gushing blood, the result of an unfortunate brush with the coral reef while surfing. A crew of EMTs, or the on-staff equivalent, descends on him. I'm not great with blood, so I sip my beer and try to find some concrete shape to latch on to out in the black hole of the night-time ocean.

The morning after meeting Claude, I'm sitting on a lounger in my villa when I see a snake S its way across the lawn. Somewhere in my welcome materials I remember reading that if I see a snake, I should alert the resort immediately. So I WhatsApp Simson. *I'm coming. What colour?* he responds. *Brown*, I tell him. It's a rice field snake, harmless. By the time Simson gets to my villa, the snake has disappeared into the landscaping. I'll google "rice field snake" later and come across all kinds of terrifying venomous creatures. But Simson knows this species of rice field snake. If it had been green, we would have had a different situation on our hands, he tells me.

Snakes, when they appear in a narrative, are almost always a metaphor. I decide that this snake represents not duplicity or the dark side but false danger, the bold adventure we think we're having, compared to the real one that Claude and Petra Graves took on. When we arrive to the luxury of Nihi Sumba, we think that there are stakes involved. But for us, the snake is always of the harmless variety.

AT BREAKFAST, I RUN INTO THE INJURED SURFER. HE AND I ARE THE ONLY two solo guests at breakfast. We are, in fact, the only two solo guests present at the resort during the several days of my visit. This isn't the kind of place to which one travels alone for any of the reasons that a person typically does so. We are a curiosity, for the honeymooners and families, and for each other. I ask him how he's holding up after the injury.

It's all right, but I can't surf anymore while I'm here. Which, if you know surfers, would be like dropping a foodie in Paris and telling her she's allergic to everything but PB&J.

Is that what you came here for specifically? I ask him.

Well. I know before he tells me that his answer will be weird. *I'm actually a therapist,* he says. *I'm here working with a couple of clients for a couple of weeks.* Not for the first time, I see that my imagination for spending money pales in comparison to that of the superrich. Imagine intentionally bringing your troubles along with you when you're getting away from it all. That's creativity.

Still, the very rich occupying the villas at Nihi Sumba differ markedly from those I encountered on, say, the French Riviera. They take their cues from start-up cofounders, not oligarchs. Lots of simple white sundresses and hair left to its own wavy devices after a near-certain keratin treatment before the trip; guys dressed just like any guy I know back home. Almost everyone looks younger than they are, except the surfers, whose time in the sun makes them appear a decade older. Still, this is a young crowd for such a pricey resort. And a relaxed one. The well-preserved faces don't have the plumped-up lips I saw everywhere on the French Riviera. That would be too overt an effort for this crowd.

Beneath the breeziness, though, Nihi Sumba is fancier than ever. In 2012, Claude and Petra sold the resort to Chris Burch, ex-husband of fashion designer Tory Burch, and hotelier James McBride. The new owners upgraded the villas, enhanced the existing amenities, and implemented new offerings, while Claude moved into a private residence that he built next door. (Claude and Petra had by that time divorced.)

The new heights of luxury manifest in things like my sunset horseback ride. I'm hoping that I'll get to take my horse, Blaze, into the ocean like I've seen in the promotional photos. But the surf is too strong, so I settle for the utterly untouched beach. I've got two guides attending to me, each on their own horse. One of them takes my camera while the other shows the way. I spend the next hour as the subject of a photo shoot.

The next day, I join a hike through the countryside to a new spa location, where treatments are lavished on me, including a cold-stone massage and the best hair masque I've ever experienced, all in a clifftop open-air room overlooking the ocean, followed by a dazzling lunch on the next clifftop over.

I don't surf, but I understand the wave that breaks just in front of the resort is fantastic. It's also private, and Nihi Sumba restricts the crowd to ten people at a time at a cost of $125 per day during the high season. Only one surfing pass is made available per villa, and it's not uncommon for a guest to rent out five villas just for the wave access. In a world where the best waves are increasingly overcrowded, this may qualify as the most luxurious resort amenity of all.

ONE AFTERNOON I JOIN AN OUTING FROM THE RESORT TO A LOCAL EN-glish school. When I arrive with five other guests, we're paraded to the front of a couple hundred local kids. They raise their hands to ask us questions, then we break out into smaller groups to go through English exercises with them. In the group I sit with, about ten adolescents exhibit the typical range of enthusiasm for schooling, with a few wanting to answer every question, and a couple others sitting at the back of the group, only half-pretending to pay attention—though they are still getting pretty good at English.

The school is one of many programs launched and run by the Sumba Foundation, which Claude Graves and a guest named Sean Downs started alongside the resort in 2001, with the two entities operating separately, but closely aligned. Claude's original idea was to divert 30 percent of the resort's profits to the community. "That didn't really work out," he says, "because we didn't have profits for all those years. So I had to kind of go to plan B." Plan B was asking guests directly for donations. In the ensuing years, they were bringing in more in donations than they were making in profits.

Today the Sumba Foundation runs on a roughly $700,000 annual budget, spearheading myriad projects on the island, one of the most notable being the malaria program it launched in 2004. The foundation surveyed the nearby villages on the island, finding that

62 percent of children under the age of five had malaria, and a third of the mothers had lost at least one child to the disease. Since then, it has distributed 12,000 mosquito nets and treated 50,000 malaria patients through its four health clinics. The effort has resulted in a 93 percent reduction in malaria infections along a fifty-mile coastal area near the resort.

In 2018, the foundation saw more than 19,000 patients total in those clinics. It has conducted 120 cleft palate surgeries and 5,000 eye surgeries. It has distributed over 15,000 pairs of glasses. In an area rife with childhood malnutrition, the foundation provides lunches three times a week in eleven primary schools. It directly treats the most acute cases of malnutrition in children. It has built wells and water stations to provide clean water for multiple villages. It has funded scholarships for higher education, including for nurses who can return to Sumba to work and further improve the island's health resources.

Even as Indonesia enacts initiatives to lift its population out of poverty and into the growing global middle class, the East Nusa Tenggara province, comprising Sumba, Flores, western Timor, and more than five hundred smaller islands, remains the country's poorest on a per capita basis. Poverty on Sumba remains substantial, but around the resort it's nothing like it was twenty years ago. A third-party assessment has yet to be conducted, so it's impossible to verify the precise impact of the Sumba Foundation's efforts, but seeing its work in action on the ground, it's clear to me that it has improved lives in the area.

When I meet with James McBride, the Nihi Sumba co-owner, we talk about the role very high-end tourism can play in developing countries. "The Sumba Foundation is a model, and philanthropy tied in with the type of tourism that we're doing I think is a very big model for the future," he tells me. "It's only appropriate and responsible that you're gonna give back to the community."

McBride believes that a business like Nihi Sumba can do more for a place than traditional economic development projects. "For a relatively small investment, not that thirty, forty, fifty million dollars isn't still a lot of money, but in the big scope of things, for what it does relatively, it's crazy. A little business can change the fortunes of a place dramatically." McBride points out that Nihi Sumba is also the biggest taxpayer on the island by far, paying about $1.2 million US annually. And the nearly 400 Sumbanese people working for Nihi Sumba have gone from making maybe $25 a month before the resort opened and hired them, to over $500 a month today. Locals now commonly own relative luxuries like motorbikes and cell phones.

Resorts like Nihi Sumba have helped to inspire a move toward the "ultra-luxury" segment of the resort market in beach areas of low-income countries, the logic being that great revenues can be produced with a smaller footprint than that generated by mass tourism. Local governments and entrepreneurs want to emulate Nihi Sumba's successes in lifting up the local population by cultivating a relationship with ultra-wealthy guests. One problem with this approach, however, is the finite number of ultra-wealthy travelers. Compared to the billions-strong middle class, just 3.2 million people worldwide have a net worth of $5 million or more, according to the data analytics firm Wealth-X—the kind of wealth generally necessary to vacation at a place like Nihi Sumba. Not every location will be able to attract them, and the question remains how far this concept can scale.

Those developers that do succeed in bringing the highest-end hotels into their localities should remember that in practice, independently run luxury resorts tend to have a more thorough relationship with local communities than resorts run by corporations, which leads to more effective philanthropic efforts. The big hotel brands typically engage in charity efforts on a broader scale that doesn't take the nuances of individual locales into consideration. Claude Graves notes that in the big companies, the general manager of a property has to answer to people in corporate who have no knowledge of a resort in the context of the community around it. Unlike them, he says, "we didn't have anybody to answer to. We could do whatever we wanted." That means Nihi Sumba and the Sumba Foundation could invest in the community in thoughtful ways that didn't need to scale. Graves used to speak at development and tourism conferences, where he encouraged adoption of the Nihi Sumba model, but usually found the CEOs of the big hotel companies unreceptive. "It just amazes me," he says, "because it's so good for business." That's what the big hotel companies don't understand.

At the time of my visit, a second high-end resort is opening on the island. I mention the place to Simson and ask if he's happy to see it. I'm expecting him to feel protective of his position at Nihi Sumba, but for him it's a no-brainer. He wants more of what Nihi Sumba has brought to the island. More jobs, more income, more opportunity.

ONE NIGHT, INSTEAD OF A FORMAL SIT-DOWN DINNER AT THE RESTAURANT, the resort puts on a "white party," which I was told about before leaving for my trip and for which I have packed a white dress, just for this occasion. Every single person in attendance adheres to the white dress code, even the guys. The dinner is buffet style and we eat at communal tables. I sit with an Australian heiress and her family on one side, and a honeymooning couple who, like me, lives in New York, on the other—she's a doctor, he works in pharmaceuticals. I wonder if the heiresses ever get sick of spending their holidays with so many newlyweds. Then again, sometimes the honeymooner faction at Nihi Sumba includes the likes of Jennifer Lawrence, who headed there with her new husband in 2019.

Later, before returning to my villa I stop at the turtle nursery to see if anything's hatching. I watch some adorable turtles begin their lives, with another honeymooning couple from San Francisco. Eventually the husband of the Australian heiress wanders over. We get to chatting and he asks me what I do for a living and I tell him. Then

I tell him I already know that he is a patent lawyer because his wife told me earlier.

His kid starts showing impatience with watching the newly hatched turtles. *They don't even appreciate they're at the best resort in the world,* he says. *My vacations were the beach across the street.*

I get it. All of my childhood vacations required a crossing of the street, as well. And then here we are, at this resort where there are no streets.

NINE

BEYOND THE SEA
Barbados and St. Kitts

BARBADOS

It's well past both sunset and dinner and the sky is pouring down rain outside the living room of our suite at Cobblers Cove, on the west coast of Barbados. A wall of slatted wooden doors are opened to reveal the water-splattered terrace, which Scott and I stare at for a while. Not ready to turn in, we then make a run from the two-story bungalow toward whatever entertainments might be available at the main house of this resort, a place tailor-made to remind the visitor that going to Barbados can be as much a voyage into a lost ideation of Englishness as it is a trip to the Caribbean. The thing we find is a backgammon table.

This romanticized Englishness involves backgammon, yes, and also chess. It involves wicker and rattan. It involves colors one rung brighter than standard pastel—mint green, flamingo pink. It involves afternoon tea served always between 4 and 5 p.m. It involves elaborately presented dinners that are fine. It involves, above all else, a conception of British people lounging in hot climates, sure of Britain's ascendancy. The aesthetic is proudly unhip. As pricey destinations in the Caribbean go, Barbados is the anti-Tulum. Some see this as falling behind global trends; others see it as a competitive differentiator. Either way, it forms a cornerstone of an industry that has come to dominate life on this easternmost island in the Caribbean for its 280,000 people.

Not until morning, with the skies cleared and the temperature pleasantly moderated, do we set off along the beach for Speightstown, about a kilometer up the shore. It's here, outside the curated environs of Cobblers Cove, that we see the engine of Barbados's economy from a slight distance, how the tourism industry has enveloped the shoreline, how it has shaped the island's personality. Each successive villa along the water comes paired with its own concrete property wall built within yards of the water, which can only have contributed to the beach's increasing narrowness over the years. At the opposite end of the bay from Cobblers Cove, we exit the beach at its public access point, where a man is waiting to offer weed to passersby like us. Continuing now along the small road directly abutting the sea, we walk for a minute or so before coming upon a sandwich sign bearing the words, "Caution: Open Manhole," next to where chunks of the road have fallen into the water.

Throughout the 1900s, sugar became increasingly less lucrative for Barbados, as guaranteed pricing was removed and mega-producers like Brazil emerged. Once the focus turned toward beach tourism after World War II, international arrivals exploded in the space of a couple of decades. In 1955, just 15,000 foreigners came to Barbados. In 1980, nearly 370,000 did. (By the 2010s, it was over 1 million.) Barbados, now populated almost entirely by the descendants of slaves, was an early adopter of the Caribbean's transformation into the most tourism-dependent region in the world.

The focus on tourism in the latter half of the twentieth century allowed a newly independent Barbados to maintain its status as one of the wealthiest islands in the Caribbean, although going first meant making the mistakes that other locations would learn from in the future. In many ways, today it's the envy of other nations striving to lift their fortunes by attracting foreigners to their beaches. On the other, Barbados finds itself on the forefront of the economic, social, and environmental realities that emerge for a country's citizens once beach tourism becomes too big to fail.

In 2019, tourism accounted for 30 percent of Barbados's total economy, and 37 percent of its jobs, according to the World Travel & Tourism Council, although it can seem even higher. As the country's 2014 Tourism Master Plan stated, "The 'tourism sector' is deeply embedded in the wider economy and society; so if tourism declines, every sector in Barbados is likely to follow suit."

After a drink at a beach bar in town, we walk along the shore road to get back to our hotel. You'd never know at most points along it that the calm waters of the Caribbean lie just yards away. You only know that on one side of the road, villas and low-slung hotels block any view through to the sea, while on the other, small, brightly colored bungalows dominate. No Bajan—as Barbadians are known—residing in Barbados permanently lives on the villa side. One can't help but wonder how they feel about this.

THE ENGLISH SETTLED AN UNINHABITED BARBADOS IN THE EARLY SEVEN-teenth century, taking years to clear the dense forest and plant tobacco, cotton, and indigo. In those early decades, British landowners brought prisoners and indentured servants over from Britain and Ireland to fill their needs for manual labor. After turning to sugar as their staple crop in the 1650s, they began importing large numbers of slaves from West Africa instead. Receiving little oversight from England, the new plantation owners would grow into a dazzlingly wealthy ruling elite—easily the richest people in British America—while everyone else on the island suffered in poverty and often-violent suppression.

Simon P. Newman describes the resulting societal makeup in his book *A New World of Labor: The Development of Plantation Slavery in the British Atlantic*: "In 1680 the 175 great planters on Barbados, drawn from no more than 159 families, controlled over 54 percent of the island's property, both real and human. Approximately 20,000 whites and nearly 39,000 enslaved Africans were on Barbados in 1680, and thus the great planters who owned half the island composed less than 1 percent of the island's white population and only one-third of 1 percent of the island's population as a whole." This structure would remain largely in place for the next 150 years, until slavery was abolished in 1834.

Prior to the twentieth century, most Americans and Europeans saw the Caribbean—and all tropical locations, in fact—as unhealthy. When they did visit, they avoided the shore, preferring the inland hills with their unobstructed trade winds and slightly cooler climate. Cuba, Jamaica, Hispaniola (the island split between the Dominican Republic and Haiti today), and Puerto Rico attracted health-seekers to their interiors while their shorelines inspired tales of malaria, yellow fever, and general malaise. Blame fell to the fetid marshes and a lack of fresh breeze at the shores.

Barbados proved an exception. With its relatively dry climate and consistent coastal breezes, it received early attention for its healthfulness. As the richest of the early Caribbean colonies, it boasted the consequent amenities to please the elite. It's no surprise that it was also considered to have the healthiest climate. As Mark Carey, a professor of history and environmental studies at the University of Oregon, explains, "The degree to which a place resembled Europe mattered in how Europeans perceived its climate." One of the earliest travelers to be thus lured there was George Washington, who accompanied his tuberculosis-stricken brother to Barbados in 1751 in the hopes that the climate might help heal him. (It didn't—Lawrence Washington died the following year.) They stayed not up in the hills but at a plantation house near the beach that today hosts both a Hilton and a Radisson.

In Barbados today, you'll notice the same breezes the early visitors did. Wind that has gained power over uninterrupted thousands of miles of the Atlantic meets land for the first time. On the eastern coast, the result can be austere. The southern coast is known for resorts that cost slightly less than the west side, thanks to a slightly stronger gust factor. On the western shore of the island, the Caribbean side, where all the swankiest resorts reside, the breeze will be light, but the air will seldom be completely still. Of course early colonists loved it. It's achingly pleasant.

Even after slavery ended, Blacks in Barbados had little opportunity to improve their lots in life, largely because wealth on the island continued to be determined by land ownership, and the vast majority of land remained concentrated in the hands of just a few white plantation owners. Small plots of land were rarely for sale, and no former slave could have afforded to buy a larger sugar estate. Only in the twentieth century, with the decline of sugar profitability and the acquisition by Black Bajans of capital via work outside of Barbados, were they able to begin making inroads. Notably, almost twenty thousand Barbadians went to work on the Panama Canal in the first decades of the twentieth century, using much of the "Panama money" they brought back with them to become landowners.

IN 2003, AN ANTHROPOLOGIST LIVING IN BARBADOS NAMED GEORGE Gmelch interviewed twenty citizens of the country working in tourism, both in the resorts and ancillary businesses, from beach vendor to housekeeping to bartender to general manager. Gmelch compiled their words in *Behind the Smile: The Working Lives of Caribbean Tourism*, providing the perspectives of a cross section of Bajans working in the country's largest industry, who viewed tourism as a positive for their country at best, a necessary evil at worst.

Some bemoaned the lack of access to their own beaches, with jetski operator Ricky Hinds saying, "Just look at all the land they took away for them big golf courses. They're pushing black people inland, right back into the bush. If you just look down this coast you'll see that hotels have taken all the land where black people once lived."

Many reported gaining skills and confidence from their work. Sheralyn O'Neale, a housekeeper at the Sandy Lane Hotel, said, "Working at the hotel has made me braver, made me feel freer to talk to people that I don't know. I think it enlightened me." But even though they mostly enjoyed their jobs, interviewees felt there was little room for advancement. Many planned to stay in their tourism jobs only until they could move on to something more lucrative.

Martin Barrow was an exception, having ascended to general manager—the highest position at a major beach resort, and one that often pays well into the six figures, especially at the higher-end spots. Despite his own success, Barrow didn't see Barbados doing enough to promote Black employees in a country with a population that was over 90 percent Black:

> In some cases there is a genuine shortage [of local qualified workers], but in others I think they're being excluded in favor of non-nationals. There are finance positions, too, where the owners like to hire expatriates. Some of the foreign companies coming into Barbados place certain restrictions on hiring—"If I'm coming to invest I get to choose my own people"—so it's a catch-22 for us. I don't think enough is being done to hire locals. In an industry that's now forty or fifty years old, there should be more local chefs being promoted to executive chefs.

A Barbadian resort chef, Malcolm Bovell, had his own theory about why Barbadians never made executive chef, saying, "You get a lot of comments from guests who say they want more Bajan foods, that they want to experience our local foods. But the hotel owners, who are mostly British, say that the guests don't want to eat local cuisine seven days a week. So they bring in chefs from overseas, mostly British and French. That prevents our local chefs from reaching the top, and I don't see that changing any time in the future."

Bovell also noted the poor salaries in Barbados's resorts: "I think people who work in hotels are very underpaid. For an industry that brings in so much revenue, they should pay their workers more. I mean, you can read the newspaper and see that this hotel made millions of dollars in profit, but the workers are not seeing it in their paychecks, and most of us are hardworking people."

Many of the employees had a story of a racist guest, but also felt that racism didn't generally factor into their work environment. A bartender at Cobblers Cove (where we are staying on this trip), Sylvan Alleyne, said that from his perspective, "All that race stuff is much bigger in the States than down here." On the other hand, Errol Sobers, the head of security at two upscale resorts, noticed a double standard. "You take a white guy dressed like a hobo, and he can walk right through this place and nobody will say anything to him, but take a black guy dressed in a suit and somebody's going to wonder, 'Who is he? Why is he here?'"

I'M SURPRISED TO LEARN WHEN WE ARRIVE AT COBBLERS COVE, ALMOST twenty years after Gmelch published his book, that the resort has a Black, female Bajan general manager. From my room at the resort, I search online for the GMs of seven other Barbados luxury resorts at random and find that three also have Black general managers. All three are employed by Elegant Hotels, a collection of seven resorts on Barbados that has publicly made hiring Bajans a priority. (Marriott acquired Elegant Hotels in 2019—whether it retains the progress made at these hotels remains to be seen.) In some cases, it seems, Bajans are now reaching the top of the industry.

In tourism jobs below the top level, though, dissatisfaction with wages remains. Paula Phillips, who works as a nanny at many resorts on the island through a local agency, feels that pay is generally not as high as it should be. Of her typical 20 dollars Barbadian hourly wage (equivalent to about $10 US), she says, "That's not really anything, and I consider myself a very good nanny." She believes a fair wage would be more in the neighborhood of 30 or 35 Barbadian dollars per hour for someone with her level of experience. I ask her if she'll ever get to that point, and she tells me that's not really how it works.

Perhaps because many tourism jobs still lack opportunity for advancement, many Bajans working in tourism aim to start their own businesses, a realistic goal in today's Barbados. While historical advantages from land ownership persist in the tourism industry—meaning that the white Bajan minority owns a disproportionate amount of wealth, land, and access to capital—some progress has been made to rectify the imbalance.* Anecdotally, it's obvious that white Barbadians run many of the larger locally owned tourist businesses, especially hotels. But Black Barbadians own many smaller ones, including restaurants, bars, and those offering water activities.

The entrepreneurial spirit, in fact, is palpable. Phillips was in the process of securing a property to open her own youth center when COVID struck, and is hopeful that she'll be able to see it through once the island's economy picks back up. Another Bajan, Antonio B. Gilkes, started working as a bartender at a popular spot in St. Lawrence Gap, a popular tourist nightlife area, when he was still in his teens, then eventually moved on to run the Coconut Court Beach Hotel's beach bar. He turned the bar from an afterthought into a buzzing success for the hotel, and he became one of the most celebrated bartenders in Barbados. Now he says he hopes to be able to open his own beach bar. "There's nothing I want more in life," he

---

* Social anthropologist Christine Barrow has noted that as of the 1980s, the many Black Barbadians who had reached the upper reaches of the middle class had done so via becoming lawyers, doctors, teachers, and civil servants as opposed to more strictly entrepreneurial pursuits that involve land ownership and access to financing.

says. Because of the following he amassed at Coconut Court, he says he's had offers of financial backing and is on the lookout for the perfect opportunity.

The locals I talk to generally enjoy interacting with tourists and meeting people from other parts of the world. Phillips remembers getting a kick out of learning her name in German from German tourists. Donovan (who preferred to use only his first name), a bar owner and taxi driver whose customers are almost exclusively tourists, says, "I make my living from them, you know what I mean. The more the merrier."

When I ask Donovan if he feels that tourists ever treat him in a way that he would consider racist, on the other hand, he says, "Not racism directly, but more along a condescending line." He estimates that 20 percent of tourists that he deals with in his two businesses are guilty of it. "It is what it is," he says. "Most locals smile, take the money, and move on."

Gilkes acknowledges the occasional bad-behaving tourist, but like the bartender at Cobblers Cove in 2003, he feels that race isn't an issue in Barbados the way it is in the States. "Our skin color may be the same, but our experiences are totally different," he says. "The struggles that you have had, which, my heart goes out to you, but those are not our struggles."

EVEN AS A TOURIST, ACCESS TO BEACHES IN SOME PARTS OF THE ISLAND AS a nonguest can feel elusive—I'm left wondering how the Sandy Lane Hotel has managed to prevent any public access point to the beach in front of it in a country where the beaches by law are public. But Paula Phillips, the nanny, tells me that she's never felt unwelcome on a beach, and often heads to one of the west coast beaches on Sunday afternoons after church. Donovan, the bar owner and taxi driver, isn't a huge fan of the beach to begin with, but he never feels that it's off-limits to him. "As with all countries, there are things that are there, but taken for granted by the locals," he says. "[The beach] is always going to be there, it's not going anywhere, it's not a novelty."

Still, a perceived lack of beach access gave a Bajan named Barney Gibbs the idea of turning a bushy, overgrown lot near a popular surf spot at Freights Bay into a public space offering both sea views and access. On this southeastern edge of the island, cliffs line the shore, and getting to the beach to surf meant navigating a treacherous stone path down through the empty lot. Gibbs was inspired by the concept of the "sea window," developed in Barbados in the 1980s, which advocates for beachfront spaces to be kept free of development as a local connection to the sea. "We would always dream about clearing it up or doing something with it. But nobody really knew who owned it," Gibbs tells me.

Eventually, through Barbados's land registry office, he tracked the owner down in New Jersey in the States. Miguel Shorui had never done anything with the parcel of land he'd inherited from an uncle who'd made his Panama Canal money, then returned with it to Barbados and bought up some land. He agreed to sell it to Gibbs at a low price on the condition that Gibbs turn it into a public space. The resulting sea window is striking in its contrast to most places along the shore roads, which provide no view of the water, much less the inviting one here.

Gibbs sees the sea window as a return of some land to those who rightfully have a claim to it. "Very few coastal properties are in local hands these days. So while on a practical level I wanted the sea window to materialize so that people could get down there and would have access to beach space and all of that, there was also a kind of philosophical or ideological level where I wanted to give a view back to the locals and visitors," says Gibbs. "So it was kind of a democratization of space project."

SPENDING TIME AT A BARBADOS RESORT CAN FEEL LIKE THE OPPOSITE OF democratizing space. The continuing Englishness of Barbados's most exclusive hotels, along with their predominantly white, foreign clientele, in fact makes for some uneasy optics in the historical context of slavery and colonialism. I notice it immediately, but Gilkes, the bartender, rejects the notion that tourism represents a form of neocolonialism. "What else do we have? Sugarcane?" he says. "The potential for what [Barbados] can make in tourism is potentially unlimited. You have this natural resource, use it. . . . If people are willing to come with their pounds and their U.S. dollars and Canadian dollars and they're going to pay for [our natural resources], then that revenue builds roads and schools and hospitals."

The tourism economy has indeed largely funded much of the infrastructure and social safety net that all Barbadians enjoy. The tap water throughout the island is highly drinkable. University tuition is free to all citizens who meet the entry requirements. The primary and secondary education system has helped maintain a literacy rate in the country of over 99 percent. Barbados also provides free health care. And when COVID shut down the entire tourism industry in 2020, laid-off Bajans could rely on national unemployment insurance to see them through a few months without too much hardship.

In 2014, Barbados released a Tourism Master Plan meant to guide the industry ahead in the twenty-first century, with a primary goal of avoiding the "middle-income trap," which can happen to a country once it has achieved a level of success that unleashes rising labor costs, which in turn makes it hard to be competitive with up-and-coming countries. When the plan came out, Barbados had experienced several recent years during which tourism declined slightly in the country, serving as a wake-up call that Barbados can't rest on its laurels and expect the industry to thrive.

The master plan also led to talk of diversifying the economy, a topic that has bubbled up over the years when external forces hit the tourism economy—an irony considering that tourism was developed in the first place to diversify the economy away from dependence on the sugar industry. The financial crisis of 2008, for example, caused tourism arrivals to tumble, which led to a cascading effect on the country's debt burden, which heightened calls for diversification. When COVID hit, the concept took on a new urgency, especially coupled with a growing fear of climate change's threat to the natural resources that make tourism on the island possible. I happen to be on the island a year and some change into the pandemic, after Barbados reopens to vaccinated travelers.

In headier times, talk of diversification addresses concerns about just how much tourism this small island can handle. Signs of strain are visible everywhere. In front of the main house at Cobblers Cove, the restaurant and pool overlook the sea from a slight elevation. They are protected first by a structural wall, and then just in front of it, by a breakwater built of boulders. Rumor has it the breakwater was installed after a particularly aggressive wave soaked guests during their New Year's Eve dinner a decade or so back. The most amazing thing about this ugly pile of rocks is how everyone pretends it isn't there—on Instagram, in reviews published in well-known magazines, among the staff, among the guests themselves. Before long, I find myself ignoring it, too.

But ignoring all of the changes to the water's edge here would be a challenge. The breakwater is one small work of coastal engineering on a shoreline full of it. The seemingly endless sandy bays of the west coast go through seasonal variations that cause beach widths to ebb and flow, but since the 1960s there has also been a documented permanent erosion of them. For decades already, Barbados has been engineering the shorelines on both the west and south coasts to ensure that the country's crucial moneymaker doesn't disappear. In the 1990s, Barbados created a dedicated department to manage the health of its coastlines, and in the 2000s, the government's Coastal Infrastructure Programme implemented a major coastal stabilization project. The breakwaters, groins, and walls have become part of the landscape.

Barbados lies outside the Caribbean's core hurricane belt, largely avoiding the direct hits that have devastated other islands nearby. But it has suffered the expected environmental damage and challenges of a highly touristed tropical island in the age of climate change: damage to coral reefs from boats and cruise ships that unleash 800,000 people onto the island annually, plus coral bleaching thanks to increasingly warm waters. It's a first stop for the sargassum blooms coming up from off the coast of Brazil. Tourists' excessive water consumption has caused scarcity of that highly drinkable tap water for locals on the island. New problems are periodically emerging, such as when major sewage leakages on the south coast in 2018 led to canceled trips and, eventually, some closed businesses.

One of the more intriguing proposals for diversification acknowledges the strain on the island and involves the very assets that drew visitors to Barbados way back in the eighteenth century: the breeze and the sun. Experts believe that Barbados is capable of becoming 100 percent energy self-sufficient within the next decade or so by building up its wind and solar power capabilities. Many expect that the country can even become an exporter of sustainable energy.

With a tinge of guilt, Scott and I enjoy the empty beaches. We take our sunset cocktails into the sea with us, and float around with them, undisturbed. Looking back to shore, we can see the mansion that Barbados native Rihanna bought a few years back. Our solitude here is as eerie as it is delightful, and we know that the presence of just two tourists on this normally coveted beach might be enough to make any country look elsewhere for its fortunes.

When I ask locals whether they'd like to see less tourism or more of it, or whether they'd rather see other industries develop, the answers invariably rest upon the assumption that the presence of tourism is a given. Diversifying the economy is a good idea, but tourism will always remain its pillar. Whether or not to cultivate it doesn't seem up for debate, only how to deal with it as an inevitability. Ask a Bajan, and he'll tell you that tourism just is.

ST. KITTS

St. Kitts, the Caribbean island fifty miles south of St. Martin in the Lesser Antilles chain, is shaped sort of like a chicken drumstick. Thirty-five years ago, the skinny end of the drumstick to the south stood empty, aside from a few foreign-owned homes and two ten-room hotels, all accessible only by boat. There were no roads. The terrain was dry and had nothing to offer in terms of sugar production, the island's main industry. At one point, salt had been harvested from a large salt pond here, but that business was long gone. Although the white sandy beaches ringing it were the stuff of Caribbean vacation fantasy, they didn't receive much attention.

Today I'm on my way to tour the area with Hazel Williams, a native Kittitian and the aunt of a friend, Sacha Phillip Wynne, back in New York. Hazel grew up on St. Kitts and recently moved back after a number of years in the States. She remembers hiking over Timothy Hill, the mountain separating this part of the island from the more northerly parts, for a picnic as a child. This time, we ascend Timothy Hill in her car via the highway that opened in 1989 to encourage development. The view from the top does the Caribbean proud—the Atlantic crashes against one side of the island, the Caribbean laps the other. Just visible in the far distance, beyond the last hills of St. Kitts and the beaches that fringe it, I see Nevis, the island that together with this one makes up the country of St. Kitts and Nevis.

We descend Timothy Hill into what is gradually becoming the mecca of luxury tourism on St. Kitts, dominated by the massive Christophe Harbour development, which so far includes a mega-yacht marina, a Park Hyatt resort, the members-only Pavilion Beach Club, a waterside cocktail bar, and a substantial array of luxury homes and home sites spread across 2,500 acres of land. A golf course is in the works, as is a concierge medical facility that might enable yacht passengers to touch up their Botox before heading back out to sea, among other services.

The previously uninhabited southern end of St. Kitts
is being developed as a center of luxury tourism.

The ambitious tourism offerings of Christophe Harbour join a mere smattering of resorts elsewhere on the island, although that too is changing. Compared to other islands in the Caribbean, tourism here is a new phenomenon. The island welcomed the occasional cruise ship starting back in the sixties, then in 1998 opened a dedicated cruise ship terminal that could dock two large ships at a time. Over on Nevis, the Four Seasons opened in 1991, but it didn't have much of an effect on St. Kitts, which wouldn't see its first large-scale beach resort until the Marriott opened here in 2003. Tourism development had been incremental and piecemeal until, two years after the Marriott opened, the state-run sugar industry shut down in the wake of long-term unprofitability. After centuries as the island's key economic driver, what remained of the sugar industry disappeared overnight. The St. Kitts and Nevis government went all in on tourism, becoming the next in a long line of island nations to replace their sugarcane fields with beach resorts.

Fifteen years later, its residents are still figuring out what it means to welcome tourism into their lives.

JUST AS DUSK SETTLES IN ON THE EVENING OF MY FIRST FULL DAY ON ST. Kitts, I head down to the shore for a swim at my resort, Timothy Beach Resort in Frigate Bay, north of Christophe Harbour. I say shore instead of beach because directly in front of the resort, there is no beach. I'll learn later that the beach here has been dealing with erosion for several decades. It's been renourished previously, and plans are once again under way to replace the sand. For now, a row of boulders keeps the land in place.

I throw my towel onto a lounger and survey the water from the ladder leading down to it. Below me, two local women are floating around and chatting with each other. Like more than 90 percent of the population here, they are Black. Of the dozens of beach resorts I've visited over the years, this will be the first swim in a low- or middle-income country that I am sharing with locals who don't look like me. Even in Barbados, where the locals by law have access to every beach on the island, I never found myself in the water with them. I hesitate, rendered cautious by the possibility that my presence as a white tourist will make them feel they need to clear out, or that by mistakenly swimming at the locals' beach, I will cause resentment from their end.

As I lower into the water, one of the women says hello to me. How are you. Very well. Unmoved by me completely. My hesitation finds no validation, and it demonstrates to me how accustomed I've grown to being isolated from brown and Black populations on beaches during my travels. Also, how accustomed I've grown to internalizing this as normal, conditioned by common beach resort practices barring locals outright at worst, making them feel unwelcome at best.

Across the parking lot of the Timothy Beach Resort, which incidentally is the only resort on the island that's locally owned, a row of beach bars and food joints known as the Strip hug the sand, Mr. X's Shiggidy Shack Bar & Grill, Vibes Beach Bar, a Mexican restaurant. At its far end, Sacha's other aunt owns Buddies Beach Bar & Grill. The Strip is a melting pot for every type of person who finds herself on the island—locals, tourists, and the thousand or so students, mostly from the States, at the veterinary school. It's known as a great place to party. I order veggie nachos and a beer one night at Mr. X's, and when they arrive, there's chicken all over them. For a vegetarian like me it's not ideal, but it's also a sign that foreign vegetarians are maybe not the only priority here.

Integration with the locals turns out to be one of the delights of St. Kitts, and something that distinguishes it from many other Caribbean beach destinations. To not feel separate from the place you have visited makes travel feel like actually having gone somewhere, which is of course how travel should be. Instead of experiencing the island from inside a sequestered resort bubble, throughout my stay in St. Kitts I mingle with locals at the coffee shop, at the beach restaurant, and at the hotel bar. I find myself mentioning to every person I meet on St. Kitts—government officials, restaurant owners, taxi drivers—that tourism development here needs to involve the preservation of this organic integration, which benefits the locals as much as it does the visitors.

The government seems aware that the country is in a position to do things differently. "We are the new players on the block," Lindsay Grant, St. Kitts and Nevis's minister of tourism, tells me when I meet with him in his office in Basseterre, the island's main city and the country's capital. "An advantage for us because we have learned from the mistakes of others, and we had basically a virgin industry to fashion how we felt it should be fashioned." It's a great situation to be in, depending on how the government proceeds.

Already some key decisions have been made. St. Kitts needed only look to a couple of its closest neighbors, St. Martin and Anguilla, to see how two divergent approaches to beach tourism have played out.

St. Martin long ago embraced mass tourism and accommodates millions of annual visitors, including those from cruise ships, and not unlike Barbados, has suffered resulting environmental and cultural challenges. Anguilla (which until 1971 joined St. Kitts and Nevis as a single British territory), meanwhile, leaned into its inaccessibility, eschewing midrange tourism altogether by opting out of the cruise-ship circuit, among other tactics. Most of its resorts fall into the luxury sector. Just under 100,000 tourists traveled there in 2019, and as a result, its beaches remain untrammeled, while its residents easily outnumber visitors at any given time.

St. Kitts decided it liked the Anguilla model better. From the outset, it pursued high-end tourists, in part to keep the industry on a human scale. "We don't want mass tourism. . . . Yes, we want tourism, but not mass," says Grant. "We don't want explosive growth, because explosive growth brings its own challenges and consequences."

For St. Kitts, focusing on the high end of the market ensures a few things in addition to preventing overdevelopment. The country won't need to import labor, for one. As an island with a population of just 35,000, St. Kitts only needs to create so many jobs. As it has for places like Sumba, going upscale will also maximize St. Kitts's income from the tourism it does develop. Better to have one couple spending $900 per day than six couples spending $150 per day—same revenues, fewer crowds, the logic goes.

The focus on luxury has helped the country's tourism industry grow robustly—by almost 15 percent in 2019 alone, far higher than the Caribbean average of 3.4 percent. And it's been great for many local businesses, like those lining Cockleshell Beach at the southern end of St. Kitts, one bay over from the Park Hyatt and looking directly across to Nevis. Here a row of beachfront spots have resisted Christophe Harbour's expanding footprint.

One of those is the Spice Mill, where I sit down with the restaurant's owner, Roger Brisbane, a native Kittitian who opened the place in 2009 after years spent working in resort hotels, including as general manager of the Four Seasons on Nevis. He does a brisk business here catering to both tourists and locals, and appreciates the type of development under way on the island. "It is a good thing that we started late [on St. Kitts], because now we only have really higher-end brands, and we can look forward to more high-end brands. High-end brands attract high-end brands," Brisbane says.

The high-end influx includes those coming onto the island via the new Christophe Harbour Marina, forged from the repurposed salt-water pond that had long ago been harvested for salt export. People on St. Kitts can be discreet, but they can't help but whisper that Jay-Z and Beyoncé docked their yacht here recently.

At first, the benefit of such a marina is lost on me, especially in the context of making the tourism industry into something that works for the locals. But later, I'll talk over lunch at the private beach club with Aeneas Hollins, who runs the operation, and it starts to make more sense. A former yacht captain to the superrich, Hollins lived on a series of luxury vessels for twenty-five years, deciding to live on land again only after coming to St. Kitts. He was drawn to it for the same reason I am: St. Kitts isn't segregated. "There are not local bars and tourist bars, there are just bars," he says.

Hollins finds the yacht-based tourism a natural fit with St. Kitts's high-end approach to tourism. "Yachts have everything you could want," Hollins tells me, "except a beach." Passengers on even the fanciest yacht have to come ashore to put their toes in the sand. Once here, they continue to spend lavishly. A Saudi royal reportedly spent some $200,000 in four days on St. Kitts, renting out a villa for his staff, hiring four chauffeured cars to be stationed around the island just in case he wanted one of them, and renting out the entire posh beach club in which we are sitting, then renting out another place on the spot when this one proved too windy that day. Hollins tells me it's not unusual for a yacht to require $10,000 worth of fresh flowers when it docks. Good business if you're the local florist, and as a middle-income country well before tourism gained supremacy here,

St. Kitts has a well-established shop that was ready to handle yachts' flower orders from the outset.

The mega-yachts coexist somewhat awkwardly alongside the cruise ships that come to St. Kitts every day, unleashing as many as 15,000 visitors on the island for the afternoon—an increasingly common occurrence since the country opened a second major cruise-ship pier in late 2019. It's the island's lone nod to mass tourism so far, and one that St. Kitts hopes will augment the revenues from its high-end industry without requiring the hotel beds to accommodate millions of additional tourists.

JUST AS MASS TOURISM COMES WITH CHALLENGES AND CONSEQUENCES, so too does the tourism of the elite. As St. Kitts reaches ever further upscale, some concerning signs have emerged for locals amid the successes. When the Park Hyatt opened in 2017 as the island's first ultra-luxury resort, it was legally required to provide public access to the beach in front of it. Because construction blocked the old public access point, the resort had to create a new one. Throughout my visit to St. Kitts, locals complain that the public access point at the Park Hyatt is unmarked and difficult to find, located near intimidating security guards and far from public parking.

The problem repeats at Sand Bank Bay, the beach that the Pavilion Beach Club overlooks, and one that locals used to be able to drive right up to. Now getting to this beach requires a ten-minute walk. As I write this, one beachfront lot in Sand Bank Bay—house to be built—is listed for $6.9 million. It stands to reason that whoever shells out that kind of money might be anticipating privacy. A Kittitian who used to frequent the beach told me she hasn't been back since they blocked the road.

June Hughes, a director in St. Kitts's Department of Environment, attributes the substandard beach access partly to the loose letter of the law here. "Our law says that you must provide an access to the beach. It does not say what type of access," she says. "It doesn't say you have to put back the equal to what was there before, and that is a challenge. We're trying to fix those little loopholes."

Roger Brisbane has run into his own challenges with the Park Hyatt. The Spice Mill lies a four-minute walk from the resort, an easy outing to a locally owned spot for hotel guests. But Brisbane tells me that in its early days, Park Hyatt staff led guests to believe his restaurant was too far away to visit without calling an expensive taxi, which would take its time arriving to the southern end of the island. Presumably, the hotel then directed its guests to one of its own, more expensive restaurants. To the hotel's credit, after being called out on the practice, guests are now encouraged to embark on the easy walk to Cockleshell Bay.

Ultra-luxury resorts like the Park Hyatt and the Four Seasons on Nevis also consume far more resources than lower-end accommodations, sometimes leaving the locals with fewer for themselves. When the Four Seasons opened in 1991, for example, its golf course alone required more water every day than Charlestown, the island's capital. This in a country where water availability poses increasing challenges. One major well that supplies the St. Kitts population has already been abandoned after its water became brackish, says June Hughes. While we discuss this in Hughes's office in Basseterre, the power cuts out and returns several times on this blindingly hot day, when air conditioners are cranked up across the island. It's an inconvenience the guests of the luxury spots probably don't experience.

WHEN THEY HEAR ABOUT THE FRUSTRATIONS OF LOCALS ON TOURISM-heavy islands like Barbados, residents of St. Kitts may not see many parallels with their own lives at the early stage of tourism development on the island, although likely there's a spark or two of recognition. To its credit, the St. Kitts government is taking steps to make the industry work for its population. Officials hope that an emphasis on cultural tourism as a complement to the beach will benefit the local community in ways that Barbados neglected when it was developing its own tourism sector.

"We have the sun, the sand, and the sea," says Lindsay Grant. "But we are fashioning our niche market . . . we focus on the culture, the heritage, the history, and the people." Part of this strategy involves heritage projects—the old sugar train has been repurposed for tours. Brimstone Hill Fortress, a former British fort built by slaves, was named a World Heritage Site in 1999 and has been meticulously restored. Romney Manor shows visitors what an old sugar estate was like. It also involves celebrating the living, breathing local culture. Locally owned bars, restaurants, shops, and other businesses are being promoted, including the ones that the Kittitians themselves hang out in.

The government considers the direct participation of the local population to be key to the industry's success and has created a community tourism program to train citizens in their options. Carlene Henry-Morton, St. Kitts's permanent secretary of tourism, says, "We are doing a lot of training because a lot of [local] people add value to the experience." She believes that the tourism industry's community engagement and inclusiveness put St. Kitts over the top in winning the World Travel & Tourism Council's Destination Stewardship Award in 2019, and wants to see it become a cornerstone of the island's appeal for visitors.

In *A Continent of Islands: Searching for the Caribbean Destiny*, the journalist Mark Kurlansky observed that "attracting tourists to one's culture rather than isolating them on a beach makes locals feel better about tourism, because it is drawing people out of a sense of pride rather than sequestering them out of a sense of shame." Ideally, St. Kitts's approach will help its people preserve their culture at the same time they benefit from it materially.

Grant says that this desire to see locals become stakeholders in the tourism industry has deterred St. Kitts from approving any all-inclusive resorts, which are well known for keeping guests sequestered on the resort grounds and away from local businesses. He also stresses that St. Kitts's cruise-ship port is the only one in the Caribbean not sealed off from the locals, who if they choose can shop at the same stores and drink at the same bars in the tourist port as the cruise passengers.

While killing some time before a meeting one afternoon, I take a stroll into Basseterre, with its colorful colonial-era buildings highlighting both the French and English elements of the island's history. At a corner, an open-air bus full of cruise-ship tourists rounds the bend. At the same time, I vaguely register two local women walking in my direction. A guy on the bus holds out a selfie stick, the camera pointed away from him, and I look to see what he's trying to capture. I don't know quite how it starts, but almost as if on cue the tourists and the two local women are whooping and hollering hellos at each other and waving their arms wildly in a manic greeting. As quickly as it flares up, the moment passes. As the bus moves on down the street, its passengers grinning, the two women pass me on the sidewalk, their workaday calm immediately restored. On one of their faces, a nonplussed expression has taken hold. The other one notices. "You have to make them feel good," she says to her, and chuckles.

I imagine everyone on that bus returning home to the States or Britain armed with this anecdote as evidence that Kittitians are some of the friendliest people they've ever come across, a common refrain from white people when speaking of brown people in the tourism-centric regions they visit. It's a simplification, of course, a tidy designation that makes a foreign place easier to process. It's also a simplification the industry encourages. If I had to guess, I'd say it's likely these women are acquainted with the training provided by the ministry of tourism.

BY AND LARGE, THE ST. KITTS LOCALS I ENCOUNTER VOICE APPROVAL OF both Christophe Harbour and of tourism development in general on their island. It's creating good jobs, after all. Hazel will ultimately go to work for Christophe Harbour as the guest services manager at the marina. She tells me she's happy she returned home.

My frequent cabdriver during my stay, who goes by Uncle Millie, used to work in sugar, but tells me he far prefers driving a taxi and meeting new people from all over. He talks about how hard the work was in sugar, that it was exciting and challenging for a while, but backbreaking as well, with its hours spent in fields in the direct Caribbean sun. I can tell he's enjoying the air-conditioning during our ride.

I ask Sacha, my friend back in New York—Hazel's niece—what she thinks of Christophe Harbour. "I'm cool with Christophe," she says. "When I was there, the staff looked pretty diverse. A lot of times, you rarely see brown or Black faces in the high-end resorts because some management think we don't convey luxury."

The recent hiring of Yvette Thomas-Henry, a Black woman originally from the nearby U.S. Virgin Islands, as general manager at the Four Seasons on Nevis provides one encouraging sign that St. Kitts and Nevis will be able to overcome the glass ceiling that Barbadians came to resent.

Also, the Park Hyatt has created about three hundred jobs for Kittitians. Anecdotally, I've heard that they pay relatively well. At the time of its opening in 2017, the Park Hyatt announced a program to train locals for senior positions. Mohammed Asaria, the vice chairman of Range Developments, the firm that developed the property, said at the time, "We would have failed in our collective responsibility if we are not staffed with Kittitians and Nevisians in senior management positions over the next few years."

When I contact the Park Hyatt to ask how far it has progressed toward that goal, a representative lets me know that the resort will not be providing any information on the subject. A quick search on LinkedIn for senior positions at the hotel gives me an inkling as to why.

Back in 1958, Hans Magnus Enzensberger wrote in his seminal

essay, "A Theory of Tourism," that "the hotel is the castle of the upper bourgeoisie. Here this new class ostentatiously usurps the lifestyle of the aristocracy in a milieu of unexcelled luxury." This mindset persists today, and to succeed within it, the luxury resort must almost by definition distinguish its guests from all other people. The local Black population of St. Kitts happens to be those other people in this scenario. This is St. Kitts's central challenge as it pursues high-end tourism, to keep the sequestering tendencies of luxury from overtaking the island's current inclusivity. The woman on the street was right: you do have to make the tourists feel good. But that should cut both ways.

TEN

A TALE OF TWO ISLANDS
Bali and Nias (Indonesia)

Let's say there's an island covering a little over 2,000 square miles of land in the Indian Ocean. It has a tropical climate with a rainy and a dry season; its coastlines boast world-class surf breaks and more than their fair share of coral reefs. Beaches abound, some in bays and coves, others fully exposed to the power of the ocean. Its mountainous interior provides not only a cooling respite from the heat at the shores, but also waterfalls, swimming holes, and villages of unique culture and architecture, housing people whose ancestors wielded great power in the region. Its local cultures are the stuff of countless anthropological studies. In its more recent history, this island became part of a Dutch colony.

Looking around, we find this place bears a striking resemblance to Bali, the Indonesian island that in recent decades has become synonymous with a certain style of spiritually plump, paradisiacal travel. If we look harder, we will find that Nias, a little-known island off the western coast of Sumatra, also fits the bill. Zoom in a bit and see Bali's overcrowded streets, its uberdeveloped shorelines, its beaches sometimes blanketed with plastic trash. Pan over and see Nias's lush jungles, its lack of traffic, its halting efforts at tourism. Nias is Bali without the tourism industry. Bali is Nias without the perpetual failure to launch. With a few twists of fate, one could have ended up the other. On both islands, it is both the best of times and the worst of times, though never in the same ways. Taken side by side, these two islands become a microcosm of the pros, cons, benefits, and challenges that come with the growth of beach tourism in a developing economy.

NIAS

I wasn't thinking about Nias in these terms yet in 2017, during my first visit to Sorake Beach, tucked into the western side of Lagundri Bay, on the island's southern shore. Scott and I were both working in Singapore and wanted to spend a few vacation days someplace new. Somehow, I came across Nias. It seemed interesting, and close.

In practice, what might have been an hour-and-a-half flight took a full day of travel. First, a flight from Singapore to Medan, on Sumatra; then another flight to Gunungsitoli, on Nias. From there, a three-hour drive on a two-lane road brought us finally past the town of Teluk Dalam, and then to the place we'd lay our heads. Sorake Beach was the only place on an island of nearly 800,000 people that offered reliable accommodation to travelers, outside of its main city. The waterfront guesthouses, or losmens, as they're called, existed because just offshore, one of the best surfing waves in the world breaks.

Each losmen generally can accommodate between 10 and 25 guests. These days, they're mostly built of concrete, with tin roofs. The losmen we stayed in, owned by an Australian named Mark Flint and his Indonesian wife, Debi, proved an exception with its traditional architecture of thatched roofs and wooden façades designed to resemble the ships of previous centuries. It also happened to charge the highest nightly rates along the shore.

Because the wave breaks where the shore protrudes into the water near the entrance to the bay, it was named the Point. Even as a nonsurfer, I got it. I looked at the wave and with no expert's help recognized its size, its consistency, the way it rolled down from the air with such poise, like a lemon twist getting peeled for a cocktail, over and over and over. Because of the way the shoreline bent, surfers could enter the water behind the wave—no need to paddle out. After the wave broke, it did a strange thing where it turned back toward land, bringing the surfer full circle back to shore.

There wasn't a ton to do at Sorake Beach aside from surfing, so Scott and I wandered. One afternoon we walked past the Point, where the bay cedes to the Indian Ocean, then kept walking. The losmens became less frequent, and as they thinned out altogether, I noticed a series of abandoned buildings. I didn't realize it yet, but I was looking at the only attempt to enter the resort market Nias has ever seen.

The Sorake Beach Resort opened in 1993, said to be funded by Indonesian investors assured that an airport would soon materialize to bring visitors directly from Singapore, Kuala Lumpur, and Jakarta. They secured the French company Accor Hotels to manage the property, with its 73 en suite, air-conditioned bungalows, most with a living room, bedroom, and front porch. We peeked into one of them and found the furniture still arranged as it had been on the day the resort closed. Up the hill, a tennis club stood more or less intact, as did the staff quarters beyond it. The main building housed a lobby bar, while down near the shore we found a freestanding restaurant with terraces on four sides. All of it was organized around the centerpiece pool, full now with water that shone a glassy green. Near the pool a bush bloomed with flaming pink flowers, a remnant of some landscaper's long-lost vision.

Back up in the open-air lobby, it was easy to see where reception

The former lobby and reception of the Sorake Beach Resort,
the only bona fide resort Nias has ever seen.

had been, where the bar was, where the concierge sat, because their
respective countertops remained, the marble surfaces retaining a
minimalist attractiveness. Behind the reception desk, I got a glimpse
through some broken glass windows of a room stacked to the ceiling with mattresses. On one wall near the concierge, someone had
recently drawn a map of local villages and other points of interest,
graffiti-style. It was hard to imagine for whom.

BALI

It's a different strain of peculiar, two years later on Bali. We're staying
in Canggu, which is enjoying a moment as the island's "It" village,
and will continue to until some not-too-distant year when another
village usurps it, the way Canggu itself usurped Seminyak, which
usurped Legian, which usurped Kuta. Then it will be that new

village's rice fields disappearing by the day to make way for hotels and their pools, cafés with their lattes and their poke bowls, bars where the smartest thing to order is always a Bintang beer, because the wine in Bali is mediocre and the cocktails are reliably among the world's weakest.

For now, it is Canggu's rice fields that are disappearing. No longer a village in anything but name, it's suburban sprawl on the beach. It's a lot like Los Angeles. The markers of hip tropical travel as it manifests in 2019 are all here—coworking spaces and English as a lingua franca and Wi-Fi as an inalienable right, because today's frontline world travelers are nothing if not digital nomads. If you go to Bali expecting to escape the stresses of life back home, your conception of Bali is perhaps in need of an update.

Canggu is a little over twelve miles from the airport, yet thanks to Bali's infamous traffic, it takes me an hour and a half to reach my hotel in a taxi. Cranes dot the sky and construction noise creates a constant background hum. Our hotel, open for less than a year, is your standard midsized resort, a single tall building, clean and colorful and concrete, with the public areas dominated by the pool and its adjacent bar and restaurant. From our balcony, I see two cows grazing in the still-empty lot next door, hemmed in by development on all sides. On their other side, a major resort is mid-construction, and beyond that, the ocean. The cows don't seem to care, but then, between the three of us, only I know that they will soon be displaced.

The beach here is fine. Provided you are not a surfer, you may find it inferior to those along the Jersey Shore. But then in Bali, unquestionably a beach destination, the beach is not necessarily the focal point, and in fact it's an open secret that its beaches don't rank at the top of all those that Indonesia has to offer. Low-key beach clubs rent chairs and serve beers. More elaborate versions have VIP areas and infinity pools and velvet ropes. But my hotel pool, which has no views and is a five-minute walk from the shore, with its loungers and food and drink service, feels like the more in-demand spot to ride out the afternoon heat.

On a map, Canggu looks sort of like a long, craggy finger pointing inland from the shore, with the cafés and shops stretching well beyond the second knuckle. The best restaurants are away from the beach, as is the social scene in general. One can easily stay in a hotel 2.5 miles from shore. And one could easily spend her week in Canggu without visiting the beach at all and not feel as though she's missed out on the Canggu experience.

I have a nice time here, but the enjoyment is fraught and coated with ambivalence. I like my healthy lunch bowls, even as I'm annoyed to find that they're no different from healthy lunch bowls in any location where yoga is a popular form of exercise. Over one such lunch, Scott and I gaze out from the restaurant's patio onto a local man working what seems to be the only rice field remaining in the town proper. The things we enjoy here are mostly derived from Western culture as they visibly squeeze out Balinese culture. None of it is unpleasant, exactly, but neither is it unfamiliar in the way I'd hoped. The driver I hire to take us around the island feels the same way. He's from Canggu. His father is still a rice farmer here, but for him, driving a taxi makes more sense. I ask him what he thinks of the developments in his home village. "For me it's fifty-fifty," he says. "It's too much. But it's good for business."

THE DUTCH "DISCOVERED" BALI IN 1597, ALTHOUGH AS ADRIAN VICKERS writes in *Bali: A Paradise Created*, "300,000 Balinese . . . were not really so surprised to hear that there was a Bali." They encountered an island of wealth and military power thanks to Bali's position along a major spice trade route. This intrigued the Dutch, as did the fact that the Hindu population had never converted to Islam, as had other islands nearby. Mostly they found the Balinese intimidating in their power and their fierce willingness to protect it.

Unable to make inroads, the Dutch instead focused on their new trading post of Batavia (present-day Jakarta) on the next island over, Java. As their role in the spice trade grew, they began to squeeze Bali out. Bali remained relevant by turning to a lucrative slave trade of its own people in which the Dutch heartily participated. This would continue, although with dwindling returns, until the mid-1800s. By then it provided one more reason for Holland to view Bali as in need of civilizing.

The Dutch finally took full control of Bali in 1908. In 1914, the new tourist bureau in Batavia extended its scope to the island, marking the beginning of official Bali tourism promotion, and the Dutch steamship line KPM published the first tourist brochures for the island. Early promotions used terms such as "Garden of Eden" and "enchanted isle," sweeping more brutal elements under the rug, not least the bloody Dutch invasions and resulting "puputans," or mass suicides, of 1906 and 1908.

KPM opened the Bali Hotel in the southern city of Denpasar in 1928 to house guests participating in organized tours that featured canned cultural stops around the island. The beaches didn't factor in. At the same time, a circle of artistically bent Westerners settled on the island, where they painted, wrote, photographed, and made films that established a narrative of the island as a spiritually evolved, artistic, erotic paradise. The inland town of Ubud became their home base, while Sanur, on a southeastern beach, became their outpost on the shore. The anthropologist Margaret Mead came for a while and brought to the Bali myth a whiff of academic authority.

The community of Westerners' version of Bali reached potential tourists back home via coverage like that by Franklin Price Knott in *National Geographic*'s March 1928 issue:

> In every man's dreams there is always one favorite spot,
> somewhere, that he hopes some day to see. . . . Some time in
> his life, the man of any imagination feels the call to far places.

So it came that I went to Bali, that beautiful but little-known island of flowers and modern Eves, lying off the beaten tourist trails, east of Java.

The term "modern Eves" reflects another key element of the emerging Bali fairy tale:

> During the years when I painted, I knew many famous models in American and European art centers, but I recall few specimens of the human race so easy to look at as the beautiful women of Bali . . . they have few physical equals among womankind.

National Geographic published twenty of Knott's photographs, five featuring topless women in Balinese dress. Western men had discovered a loophole in the times' standards of propriety, and photography like Knott's stoked widespread interest in Bali.

Then, in 1936, an American couple, Robert Koke and his eventual wife, Louise Garrett, built some beachfront huts and opened the Kuta Beach Hotel. Koke, who had lived in Hawaii, sent for his surfboards and introduced surfing to Kuta tourists. Their operation contributed to a small but enthusiastic tourist scene. In 1929 about 1,400 tourists visited Bali. By 1940 that number had grown to a still-modest 3,000, as Bali became a common stop on the circuit traveled by a few wealthy Europeans.

Meanwhile, the Balinese themselves struggled with their new reality. Dutch authorities reorganized local governance, grouping villages under broader administrative oversight, which sowed confusion and resentment. Many former Balinese royals went into exile, while others stayed to work within the Dutch system, regaining power at the expense of the greater Balinese population. The Dutch codified the formerly fluid caste system, sowing further frustration. Alongside the political shakeups, the Dutch undertook a program to reinforce Balinese culture as they saw it, or wanted to see it—they called it "Baliseering," literally the "Balinization" of Bali as conceived by the Netherlands. This is the Bali the early expats conceptualized, and the one that would capture the tourist imagination.

NIAS

The Nias Heritage Museum in Gunungsitoli, the island's main town, sits on the eastern shore near the port, founded by a German missionary who arrived in the 1970s. Its collection of artifacts dates back centuries, among them a series of fine porcelain dishes acquired from the Chinese in return for slaves. Likewise the gold jewelry from the Acehnese on Sumatra. Both serve as reminders that at one time, although at the expense of human bondage, considerable wealth flowed through Nias.

The Dutch took an interest in Nias beginning in the 1660s. In 1693, the Dutch East India Company and Nias chiefs entered into an agreement for the sale of slaves and produce, and the protected anchorage of Dutch ships. This brought a measure of cosmopolitanism while prompting a defensive, battle-prone mindset. Villages were built atop hills, with a view of the sea to monitor the approach of potential adversaries. Like the Balinese, the Niassans too were known for their ferocity.

Nias never factored heavily in spice trade routes, which solidified farther east in the protected waters of the Malacca Strait. As the appetite for slavery diminished, Nias, especially in the south of the island, maintained some wealth through the export of crops. Despite this, in the nineteenth century the outside world lost interest in Nias. The Dutch put up a fort in Lagundri Bay, but after it was destroyed by flood—likely a tsunami—in 1861, it was never rebuilt.

As in Bali, Islam never made its way to Nias, leaving the island open to the influence of Christian missionaries. Today, more than 90 percent of Nias's population practices Christianity—this in a country that is almost 90 percent Muslim. On both Bali and Nias, the practice of minority religions smoothed the path to beach tourism development—no cultural hurdles with booze or bikinis.

The Dutch took control of Nias in 1906, and the West gradually took some interest in it. In 1931, Mabel Cook Cole, an anthropologist and contemporary of Margaret Mead, traversed the island on horseback with her husband in tow for *National Geographic.* "Here primitive people built great cities with paved streets, carved enormous stones where ghosts of their ancestors are wont to sit," she wrote. "Yet comparatively few people have ever heard of the island of Nias." Unlike her male peers writing about Bali, Cole managed to avoid defining Nias by an appraisal of local women's assets.

Between the world wars, Nias began to make appearances on tourism itineraries. In 1935, the *New York Times* alerted readers to a new sightseeing cruise taking travelers to Bawamataluo, just inland from Lagundri Bay on "primitive Nias," which "rivals Bali for strange customs, royal processions and festive dress." As in Bali, the beaches were not a key attraction. The cruise must have proven a success, because two years later, the *Times* reported on another one. Nias even seeped into Hollywood pop culture, making a cameo in the 1933 film *King Kong.* As the group from New York comes ashore on Skull Island, they hear chanting. "It sounds something like the language the Nias islanders speak," says Englehorn, the ship's well-traveled captain.

Leading up to World War II, Nias saw the beginnings of a tourism industry, although almost all visitors stopped off on day trips from cruise ships. It seems even a "ring road" was built around Nias sometime in the 1930s, infrastructure that might foster tourism on a larger scale, with maybe even some hotels on the horizon.

BALI

By the end of World War II, the Kuta Beach Hotel had burned down, almost all Westerners had left, and tourism had ceased completely. In a newly independent Indonesia, the Balinese would confront a reckoning over their future, divided between the nationalist party of the first president, Sukarno, and factions that opposed national rule. The tensions culminated in 1965 and 1966 with the massacre by the Indonesian military of at least 500,000 suspected communists, 80,000 of them on Bali—5 percent of the island's population. The slaughter was led by a military general, Suharto, who soon wrested control from Sukarno and assumed the Indonesian presidency, which he would hold in dictatorial fashion for the next thirty years.

These were hardly the conditions for a resurgent tourism industry, and in the late 1950s, barely a handful of tourists came to Bali. Still, the island maintained some advantages. A simple airstrip built by the Dutch in 1930 and expanded during World War II became an international airport just a couple of miles from Kuta Beach and eight or so miles from Sanur. Bali became its own province in 1958, enabling direct appeal to the central government for investment and loans. Also, it continued to benefit from its proximity to Java, sometimes tangibly—in 1989, two underwater cables would bring reliable electricity from Java's advanced power grid to the entire island of Bali.

The national government opened the Bali Beach Hotel in 1963, bringing the first true beach resort and only the fourth hotel to the island. In 1968 Indonesia requested assistance from the World Bank for tourism development on Bali. This led to a $16 million US ($83 million in 2019) loan in 1974 for the construction of 2,500 hotel rooms in a new, self-contained resort area of Nusa Dua, plus infrastructure improvements and hotel training facilities. A further 1,600 rooms were planned for elsewhere on the island. All of the major contracts went to foreign firms—Bali's own government was not involved in the tourism plan.

Perhaps most importantly, Bali's reputation as a lush, artistic, Edenic island with some of the friendliest people on earth endured. Never mind that this image was a Western construct, or that the Nusa Dua area was cleared of locals to make way for large hotels, or that what the tourist perceived as friendliness was as likely as not a refined application of basic customer service principles.

In 1971 the airport expanded to accommodate large jet planes, while surfers discovered a wave at Uluwatu, near the southern end of Bali, that quickly rivaled the waves of Hawaii's North Shore as the best in the world. An explosion of tourism kicked off that would run unabated for the next four decades. In 1970, there were fewer than 500 total hotel rooms on Bali. By 1995, there were 30,000, and by 2019 a full 60,000 rooms dotted the landscape. The correlating numbers of foreign visitors grew from 30,000 in 1970, to a million in 1994, to almost 6.3 million in 2019.

NIAS

There is astonishingly little information available about Nias in the decades following World War II. The island grew so deeply isolated during the war that, although occupied by the Japanese, it's said to have taken two weeks for news of their surrender to arrive. After its 1937 article, there would be no further mention of Nias in the *New York Times* until the late 1970s.

Its isolation perhaps contributed to Nias's reputation on Sumatra and beyond as a culture of laziness, its inhabitants interested only in putting on huge feasts, a stereotype that continues to this day. There was little to no infrastructure development during this time, and the ring road was long gone.

Niassans continued with agricultural production, with coconut and rubber plantations and some rice fields around Sorake Beach. In 1959 reports emerged that "huge quantities of copra" ready for export were languishing on the island after the Dutch shipping line KPM suddenly ceased operations in Indonesia. This suggests that the Nias people suffered more from a lack of infrastructure and access than of motivation. When Indonesia created its provinces, Nias was tacked on as a regency of North Sumatra. In contrast to Bali, this meant that Nias was overlooked by its regional government for investment funds, infrastructure projects, and educational advances, and was unable to appeal directly to the national government.

This was the situation when two Australian surfers, Kevin Lovett and John Geisel, discovered the spectacular wave off Sorake Beach in 1975. After seeing the wave, they set up camp on the shore, surprising people from Botohili, the village up the hill, who avoided the waterfront, having seen those who did frequent it come down with a deadly sickness or succumb to the dangers of the water itself. The area just behind the beach was a marsh with a flourishing mosquito population.

"I was amazed. I'd never seen a person riding the waves," said a local named Ama Dolin in *The Golden Pig*, a documentary from 1996 about the wave at Sorake Beach. "To people here, if someone enters the water, they're destroyed, dead." In the end, both Australians contracted malaria on Nias, and John Geisel died from it nine months after finding the wave.

Word of the wave trickled out to the surfing community. William Finnegan, the *New Yorker* writer who won the Pulitzer Prize for his surfing memoir, *Barbarian Days*, surfed it in 1979 (and also contracted malaria). Soon after, *Surfer Magazine* ran an article with the first published photo of the wave, and Lagundri Bay immediately became Indonesia's second great surfing destination.

In 1980, Mark Flint showed up. Sorake was one stop on a round-the-world surf trip, but once he experienced the wave, he concluded he wouldn't find anything better than the Point. Forty years later, he was still in Lagundri Bay and we were staying in his losmen, enjoying his encyclopedic knowledge of South Nias and tendency to talk about the past in the present tense. He used to work as the general manager of the Sorake Beach Resort and showed me photos of the place in its heyday. The pool, especially, looked wonderful.

The local elite didn't pay much attention to those early surfers, but poorer villagers started coming down to the shore out of curiosity. They noticed that surfers loved a refreshing coconut after a session, and started selling them. "The people that were coming down and climbing the coconut trees didn't generally own the coconut trees," Flint tells me. "All of a sudden they learned a spattering of English, watching the surfers." On occasion, a surfer would hire someone to build a bungalow for the following year's trip. Some enterprising locals took sand from the beach to fill in the swamp behind the shore, creating new land that they by default owned and built losmens on. Over the course of the 1980s, a row of them went up. Economic clout began to shift toward locals previously at the bottom of the rigid village hierarchy. Over the following decades, the local socioeconomic pecking order would reorient.

Elvira Wau's family was part of this shift. Today they own the Hash & Family Surf Camp, right on the Point. Its first-floor restaurant is a popular spot to get a beer and watch the wave. During our first trip, it was clear that the then twenty-two-year-old Elvira, daughter of "Hash," was running the show, organizing the reservations and meals and interacting with guests.

When we return to Sorake in 2019, Elvira explains to me that her family was one of the first to move down from Botohili, pivoting early from rice farming to the far more lucrative tourism business. She doesn't know exactly when her father and his parents came down, but Hash spent his teenage years living on the beach. Her grandparents owned and rented out some bungalows a few plots down from the Point. Elvira has lived on Sorake Beach her entire life.

BALI

We've been told by everyone, including our driver here in Bali, to avoid Kuta, but head out one afternoon to see it anyway and encounter block after block of bars promoting drink specials, restaurants serving pizza, burgers, and, occasionally, Indonesian food. Every shop sells the same round straw purses and flip-flops. It's built up in the same way that certain neighborhoods in Manhattan are, dense and chaotic. Aside from the beach itself, the main tourist attraction seems to be the empty lot that is the site of the nightclub bombing in 2002 that killed 202 people, and the memorial across the street.

The beach itself, across a busy street and on the other side of a wall from the buildings, seems unrelated to that packed neighborhood. It's pleasant enough—the sand is wide, and during this dry season, clean; the breeze is gentle. The waves echo those of Waikiki—too easy for today's expert surfers, but great for learning and perfect for the longboarders of yesteryear. Out on the beach, it's possible to forget the overdeveloped mess we've just left behind, but still, this is not the beach of vacation dreams. It's more like an urban park.

Kuta traced a familiar path for beach resort areas. In the late sixties, Australians started checking out the waves here again. While the government was preoccupied with the creation of high-end Nusa Dua and further development at Sanur, the free spirits flocked to Kuta. Around them an informal industry of losmens and restaurants popped up. As such, it also became the party beach. After the surfers and the hippies show up, the government and international companies tend to swoop in. Kuta was no exception. On the site of the old Kuta Beach Hotel, today we find a 418-room Hard Rock Hotel.

The vacationers who stay in Kuta today are looking for a deal, or they're here mostly to party, or they want a place close to the airport, or they know of Kuta's fame but, until they arrive, not its overdevelopment. The area has few defenders—it's best known instead as an example of what not to do in beachfront development.

Other tourist areas of Bali reflect Kuta to varying degrees. It's hard not to see Canggu as Kuta thirty years ago. Sanur and Nusa Dua fulfilled their destinies as self-contained areas for large, expensive resorts—nice, but no different from any other beach resort area around the world. The area around Uluwatu has fully embraced surf culture— it's less developed and more specific in its appeal than other areas. One afternoon, we head to Single Fin, one of the surfing world's famous bars, perched on the high cliff above the wave. The beers here cost twice what they do elsewhere in Bali, the price of admission for a prime view of the elite surfers. We arrive at low tide, even lower than normal because of a full moon. As such, the reef is exposed near the shore, and with intense jealousy I watch a couple swimming in a tide pool. The overall vibe is more Hawaii's North Shore than Bali.

Thirty years ago, media coverage of the island tended to mention both its excessive development and the Balinese magic that endured in the face of it. Bali was beginning to deal not only with unsustainable numbers of tourists, but with growth in the permanent population moving here for work, from 1.8 million in the early sixties to 4.2 million in 2014. Stories started to emerge of certain beaches washing away, such as at Kuta, after a runway extension into the water blocked the flow of sand, and of certain coral reefs dying, such as those near Sanur, thanks to activity on land to the south of it. Traffic was starting to overwhelm the roads. But one could still squint and pretend it wasn't all going sideways.

At the same time, life was changing for the Balinese. Residents saw gains in education, income, and access to health care. By 1995, every village on the island had electricity. On the other hand, skilled workers from Java often took the best jobs, meaning that, yet again, the benefit for the Balinese wasn't as great as it might have been, and revenues from tourism did not benefit all—inequality was on the rise in Bali.

NIAS

Entering the 1990s, it seemed like tourism in Lagundri Bay was taking off. The shoreline got hooked up to the electric grid (a few years before the village up the hill), the Sorake Beach Resort opened in 1993, and the following year, the Point hosted its first international surf contest, prompting road improvements, a renovated judges stand, new shops, and periodic spraying to keep mosquitoes at bay. The community anticipated the opening of the airport.

But by the late nineties, the optimism began to fade. The airport had made no progress. Mark Flint heard rumors of an official using government money to buy land near the proposed airport in his own name, hoping for a big profit as things developed. I found another report of locals who suspected the resort owner of maneuvering to secure the airport contract for himself and who grew suspicious of the whole endeavor.

Into the 1990s, Sorake was a classic sand beach dotted with palm trees. But as concrete replaced traditional building materials, locals systematically shoveled sand from the beach to mix with the cement. As the sand disappeared, the shore's palm trees, one by one, tipped over into the ocean. Today the shoreline at Sorake Beach could not be described as a beautiful one.

Then the Asian financial crisis brought government investment to a halt. The following decade, other waves on some smaller islands near Nias were discovered, with losmens going up there to serve the surfers and bringing increased competition for their business. The Sorake Beach Resort proved less of a draw than hoped for, and before long Accor severed ties with it.

The day after Christmas in 2004, a magnitude 9.2 earthquake struck with an epicenter about three hundred miles north of Nias. It was the strongest quake globally in at least forty years, and at eight to ten minutes, the longest in recorded history (most last under thirty seconds). Sorake Beach lost most of its buildings but was spared the worst of the ensuing tsunami that killed at least 225,000 people worldwide.

Three months later, on the night of March 28, another earthquake struck, this one with a magnitude of 8.6. On our second trip to Sorake, we are staying in a losmen run by a man named Site (pronounced *see-tay*), whose family also migrated from the village and owns this land. He tells me that on the evening of March 28, at home in his losmen, he got a spine-tingling feeling out of nowhere, and walked immediately up to the village to see his parents. He returned around quarter to eleven and noticed that his sister's house across the street was bustling. He joined the group there watching the film *Volcano*. Wrong natural disaster, but in hindsight easy to take as a sign. Fifteen minutes later, the earthquake struck, flattening the losmen he would normally have been sleeping in at this time of night.

This earthquake changed the very geology of Nias, permanently elevating it two meters in one fell swoop. The coral reef lining the shore by the Point was suddenly well above water during low tide and soon died. Sorake Beach found itself in the strange position of no longer needing to worry about sea level rise. As the ground settled, it became clear that the quake had made the wave even better. For the first time, the island received attention from the international community. Aid poured in and propped up a tourism industry for which there had been little market, and for which recovery would be slow.

But it would happen. By my second visit in 2019, I am able to choose from a number of losmens that seem entirely comfortable. We are more than pleased with the one we're staying in, largely thanks to Site. He has the universal mannerisms of the surfer, a nonchalant demeanor pierced only when talking about the waves, at which point an intensity of character kicks in. Surfing got Site to Bali, where he became a surf instructor in Kuta. There he met a Swiss woman, married her, and followed her home. The marriage didn't last, but Site stayed in Switzerland and eventually met Petra, who recently followed him back to Nias. She's running the losmen's marketing and customer service and also its new drone, which is great for capturing footage of their guests surfing.

Site brought a knowledge of Western dishes back from Switzerland and knows how to interpret Indonesian dishes for Western palates. Thanks to him, we eat very well here—vegetable coconut curries and perfect omelets. There's good air-conditioning in the bedroom and reliable Wi-Fi. This would have been unthinkable even a decade ago.

BALI

Today there are more than four thousand hotels and guesthouses in Bali, according to government figures. They've transformed villages and led to a perplexing urban milieu. In Canggu, roads run perpendicular to the beach, with few or no connecting streets between them, like ladders with no rungs. Getting to a café just one block over can mean a mile-long trip. "Shortcut" roads have been built in a couple of places between Canggu and Seminyak, the next village over, single-lane affairs not only with no shoulders, but raised several feet above the rice fields they traverse. Cars and motorbikes regularly fall over the abrupt edge.

The roads can't accommodate all the cars and motorbikes. The landfills can't accommodate the 1.6 billion tons of trash produced every year. From that, 33,000 tons of plastic make their way into the ocean annually. During the wet season, much of that plastic washes back onto the shores, blanketing the sand.

Ketut Putra, who grew up in Bali's central valley, is the executive director of Conservation International in Indonesia. He tells me that instead of providing an economic boost, the beaches today have become a money pit. "Our environment is supposed to be helping us, but now it's a kind of cost for us to maintain the good nature," he says.

So much water has been extracted from the ground for tourists' showers and swimming pools and golf courses that the water table has lowered and salt water is now seeping in. Rivers have dried up. Rice fields sometimes turn brown.

"The way we develop our island is based only on the economic, but not based on the real culture required to maintain our own beliefs, our own island, and the ability of our island to be resilient," Putra says. "If you don't really secure the environmental quality that you have on the island, I don't think you can secure your economy."

This is all connected to how unpleasant Bali can be on the ground in certain moments. For the tourist, simply getting a taxi can be a fraught experience, as local cartels control certain zones and allow neither Ubers nor metered taxis from outside the zone to pick up passengers. Flouting their rules can result in violence. In Canggu, there are few sidewalks and lots of motorbikes. The only Balinese people I interact with are those selling me things. The sound of construction often precludes relaxation. The beaches are often dirty. Matters of money seldom feel straightforward.

On the flip side of the equation, the Balinese have continued to gain in prosperity thanks to tourism. The island's official poverty rate is below 4 percent and per capita GDP is over $17,000 US, many times higher than most other islands in Indonesia. Then again, it's been estimated that 85 percent of Bali's tourism economy is controlled by entities or people outside of Bali. When large-scale resorts became common in the 1980s and 1990s, wealthy Javanese firms often developed the properties and brought international companies in to manage them, an arrangement that became the standard. For local populations, prosperity derived from beach tourism never seems to grow in a straight line.

NIAS

On Nias, I encounter everyday local life without even trying. Women do laundry in one river. Kids swim naked in another. A wedding gets under way with half the seating on one side of the road and half on the other, the guests dressed in their shiny, colorful best. On a front porch, two women get their hair done. A local takes us to a tofu factory in a shack at the end of an alley just outside Teluk Dalam. I find certain elements uncomfortable, like the cockfight in progress at the side of the road, two roosters duking to the death inside a metal barrel while ten or so men look on. Or the restaurants marked with a "B1," which means dog meat is served.

One afternoon, Scott and I walk down to the bottom of the bay, where we spent a late morning two years previous swimming in the sandy-bottomed water and paying a local boy the equivalent of fifty cents to climb a palm tree and retrieve two coconuts for us. His father had named the price, and when the boy returned with the coconuts, his father cut them open and served them to us with straws and spoons. In the early days of tourism here, bungalows lined this beach. During this visit, a couple of them still stood, abandoned. A single losmen accepted guests.

Since our last trip to Nias, two government-sponsored hotels have begun to go up. We try to find someone to sell us coconuts again, to no avail. While we sit facing the water, two sets of guys shovel sand into wheelbarrows and when they're full, haul them away to be mixed with cement for the hotels, destroying the very attraction for which the hotels are being built. Mark Flint tells me that the beach here used to be fifty meters wide. In a repeat of what happened to the beach at the Point, palm trees here topple into the water as the sand that supports them disappears. Several rows of palm trees have already vanished. What had been one of the best beaches I've ever seen no longer exists at high tide.

On the way back to our losmen, I stop to take a picture of an old house that has recently collapsed onto the beach, another victim of illegal sand mining. In front of it, flies swarm a newly dead dog. I will notice only later, after downloading the photo to my laptop, that the dead dog is in the frame.

On Nias, the progress comes in fits and starts, as does the environmental mismanagement. The new hotels are going up at the expense of the beach in front of them. The strip of losmens is hooked up to an electric grid, but it's powered by diesel fuel—hardly a sustainable solution.

In 2016, just 3,143 foreign tourists came to South Nias, millions fewer than came to southern Bali. (The numbers are not broken down further, but almost all of those likely came to Sorake Beach.) To grow the industry, they'll need to expand their pool of guests beyond surfers. To this end, Nias has been making strides toward becoming its own province. Mark Flint thinks the move is necessary for further development—it will enable implementation of a local tax structure and ease the way for investment and loans from outside.

For now, poverty in South Nias is over 16 percent, and GDP per capita just $478. Still, these numbers are far better than in other areas of the island. Anecdotally, locals have benefited from the small tourism industry here. I spend one afternoon at a new health clinic set up by an Australian doctor who surfs on Nias periodically. The clinic serves local residents free of charge, and demand is high.

Elvira Wau's brother is at university in Jakarta, and Elvira is in pharmacy school in Medan while continuing to help with the family's losmen. She and her other siblings have the opportunity to see the world outside of Nias, and to bring their education back home for the benefit of their community, all thanks to the losmen on the Point. Site represents the next wave of this progress. And because the tourism here has been created by the locals, the people of Lagundri Bay still inhabit their land on their own terms.

ON THIS SECOND TRIP, WE RETURN TO THE ABANDONED SORAKE BEACH Resort to find that it has deteriorated significantly. The roof of the freestanding restaurant has caved, its floor crumbled. The flowering pink bush is gone. A family has moved into at least one of the bungalows, reclaiming the land that had been taken for development by outsiders. This resort on Nias didn't work, while so many just like it on Bali found success. In the end, a few small factors going back centuries made the difference—spice routes, proximity to the center of power, Margaret Mead, the whims of a *National Geographic* writer, an airstrip built during World War II.

The rise of beach tourism brings quantifiable benefits at the same time it hurts communities in less tangible ways. On Nias, people struggle for education and health care, yet their culture remains their own. Life on Bali has become busy and anonymous, but its people can usually get the things they need. Ambivalence is built into the game, either way. One day a group of young kids follows us through Botohili, their village, while we're on another of our wanders from Sorake Beach. They're excited we're here, and right before we leave the village, they bid us to take their picture. They huddle together in self-conscious poses and I'm thinking what a great interaction this is, between us, the tourists, and them, the locals. Then, just as Scott snaps the photo, the little girl in the center gives him the finger.

ELEVEN

GHOSTS IN THE MACHINE

Baiae, Rockaway, and Acapulco

BAIAE, FIRST THROUGH FOURTH CENTURIES

Near the western edge of Italy's Bay of Naples, some fifteen miles from the city of Naples itself, the town of Baiae presents a blink-and-you'll-miss-it affability. At the water's edge and fronting a smaller bay within the larger one, a row of restaurants and cafés serves customers out of semipermanent tents next to a marina filled with boats, some of them impressive. Just behind the tents, the main street traces the outline of the shore as it morphs from beach to hills to cliffs. A few dive shops share the colorful stucco buildings with low-key restaurants and a bar or two, plus the businesses that signify local life—a pharmacy, a grocery, some residential buildings.

Despite its seaside charms, Baiae barely registers in guidebooks, if it does at all. Most tourists to this region, in fact, have never heard of it, busy as they are swarming to blockbuster locations nearby: Naples, Pompeii, Positano. Baiae, instead, is pleasant and unassuming.

There's little indication, in fact, that two thousand years ago this was the world's first full-fledged seaside resort.

Unlike many other cultures, the Romans had a thing for the sea, and throughout the empire those of means built villas near the water, as far away as the island of Mersea in present-day England. Both Augustus and Tiberius had villas on Capri. But no other location came close to the collective ostentation on display at Baiae. In the first centuries AD, emperors and aristocrats sequestered themselves here from the dirt, the chaos, the responsibilities, and the constraints of everyday life in the city 150 miles to the north. And they had a good time doing it. This was no ancient Newport, full of rich people behaving themselves. It was more like a Las Vegas-by-the-Sea, or a nineteenth-century Monte Carlo, but even more over the top, rife with beach parties, boat parties, music, booze, orgies, and opulent banquets—featuring the world's best seafood, some of it sourced from substantial fish ponds of both salt water and freshwater within the villas. As the Roman Empire barreled toward its peak and decline, the party in Baiae only got crazier.

I'm here to see what's left of it. A swath of hillside ruins directly above the main street comprise the Archaeological Park of Baia, while an additional few buildings mingle with the houses and shops and cafés. These ruins are spectacular, yet they're only the second most intriguing excavation here. The real showstopper, and the thing that differentiates Baiae from the hundreds of other spectacular ancient sites in Italy, lies literally beneath the surface. Today more than half of ancient Baiae—about 437 acres—sits underwater. In Roman times the shoreline here extended 1,300 feet farther into the bay than it does today, and was some of the most coveted real estate in the Roman Empire. The only way I can see where the heart of the social scene was set, and where the most extravagant parties took place at the old resort, is to head underwater.

And so, for the first time in my life, I go scuba diving.

———

NEITHER THE NAPLES METROPOLITAN AREA'S PUBLIC TRANSPORTATION managers nor its tourism operators have prioritized easy access to Baiae, unlike, say, Pompeii, which lies a similar distance from central Naples in the opposite direction and where the train stop is just a five-minute walk from the ruins. Pompeii receives 3.5 million visitors every year. By comparison, Baiae feels half-forgotten.

To get there, I take a commuter train to Fusaro, a twenty-minute walk across the peninsula from Baiae. On this sunny, otherwise superlative morning, the train stalls halfway through the trip, and as I follow the other passengers off, I admire the sheer comprehensiveness of the graffiti covering the train cars. We are herded onto a replacement bus and now I know I'll be late for my dive. Once at Fusaro, in my hurry to condense the remaining twenty-minute walk into ten, I step in dog shit in the middle of a roundabout, and just like that I've checked off two rites of passage for the tourist to Italy.

By the time I arrive at the dive shop on Baiae's main street, the scuba orientation has begun, and I spend the next half hour playing catch-up. After, I get suited up and then I'm on a Zodiac boat with inflated sides, on which the other divers and I sit facing each other. Because I'm a novice, my dive instructor, Ornella, will stick with me every kick of the way, adjusting my oxygen and other controls on my suit that I don't understand. With my oxygen tank on my back, I fall backward from the Zodiac into the sea. Ornella joins me, and after practicing breathing underwater at the surface, she adjusts a gauge or two and we sink to the seafloor.

While I'm waiting for the onset of claustrophobia, I focus hard on my breathing, which is a weird way to breathe. Then Ornella takes my hand and we begin to swim, coming almost immediately upon a series of statues arranged in a U-shape. These statues lined a nymphaeum, a sanctuary room dedicated to water—a fact I'll learn later in the day when I meet Barbara Davidde, the archaeologist leading the underwater excavation here. I'll also learn that the statues I'm looking at are replacements for the originals, which were removed to protect them from degradation at the hands of the ocean.

In the pool at the nymphaeum's center, guests gathered for gluttonous meals served on large floating trays. These gatherings were likely hosted by none other than the emperor Claudius, who reigned over the Roman Empire from 41 to 54 AD and owned the villa to which this nymphaeum belonged. Later it belonged to Nero, an emperor known to enjoy an indulgence—his parties were legendary throughout the empire. This villa and others were arranged around a small, oval-shaped harbor open to the sea at a narrow channel— which was probably the crater of an extinct volcano; it was absolutely one of the toniest addresses around.

Ornella points out old brick walls and inlaid marble floors. We make out the outlines of rooms everywhere via their intact walls. We swim down what's either a hallway or a narrow street, I can't quite tell. At one point Ornella swims down to the seafloor and starts clearing the earth, gradually uncovering a black-and-white tile mosaic portraying two men locked in battle, one seeming to be attacking the other's skull. It's gorgeous, and complemented by a red starfish hanging on a nearby wall. This mosaic once served as the floor of a sort of locker room—known as such because of extant hooks and partitions typical of such rooms. When I'm done taking it all in, Ornella covers the mosaic to protect it from the elements of the ocean.

We swim above a road made of cobblestones so big I want to call them boulders—this is the Via Herculanea, the major thoroughfare of ancient Baiae. Ornella shows me a series of holes in a wall where hot water or perhaps steam once entered a spa room. The patrons of Baiae had been attracted to these shores in part because of the volcanic activity beneath them, which enabled villa owners to build elaborate thermal baths, saunas, and steam rooms merely by exploiting the natural elements.

———

AFTER MY DIVE I HAVE TROUBLE FINDING A RESTAURANT THAT ISN'T closed, so I skip lunch and walk up to the archaeological park entrance at the top of the hill. This is mid-September, hardly the low season in Italy. I'm sure Pompeii is packed, yet I have the ruins here to myself, save for a couple who enters a few minutes after me, and then a father-son duo who enters just before I leave. Also, a few resident cats. This is a delight, but it also confounds me, considering how great these ruins are and how well they evoke that topic of timeless fascination, the lives of the rich and infamous. Improved signage or maybe even an audio guide would help, but this feels like the foundation of a major tourist attraction. The ruins of Baiae, in fact, are three times the size of those in Pompeii (although both sites remain only partially excavated).

The centerpiece is a villa built over six terraces in the hillside, with intact rooms, mosaic floors, wall frescos, living quarters, gardens, and possibly a theater. Another highlight: the so-called Temple of Mercury, which is not really a temple at all, but a domed swimming pool. With its 71-foot diameter, this was the largest concrete dome in the world until the Pantheon was completed in Rome. Inside, the pool is still there, filled with water. Baiae also boasted the largest freshwater cistern in the entire Roman Empire, one more way to keep the republic's most prominent citizens comfortable during their time here.

Later in the afternoon, I sit down with Barbara Davidde at one of the cafés lining the marina. I'm the only customer in the place when I arrive, but before long a crowd will start trickling in to watch a major soccer match between Naples and Liverpool. Davidde has been the head archaeologist working on the underwater portion of Baiae since 2011, though she's been involved in the project since 1992, when she helped excavate an underwater statue in a garden of one of the villas.

At that time, she tells me, most of these cafés and restaurants hadn't yet opened. As with many small municipalities in Italy, recent decades have not been kind to Baiae. The town suffered from a lack of opportunity for young people especially; they were decamping in large numbers to the country's major metropolises or, just as often, for opportunities in other EU nations. For the last several years, in fact, Italy's total population has been falling. Well under half the population of Bacoli (which encompasses Baiae) today is under the age of forty.

Along the stairway up from the main street to the bigger road that takes cars in and out of town, elderly women climb the steps in spurts, stopping after every few paces to gossip with a friend, or if no one's around, just to scowl at the remaining stairs ahead of them. Men and women living in the houses on the hill keep the street cats well fed. Down on the main street, only the occasional car rolls by. But the traits that made Baiae attractive to the Roman elite are still intact. The natural beauty of the landscape is a fact of the place, inspiring the Roman poet Horace to say of it in the first century BC, "No bay on earth outshines the lovely Baiae." The volcanic activity enabling the thermal baths sealed the deal.

In addition to its earthly splendor, Baiae was also conveniently located just across the harbor from Puteoli, the most important port of the day. "Puteoli was the harbor that connected Rome with all the [goods] from the Near East, Alexandria, Egypt," Davidde says. "The very rich people involved in trade had to work in Puteoli." Everything that made the good life good—spices, fine silks, ivory, jewels—came easily to Baiae. It proved the perfect spot for the second homes of the elite.

There may be no beach resort of our times—not Monte Carlo, Atlantic City, South Beach, or even Cancún during peak spring break—that can rival Baiae for complete creative decadence. Likewise for exclusivity. Baiae became synonymous with indulgence—all manner of escapism included. In addition to Claudius and Nero, Julius Caesar, Brutus, Cicero, Augustus, and other emperors and elite Romans had seaside villas there. The philosopher Seneca also visited, describing it disapprovingly in a letter as "a hostelry of vices" and "ill-adapted to excellence of character."

This was no place for the rote demands of everyday life. Rather, people came here to disregard them. Davidde tells me that while they've discovered likely evidence of shops and other daily conveniences along the main road, archaeologists have yet to uncover evidence of public buildings, such as a forum, temple, or marketplace. Baiae was devoid of the types of buildings that are suggestive of accountability.

On at least one occasion, decadence descended into malevolence. Nero acquired a second villa and used Baiae as his personal, depraved playground. Here in the year 59 AD, the emperor masterminded the murder of his own mother, Agrippina, who had herself masterminded Nero's rise to the throne, but lately had grown apart from her son. She traveled by sea to meet him in Baiae sometime in March, and he welcomed her with one of his elaborate banquets. When it was over, he put her on a boat ostensibly to take her to her own villa for the night. But the boat had been rigged to self-destruct in the water. When it fell apart, Agrippina swam away from it and was rescued, only to be murdered later in the night by one of Nero's men.

Matricide was extreme even for Baiae, but in general its shores became a place where powerful people generally got up to no good, using their distance from Rome as a rationalization for indulging in all kinds of vice and scheming. It was a custom that would be replicated in modern times at the casino in Monte Carlo, at the offshore banks in the Cayman Islands, at nightclubs in Cabo, and even at Mar-a-Lago in Palm Beach.

THE VOLCANIC ACTIVITY UNDERGROUND MADE BAIAE AN EXCELLENT RE-sort, but also spelled its doom. The ground here sank about sixty feet starting in the fourth century, thanks to what's known as bradyseism, a phenomenon in volcanically active areas in which underground magma chambers empty out or fill back up, causing the ground to sink or rise accordingly. The former caused half of the ancient resort to sink into the sea. By the 1500s, Baiae had been abandoned entirely. This wasn't climate change, and it wasn't sea level rise, but the result was similar and provides a startling preview of what the future might hold for beach resorts the world over.

Gradually, the magma chambers partially refilled, raising the land again. In the past three decades, the ground under Baiae has gained six feet of altitude, bringing the underwater ruins back to within fifteen or so feet of the surface. The submerged portion of ancient Baiae gained official protection in 2002 with the creation of the underwater archaeological park. Larger ships coming to the industrial port in this harbor had already caused considerable damage to the ruins, especially surviving walls, so to protect them from further damage, the government moved the port elsewhere in the Bay of Naples, and opened the marina for leisure boats instead.

The marina has helped the potential revival of the area. Many, including Davidde, hope to see the ruins of Baiae further the area's appeal as they are documented and made more accessible. In addition, the shoreline is great, many of its beaches lovely. A tourism industry could feasibly build up around them and might entice young people to stick around. On the other hand, it takes little stretch of the imagination to see how its popularity might play out. The underwater ruins would be threatened by too many boats and too many divers. The aboveground archaeological park would become something like that of Pompeii, visited by millions of people every year, some of whom cause damage to the site, mostly incidental, sometimes intentional. People would complain about all the souvenir shops, and talk about how much better the place was back when. Eventually the town would cede to calls for limiting access to its ruins. The tourism development cycle would strike again.

That's the hypothetical. For now, Baiae remains the world's first known seaside resort, and also the first to have disappeared. Toward the southern tip of the peninsula that marks the edge of the Bay of Naples, a fifteenth-century castle stands out against the sky, timeless and majestic. Today it houses an archaeological museum showcasing relics from the area, including the original statues retrieved from underwater for safekeeping. The castle is more intriguing for the likelihood that Julius Caesar's seaside villa lies buried beneath it, one of the scores of Baiae holiday villas that may never be unearthed.

ROCKAWAY: NINETEENTH THROUGH EARLY TWENTIETH CENTURIES

I wasn't among the first gentle wave of Brooklynites to descend on the Rockaway Peninsula in Queens, New York, in the early years of this century. But I wasn't far off. On the first day of 2012, Scott and I rented an apartment on the second floor of a ninety-year-old house in Rockaway Beach, a block up from one of the area's two surf breaks. The Rockaways, or just Rockaway, as the neighborhoods of the peninsula are alternately known, are lined by a ten-mile sandy beach on one side and the expansive Jamaica Bay on the other. A boardwalk spans five and a half miles of the beach. There's water all around. That such a natural phenomenon exists within New York City has shocked and delighted more than one newcomer, who can never resist musing over why the place isn't better known. I counted myself among them.

I bought a boogie board. Once the weather got hot, I went for morning swims. Scott kept buying new surfboards, which were absorbed into the apartment's décor. We rode bikes up and down the peninsula, where we found no uniform aesthetic to the place. Instead we'd ride through housing projects, then streets with the manicured lawns of the upper middle class, through high-rises built for the middle-income crowd, then deserted stretches of beachfront land and a parking lot that was built to hold 9,000 cars at once. Beyond this was Fort Tilden, a former army installation, and then a final gated community of bungalows at the tip of the peninsula. Three or four different urban milieus might be represented in the space of a block. All of it within a couple minutes' walk of the beach.

To gain a foothold here, I got a summer job at Rockaway Taco, the peninsula's seminal hipster joint. Before it opened in 2008, the surf scene in the Rockaways remained a fairly well-kept secret. The city had designated the first surfing-only beach in 2005, at Beach 90th Street, and once in a while you might see a guy on the A train with a surfboard, and smile at the dissonance of it; where was he even going with that thing, et cetera. But after Rockaway Taco, all of Brooklyn started crowding into those same A train cars on summer weekends. On an 83-degree Saturday, the line for fish tacos stretched out of the shack that housed the business, then down and around the corner, then halfway down the next block, too. You could easily spend an hour in line before placing your order. Coming to Rocka-way Taco became as much a part of the Rockaway experience as lying on the sand.

By the 2010s, word of a renaissance was seeping out. Rockaway seemed ready to become the next Williamsburg, a neglected pocket of the city transformed first by some pioneering group, in this case surfers, then by the hipsters in their wake, and finally by the mon-eyed classes swooping in to capitalize on the new cachet. Patti Smith bought a bungalow and made it her permanent home. The lead singer of MGMT bought a house near the surf break and subjected it to a high-design renovation.

A renaissance, by definition, requires something that came before to be revived. In the case of Rockaway, the previous era remained hazy, but usually pointed to things that living people could remember firsthand, like Playland, the amusement park between Beach 97th and Beach 98th Streets that opened in 1902 and didn't close until 1985. An entire generation of working-class New Yorkers seems to have fond memories of the thousands of summer bungalows that once covered the peninsula, simple dwellings whose charm lay in their lack of pretension, and pockets of which remain to this day.

As the surfboards and trend pieces proliferated, nobody in the media or in Rockaway itself seemed to recall the gilded history that came before the bungalows and roller coasters. Collective memory can be alarmingly short when not a single physical relic remains to remind us. That was the case with Baiae, and similarly, what's been forgotten here is that in the nineteenth century, hundreds of hotels dotted the Rockaways, many of them as vast as they were grandiose. For a time, there was no more prominent place in the country to retreat during the summer, and when writers covered the great resorts of the age, Rockaway not only made the cut but often topped the list.

EUROPEAN SETTLERS PURCHASED THE ROCKAWAY PENINSULA IN 1685 from the Native American Canarsie (whose "Reckouwacky" means "the place of our own people"), after which the first white family—the Cornells—built a house in present-day Far Rockaway in 1690. For the next hundred or so years, the land remained sparsely populated, used for farmland and livestock grazing. But toward the end of the 1700s, a few shorefront residents started to let out rooms and create rudimentary bathing establishments. A letter in *The Literary Magazine and American Register* in 1803 chronicled a stay in a lodging house in Rockaway that could accommodate 20 or 30 people.

The Cornell house would be demolished in 1833 to make way for the Marine Pavilion, Rockaway's first major hotel. Financed through a partnership that included at least one ex–New York City mayor and one ex–New York governor, the 160-room Marine Pavilion immediately became one of the most fashionable hotels on the East Coast. In an old sketching, it looks sort of like the White House. Henry Wadsworth Longfellow and Washington Irving both stayed there, as did any number of movers and shakers from New York and beyond. In 1853 the *New-York Daily Times* (as the *New York Times* was called until 1857) described a summer scene at the Marine Pavilion where "storekeepers from the city, bank-clerks, brokers, and clerks in large importing houses, play the aristocrat for a week, at from two dollars to two and a half per day . . . and have the pleasure of being in the same house with some celebrity occasionally to be found there."

The Marine Pavilion followed the English model. Despite the celebrity influence, the clientele seemed dedicated to good behavior, never dancing to "an excellent band of music" that played nightly and comporting themselves "with true aristocratic frigidity." An 1839 history of Long Island notes the apparent healing benefits of a stay: "The atmosphere here is fresh, cool and delightful; invalids soon find themselves benefited, and all experience fresh inspiration and increased vigor by repeated plunges in the ocean."

Like so many other nineteenth-century resorts, the Marine Pavilion would burn to the ground, in this case in 1864, but not before it kicked off an era of grand hotels, puffed-up social strata, and elaborate sea-bathing in the Rockaways. Almost all of the earliest tourism centered on Far Rockaway—the section closest to the mainland of Long Island—while the slender peninsula farther out remained empty—early maps refer to it simply as Sand Hills, with dunes as high as fifty feet. Reminiscing in later years, the *New York Times* observed, "Among the Summer resorts that were once the most cherished by the wealthy, the aristocratic, and the fashionable families of New York, Far Rockaway was, perhaps, the most beloved."

The success of the first beach resorts all but guaranteed that the concept would creep over the rest of the Rockaways—which were, incidentally, gaining acreage as sand accreted and increased the length of the peninsula. The land on which Jacob Riis Park sits today, for example, emerged sometime around the 1860s. (Today a third of Rockaway stretches beyond even that point.) Two train lines—one on the ocean side and one on the bay side—gradually extended westward through the peninsula, making access from the city and elsewhere feasible. As the hundreds of hotels went up, so did restaurants, amusement rides, theaters, dance halls, Turkish baths, swimming pools, train lines, boardwalks, and steamboat piers, the entertainments now as endless as the beach itself.

ONE SPRINGTIME AFTERNOON, SCOTT AND I DRIVE TO BEACH 20TH STREET and Plainview Avenue, in the heart of Far Rockaway. Today it's a frenetic area, urban but not quite cohesive in its layout and vibe. We pull into the parking lot of a cramped shopping center, creeping past a Subway, a Dunkin' Donuts, a CVS, and a Caribbean seafood spot called Just Taste It. We are now at the top of a slight hill. Almost two hundred years ago, instead of a shopping center parking lot, here sat the Marine Pavilion, arguably the finest seaside resort in the United States. I look past the traffic and urban surfaces and I can see how this spot, with its ocean view and breezes, might have been ideal.

We go exploring the Edgemere section, running from present-day Beach 32nd Street to Beach 56th Street. The Edgemere Hotel,

The Edgemere Hotel once stood on this stretch of land in Rockaway, New York.

built in 1895, gave the area its name and could welcome 400 guests at a time. At its height, this land boasted over 60 hotels. Today these are the emptiest blocks in New York City, razed in the 1960s and left to nature, which has reclaimed them. A few years back, the set for *Boardwalk Empire* included a replica of the Atlantic City boardwalk built between Beach 32nd and Beach 35th, the area so little visited that hardly anyone knew about it—this long-abandoned beach resort, however briefly, regained its glory by dressing up as another resort, in another time and place altogether.

Where the Edgemere stood, with its stately air and tennis courts and long, wide verandah, a crumbling paved street now intersects a dirt road. The usual assortment of trash sullies the shrubbery to each side, tires and crumpled aluminum foil among full black garbage bags that have been dumped here. Near the ramp leading up to the boardwalk, a bloated brown recliner faces the ocean. Well-maintained street signs point out that we are at the intersection of Beach 35th Street and Sprayview Avenue, and indicate that the city expected these streets to be used, and possibly still does. The periodic fire hydrant peeking out from the brush will also drive that point home. On Beach 35th Street, closer to the main road, there's the still-operating Public School 106, the only building remaining in these would-be beach blocks, like the only building left standing after an air raid, or a hurricane.

Farther west, there's a bizarre apartment complex with tiny windows, no outdoor living space, and a beachfront given over to its dumpsters. Past it are the first buildings of Arverne by the Sea, a massive residential development that went up in the aughts, mostly buildings a few stories high with gray or beige siding and white trim that feel appropriate to their oceanfront location. Here at Beach 69th Street was the 300-room Arverne Hotel, built in 1888 (and burned down in 1935), with its Italian gardens and saltwater swimming pool, another hotel that gave the neighborhood its name. Around the Arverne Hotel, some 40 "cottages" stood, owned by various New

York City luminaries—cottages in the same way that the mansions of Newport were.

The Rockaway of yore had more hotels than Cancún does today.[*] And it had one that for a split second laid claim to the title of biggest hotel in the world. The Rockaway Beach Hotel once spanned the entire seven-block stretch of beachfront between what are now Beach 112th and Beach 119th Streets. Built by a crew of 1,500 men to be ready for the 1881 summer season, its endless red roof and series of conical cupolas promised a new cultural landmark. In the summer of 1880, visitors to Rockaway got their first look at its four stories, with a 125,000 square-foot footprint, 650 bedrooms, and a capacity to feed 10,000 people per day in its restaurant.

The Rockaway Beach Hotel was insolvent from the start, and never opened to full capacity. In 1883, suppliers went unpaid and complained to the press, a sure sign of financial trouble. Later that decade, the hotel was torn down and sold for parts. Today, in its place, you'll find the Sand Bar, a boardwalk concession bar that Hurricane Sandy shuttered in 2012. Next to it you'll see the terminus of Beach 116th Street, a main shopping thoroughfare perpetually on the verge of revitalization. Across the street, you'll see a new apartment complex looking to force the area a notch upmarket. Venture a block east and find a meticulously restored but shuttered bed-and-breakfast sharing a block with some down-and-out SROs straight out of 1970s Times Square. Along the beach, there's the Promenade Rehabilitation and Healthcare Center, the Park Nursing Home, and the Beacon Nursing Home. It's an area that fared poorly when the coronavirus pandemic took hold—one of three Rockaway

---

[*] Here is a partial list of other hotels in Rockaway during its heyday: The Atlantic Park, the United States, Holland House, the Seaside House, Hemberger's, the Prince George, the Caffrey Kuloff, the Tackapousha, Faber's, the Hotel Lyndeman, the Hotel Lorraine, the Grand Embassy, the Hotel Frontenac, the Holmehurst Inn, the Colonial, the Hotel Majestic, the Hotel Britain, the Hotel Jerome, the Hotel Pasadena, Hammels Hotel, the Oceanview, the East End Cottage, the Holland, Emmerich's, the Shirley House, and McCarthy's.

neighborhoods that ranked among the top eleven in the city for COVID death rates by the late spring of 2020.

For a fleeting moment in the nineteenth century, the purported largest hotel in the world dominated this shoreline. In its failure, the Rockaway Beach Hotel perhaps succumbed to the limits of America's emerging bigger-is-better ethos, but it did little to slow enthusiasm for the Rockaway Peninsula as a summer destination. The decline would come during the following century.

ENTERING THE TWENTIETH CENTURY, ROCKAWAY'S POPULARITY AS A SEA-side resort continued apace. New hotels opened, while next to them small bungalows and seasonal tent colonies went up and began catering to those on a tighter budget. Playland opened alongside other, lesser-known amusements. A series of boardwalks teemed with all manner of entertainments.

Formerly part of the town of Hempstead, Long Island, in 1898 the Rockaways joined the borough of Queens when it in turn joined New York City. This opened up access to the city's considerable resources, but would also make Rockaway victim to its whims, including those of the singular force that was Robert Moses. The notorious New York City parks commissioner came to power in the 1930s and took a particular interest in Rockaway. He wanted to turn the peninsula into a healthful place for people to live, but also a parklike span of leisurely beachfront for the masses. As Lawrence and Carol P. Kaplan put it in their book *Between Ocean and City: The Transformation of Rockaway, New York*, "for approximately thirty years Moses played the single most important role in determining the fate of the peninsula."

Well before Moses's arrival, signs of trouble were emerging in Rockaway. Where once the action had spanned both the ocean side and bay side of the peninsula, by the 1920s Jamaica Bay had become too polluted for recreation, rendering the many hotels facing it undesirable, and most of them closed. Throughout Rockaway, the elite travelers who had given Rockaway its sterling reputation were decamping to less crowded beaches farther afield. Still, in the 1930s over 100 hotels dotted the peninsula. But bungalows, rooming houses, and year-round homes were gaining ground. It was gradually becoming clear to local leaders that Rockaway was transitioning to a year-round community. By the end of World War II, only about ten hotels remained.

Instead of drawing visitors from all over the eastern United States, Rockaway now hosted working- and middle-class residents of the tristate area. The peninsula was less prestigious, but busier than ever. In the summer of 1950, an astounding 48 million people visited Rockaway during the summer season. This would be the peak. That summer, the wooden trestle that carried Long Island Rail Road trains over Jamaica Bay from Manhattan to Rockaway burned, cutting off a crucial transport link. At the same time, American vacation habits in general were beginning to change—air-conditioning and suburban swimming pools made summers at home less brutal, while accessible plane travel, mass car ownership, and the advent of paid time off enabled travel to more distant beach resorts.

The new generation of prosperous travelers had expectations for their accommodations that the old bungalows and rooming houses of Rockaway couldn't meet. Even before the trestle burned, summer rentals were decreasing. Rockaway's seasonal population dwindled from its high of 225,000 in 1947 to 106,000 in 1952, just five years later.

Robert Moses was here for it. He recognized the current moment as his opportunity to fulfill his Rockaway vision. Many wanted to see the peninsula transition to a modern beach resort, but time and again they ran up against Moses, whose power was such that he could prevent any projects that would have commercialized Rockaway or reserved its shorefront for moneyed private interests.

While he would make some improvements to the peninsula's

public transportation options, Moses's true allegiance lay with the automobile. He elevated the existing train tracks to make way for a thoroughfare for cars underneath it. He built the Marine Parkway Bridge connecting Rockaway and Brooklyn. He renovated Jacob Riis Park in Rockaway's western section, building the parking lot for 9,000 cars there. In 1939, Moses unveiled Shorefront Parkway, running from Beach 73rd Street to Beach 108th. A road along the beach was considered—by Moses in particular—an upgrade over the concession stands, bathhouses, ramshackle hotels, and houses he tore down in order to build it. He meant it to be the first leg of a parkway that would run all the way out to the Hamptons along the barrier islands of Long Island. Never completed, Shorefront Parkway became known as a road to nowhere.

The train reopened six years later, now as part of the New York City subway system, thanks to Moses. In the summer, the city offered a daily "Rockaway Special" train from Manhattan to Rockaway. But riders found that the trip had become longer and the system less reliable, nothing like the half-hour trip on the old LIRR. In 1959, the city cut Rockaway Special service to weekends only. At some point it disappeared completely.

In the late 1940s, New York City suffered a serious housing shortage, thanks to an influx to the northern United States of African-Americans and Hispanics, plus the return of servicemen from World War II. Moses proposed a short-term solution of winterizing Rockaway's summer bungalows in order to house veterans. In the longer term, he wanted to tear them all down and build large-scale residential buildings.

In reality, the city soon shifted its focus in the Rockaways from housing veterans to finding placement for its neediest residents. The Rockaways' seasonal nature meant a weaker local community to put up resistance. The decline of the summer bungalow crowd meant, too, that empty housing was instantly available, even if it wasn't winterized and often involved shared toilets and outdoor showers. In 1949 the commissioner of welfare explained that the former criminals, drug addicts, and single-parent families being rehomed in Rockaway were not expected to find work, so its remoteness wouldn't be a problem. The undertone of racism in these policies was not well concealed. The bungalows became some of the worst welfare housing the city has ever seen, as landlords welcomed the guaranteed rent payments while enjoying little oversight for maintaining the homes to a livable standard.

The first big publicly funded apartment buildings opened in 1950 on previously empty marshland toward the bay side of the Arverne section. After this, slum clearance became part of the development equation. In 1953 the city cleared fourteen acres in the Hammels section—historically one of the few areas Blacks were welcome—and built subsidized housing on it, but made no arrangements for the displaced residents, who simply moved into extant summer bungalows in Arverne. In 1956, Moses presented his plan to raze the 3,613 "dwelling units" between Beach 90th Street and Beach 74th Street and replace them with 28 high-rise apartment buildings.

A number of additional housing projects would go up across Rockaway in the name of improvement. In effect, many simply became slums in different form, with uninspired high-rise architecture that set them apart from the Rockaway community at large. By 1975, Rockaway would contain 5 percent of Queens's population, but 57 percent of its low-income housing. Then came homes for the mentally disabled and low-rent nursing homes, following the same template. Only a few well-organized and affluent neighborhoods, mostly on the western end, managed to keep change out.

In the 1960s, more than 4,000 houses and bungalows were razed in Arverne and Edgemere. But thanks to a combination of complicated local politics, changing attitudes toward slum clearance and public housing, the federal government's moratorium on federal housing subsidies in the early seventies, and a national recession that hit New York City particularly hard, redevelopment didn't materialize for more than thirty years. In the first years of the new millennium, homes finally went up in the Arverne section—the first residents moved into Arverne by the Sea in 2004. The Edgemere section remains empty but for Public School 106.

Today, over the entire span of Rockaway, not a single one of the great old hotels remains.

LESS THAN A YEAR AFTER WE RENTED OUR PLACE IN ROCKAWAY, HURRI-cane Sandy struck in October 2012. When we got out to the apartment a couple of days after, a section of the boardwalk sat in our front yard. Hundreds of bungalows had burned down. Sand covered the land from ocean to bay. Down the street from us, a streetlamp drove straight through the first floor of a house. The damage across the peninsula put the renaissance on hold, as Rockaway's basic survival seemed no longer assured. This could have been the end of it—the state government offered to buy residents' homes and return the properties to nature. But few took the government up on the offer.

Eventually the boardwalk was rebuilt, now made of durable concrete instead of wood. Dunes were created to serve as a buffer between the ocean and community. Businesses reopened. Rockaway Taco, after a dispute among the owners, moved and became Tacoway Beach. It's as popular as ever. We spent another summer with our beach apartment, and then another. And now, improbably, a major resort hotel has just opened. The 61-room Rockaway Hotel counts itself the first here in nearly a hundred years.

ACAPULCO: TWENTIETH CENTURY

Tony Rullan is keeping me waiting. But then, eight thirty in the evening in retrospect may have been an unreasonably early time to schedule dinner with him. After fifty years in the Acapulco nightlife business, Tony is a guy who still regularly stays out until dawn. He makes a point of waking up in time to have lunch with his wife every day, but then lunch is at three or four o'clock. So I sit at a prime table in his eponymous restaurant, Tony's Bistro, and sip a glass of white wine while gazing out toward the incredible Acapulco Bay, surrounded by the foothills of the Sierra Madre. The bay gives Acapulco its dramatic natural edge over other resort towns. It makes me want to look good against it, which, I suspect, played some part in the emergence of Acapulco's midcentury glamour.

When Tony finally walks in, he's profuse with apologies. In wellpressed black slacks and a partially buttoned up black button-down, he looks well rested and ready for an eventful night. I forgive him for keeping me waiting, swayed by the charm I assume he uses on the parade of celebrities who join him at the various night spots he's run over the years. We end up sitting for a couple of hours, eating dinner and chatting over the beats of a downtempo EDM soundtrack. Tony interrupts me periodically to clink glasses, his whiskey to my wine. *Salud*, he says, every time.

Tony came to Acapulco for a visit from Mexico City in 1967 at "more or less" the age of eighteen and never left. He ended up running PR with his brother for the Villa Vera Resort. Specifically, for its daily pool scene—"*The* place to go"—with its swim-up bar immortalized in a series of Slim Aarons photographs. He soon started running the discos that put Acapulco firmly on the global nightlife circuit, starting at what is generally recognized as the first one in all of Latin America, Tequila Go Go. He hasn't slowed down since then—up the hill from Tony's Bistro is his Palladium, one of the most notable Acapulco clubs of the past couple of decades.

Tony shows me photos he's taken over the years during his nights out, with Frank Sinatra, with Elizabeth Taylor, Sissy Spacek, Sly Stallone. *I guess it's not good to show you OJ anymore*, he says, and swipes past him. A moment later he shows me a snap of himself with Michael Jackson. I try to picture Michael Jackson on a beach and can't.

I've been here a day, but Tony Rullan is in fact my second run-in with the stubborn glamour of Acapulco, the first coming when I arrived at night to the Hotel Las Brisas up on the western end of Acapulco Bay and saw, from the lobby's wraparound glass windows, a blanket of glittering stars hugging the bay. From a distance this crowded, flawed city looked like magic. Up close, I'd see later, it can be a big old mess. Cher Horowitz's "full-on Monet" comes to mind.

From the moment it opened in 1957, there was no more sought-after address than Las Brisas for Hollywood A-listers and honeymooners alike, but that was a long time ago, and I wasn't expecting to find the original allure intact. But find it I did. My room is a free-standing casita and a midcentury reverie, with its chevron tile floors and wicker egg chairs, its slatted sliding doors that open onto my own bean-shaped pool and a view that beats even the one I'd taken in at reception. The exterior white stucco was accented with hot pink trim, and I considered it something like fate that I'd brought along a bikini that matched it exactly.

I have paid $130 per night to stay here in the first weeks of the high season, evidence from the outset that things are not as they were in Acapulco. This same casita went for $340 per night back in 1981—$950 in 2020 dollars. It was partially this bargain rate that kept my expectations low, but also Acapulco's contemporary reputation as a complete has-been, smothered by its overdevelopment and rendered almost unvisitable by its ongoing problems with organized crime. Instead of anticipating delight, I'd been preoccupied with ensuring my safety in Acapulco, about which every recent U.S. article has emphasized a murder rate that is the third highest in the world.

But then, the standard narrative of Acapulco doesn't always stand up to scrutiny. It wasn't as perfect as it is remembered, and it isn't as doomed as is currently reported. Lawlessness and celebrity and power have always made for a potent cocktail here, even if the exact measurements aren't always the same. That no one is fond of discussing the details makes it a hard place to know.

From my patio at Las Brisas, I periodically hear an echoing boom coming from the mountains. I mention this to Tony Rullan.

They're fireworks, he says.

But not during the day, I press on, quite sure that what I heard was not fireworks.

They're gunshots, he says, trying a different tack. Wrong again, I'm sure.

I'm getting nowhere with this line of questioning. I shoot him a look.

Boom boom boom, he says, and touches his whiskey tumbler to my wineglass. *Salud*.

PRESENT-DAY ACAPULCO'S TOURISM AREA HAS FOUR DISTINCT SECTIONS. First, where I'm staying, Las Brisas, which is the name not only of the hotel but also of an entire neighborhood of drool-worthy villas cascading down the hill at the eastern end of Acapulco Bay. This was and is the elite section, sequestered behind guards and gatehouses. Lining the bay itself is the Zona Dorada, the Golden Zone, with its rows of high-rise hotels and chain restaurants along the six-lane, bumper-to-bumper Costera road. When people speak of overdeveloped Acapulco, they have this stretch in mind. Beyond Las Brisas in the other direction, Acapulco Diamante contains the newer, higher-end mega-resorts and a good number of condos on a beach fronting a flat expanse of land that is far less compelling than Acapulco Bay. Then, over at the opposite end of Acapulco Bay from Las Brisas, there is Acapulco Viejo, Old Acapulco, where a small, isolated port town first evolved into a resort, and where I am currently sitting at a table overlooking Caleta Beach with my lunch and a Corona. Across from me is Hector, the manager of this restaurant, La Cabana de Caleta.

This is the most famous beach in all of Mexico, he says, looking out at the weekend mayhem on the sand. While his thirty years working here have probably biased him, Hector's statement isn't hyperbole.

Caleta Beach, along with its smaller neighbor Caletilla, were indeed the first in Mexico to attract sunseekers. Beach tourism in Mexico started right here; this restaurant has been here since the 1930s. They're diminutive beaches, and essentially perfect natural creations, side-by-side crescents with a small rocky island between them. For swimmers, they're protected by Roqueta Island, farther offshore. Nearby hills partially obscure the big bay in the background. They remind me of La Garoupe, back in Cap d'Antibes.

Mexicans have remained loyal to Caleta and Caletilla even as international tourists have long since moved on. At this midafternoon hour, substantial crowds have settled in. I suspect that earlier there was jockeying for the best tables, but now a stupor has set in beneath beach umbrellas set so close to one another that they form an unbroken stretch of shade. Straight ahead in the water itself, a man wades alongside a canoe filled with trinkets for sale. Another walks down the beach trying to sell two children's lawn chairs, while yet another is wholly subsumed by his offering of inflatable water toys. A five-person brass band wanders the beach, paying visits to each party.

Legend holds that Hollywood luminaries like Errol Flynn and John Wayne just happened to stumble upon this unknown place and found it so beautiful—and so devoid of societal rules—that they stuck around, partying on their yachts and opening some little hotels for themselves and their famous friends. The truth is that by the time the first American celebrity laid eyes on this land, the Mexican government had already positioned Acapulco to strike straight for his heart.

The first step came in 1927, with the completion of a highway between Mexico City and Acapulco. It was fully paved in 1934, the same year the first flights arrived from Mexico City. Before the highway, Mexican tourism had followed the railroads, none of which made their way to Acapulco. After the highway was in place, the government began explicitly recommending Acapulco to tourists, and new hotels followed, notably the Miramar in 1928 near the old town square, with the unprecedented offering of a room with private bath. By 1933, four hotels welcomed guests, and locals had established a series of food kiosks on Caleta and Caletilla Beaches that also rented changing rooms and storage to visitors.

It really was perfection—the temperature rarely fell below 75 degrees Fahrenheit or exceeded 90 degrees. Between the months of November and April, one could expect about four days total with any rain at all. The bay itself was almost ridiculous in its visual appeal. The seawater, year-round, remained an ideal temperature for swimming.

Early Acapulco hotels set the precedent of placing the most coveted addresses high above the water in the hills and on cliffs. These hotels had views for days, but not their own beaches, so guests would get a taxi down to Caleta for the morning or afternoon. At the same time, a dual hotel market emerged, with hotels marketed to Americans charging roughly double those aimed at domestic tourists—which clustered in the old town or near the water by Caleta Beach.

Mexico's federal government saw how quickly its minimal effort had sparked a tourism industry, and in the early 1930s began a more structured effort to take advantage of Acapulco's potential. It laid out the first subdivisions, intended for the second homes of the wealthy. It improved the roads. State tourism literature began promoting Acapulco's beautiful bay, warm waters, and reliably awesome sunsets. The efforts would get a boost from the onset of World War II in 1939, which cut the jet set off from its beloved French Riviera and Waikiki. As a stand-in, Acapulco would do just fine, if not better.

To clear the way for beachfront development, Mexico engaged in a systematic dispossession of locals who held waterfront land but little power; the government took over collectively owned farms known as ejidos, sometimes using violence, including by burning houses and crops and offering little compensation. Displaced locals were left to find new homes and livelihoods. In one example, the Icacos ejido, located near the western end of the bay just below present-day Las Brisas, gave way involuntarily to a golf course and a new subdivision. The farmers received no monetary compensation; the new owner was only required to make "civic improvements" equal to the value of the land. Locals then settled in the precursors of hillside slums above the main city that today comprise a fifth section of Acapulco. From the moment the government began expropriating land from the ejidos, Acapulco's local population has struggled with poverty and with efforts to have a say in their situation.

In 1949 the Mexican government opened La Costera, the road stretching around Acapulco Bay, enabling resorts and tourism in general to extend well beyond the original Acapulco at the western end, the catalyst for the notorious overdevelopment to come.

THE ORIGINAL ACAPULCO RESORT TOWN IS STILL HERE, ASSUMING YOU'RE willing to look for it. Acapulco is not a walkable place—first the hills and later the Costera made sure of it. I have a private driver for the afternoon, who takes me through the steep roads of old Acapulco, where paint jobs and landscaping have gone largely overlooked in recent years. Then the road flattens out and we drive alongside a pink wall marking the property of Los Flamingos, a clifftop resort opened in the thirties. The height of its fame came in the 1950s, when John Wayne and Johnny Weissmuller, who played Tarzan in films, bought the hotel and turned it into a private hideaway for their famous friends.

When I visit, a few men sit in a row against the wall next to reception, like men do in hot climates. One of these men is Adolfo Santiago, who now owns Los Flamingos, which, like the neighborhood we came through to reach it, could use a little sprucing up. Santiago worked as manager of the hotel for years, then inherited it from

John Wayne. The richest man in Mexico has apparently expressed interest in buying the property, but Santiago will wait until his days are out and let his four children decide its fate.

Despite the disrepair, Los Flamingos is a spectacular spot from which to look out at the world. When the cruise ships come into port, which everyone tells me will happen just after the holidays, the bar will be packed with day-trippers ordering coco locos, the cocktail invented here. On this afternoon, though, it's mostly empty. I wander the grounds along a path running parallel to the cliff's edge. You can tell how recently or not a property has been renovated by its pool. If it's not an infinity pool, it's often been a while. The Flamingos' pool is well kept, but yes, it's been a while.

My next clifftop stop, El Mirador Hotel, is home to the famous Quebrada cliff divers. Opened in 1933 by a retired Mexican oil company accountant named Carlos Barnard with twelve guest cabanas, the hotel quickly expanded as Americans poured in. Early staff members at El Mirador became the first cliff divers and started a tradition that has today become the most recognizable symbol of Acapulco. I pay ten dollars to enter the hotel's La Perla restaurant. The price of admission includes a quickly melting frozen margarita, some shade, and the best vantage point from which to watch the show, which is as amazing as advertised. The divers climb the vertical cliffs barefoot, then one after another soar through the air.

After El Mirador, my driver offers to show me a hotel he likes, and we head to the Hotel del Monte, which I've never heard of. When we get there, it's virtually empty. The del Monte was popular with Americans in the 1940s, just as popular as El Mirador and Los Flamingos, perhaps. But it had no John Wayne or cliff divers to secure its continued relevance. In the lobby bar, the furniture is basic, but the view over the bay remains spectacular. The pool itself hasn't changed a bit since the 1940s, but around it, the fancy lounge furniture and palm trees that would once have provided tropical glamour have long since vanished. When we head out, I see that directly across the street

sits the former Hotel Casablanca, for a time also the "it" spot in Acapulco. It's now apartments, no longer on any tourist's radar.

I'VE JUST ORDERED A VEGGIE SUSHI ROLL AT LA PLAYITA, A RESTAURANT ON
the beach along the Costera. This is merely the latest installment in
my struggle to consume Mexican food in Acapulco, where in addition to sushi I've so far eaten pasta and salads and a veggie burger. La
Playita sits squarely in the heart of the Acapulco Bay hotel strip. This
is where, out on the street, Walmart neighbors McDonald's, which
in turn neighbors Baby'O, arguably Acapulco's most famous nightclub. My driver points out that at least there's no Taco Bell.

I'm struck by the cordoned-off beauty of the beach itself. The
concrete and the traffic and the noise and the lights stop abruptly
where the sand starts. The beach here is like the freeway during a
wildfire—the last defense against a stark reckoning, a non-landscape.

I'd been told to expect a lower-middle-class Mexican crowd in
this area, but that's not my experience. I pop some sushi into my
mouth and watch a group of beautiful Mexican twentysomethings
take selfies with their latest-model iPhones, then tuck their iPhones
away to pose for the one guy in the group who brought his Nikon
DSLR along; they pull their Ray-Bans down their noses to look
closer at the menu, then look back up, deliciously bored. The women,
I notice, drink Coronas over ice. This seems like a fantastic idea.

Before I leave, I chat with the owner. *This is the real Acapulco*, he
tells me. Only later do I realize I don't know exactly what he meant
by this. This is, after all, the Acapulco that today has a bad name. It's
the Acapulco where one constantly sees the federal military police.
It's the Acapulco of overdevelopment, and undistinguished high-
rise hotels. It's not the original Acapulco, or the one that hosted the
golden-age movie stars.

I'm certain he doesn't mean this is the Acapulco of alarmist media coverage, that is, "The Mexican Government Wants You to Think

Acapulco Is Safe. But Is It?" (*Daily Beast*, May 4, 2019); "How Acapulco Became Mexico's Murder Capital" (*Washington Post*, August 24, 2017); "From Glamour to Gunfire: The Tourist City of Acapulco Torn Apart by Violence" (*Guardian*, December 16, 2016).

The real Acapulco is a hard concept to pin down. The violence is certainly part of it, and the city can indeed be a dangerous place for the people who live here. Especially since its dominant drug cartel splintered, criminal activity has devolved into petty rival gang schemes. Where once the violence was contained to those involved in the drug trade, today average citizens find themselves swept up in it. The new, smaller gangs have become well known for extorting everyone from restaurant owners to taxi drivers. But the media's framing of this as the cause of Acapulco's decline as a resort overlooks both the fact that it had already declined as a destination for U.S. tourists before the criminal activity exploded, and the fact that Mexican tourists are coming here in larger numbers than ever.

By the early 1960s, Acapulco had been declared over at least once by the fickle jet set. This in the era that saw two future U.S. presidents (and three winners of the popular vote) honeymoon here. Later in the decade, the jet set was back, if it had ever really left at all. That's when Tony Rullan showed up—the discos were getting started. For a time in the 1960s and early 1970s, foreign visitors to Acapulco outnumbered Mexican tourists. But by 1975, the domestic market had retaken the lead as international tourism began to decline. In 1981, at least two airlines, Eastern and Aeroméxico, offered direct flights between New York City and Acapulco, but those numbers would soon dwindle, too. Today that trip invariably involves a lengthy layover in Mexico City.

The recent drug violence narrative also ignores Acapulco's longer history of lawlessness, starting with pirates intent on looting shipments of silver headed for Asia centuries ago. In the early twentieth century, the isolated geography of Guerrero, the state where Acapulco is located, hindered efforts by the national government to control it.

Powerful landholders held sway over the peasants who relied on them and could even call them to arms on occasion, while bandits and rebels perpetually challenged the default political order. Illicit behavior was part of the original appeal.

Even in Acapulco's heyday as an international hotspot, violence could on occasion infiltrate the bubble of resort life. Teddy Stauffer, the bandleader turned nightclub impresario, recalled one such incident in 1948, when he was managing the glitzy former Hotel Casablanca. A local fishing boat captain who'd been barred from the hotel after drunkenly trashing the pool bar returned to it a few days later with a hired gunman, who proceeded to shoot at Stauffer.

Overdevelopment in the seventies did not stop more development from coming in. During the eighties, twenty-seven major hotels went up along the already crowded bay. The resulting version of Acapulco lost ground when Cancún, Cabo, and Puerto Vallerta came on the scene. In 1986, more foreigners headed to Cancún than to Acapulco for the first time. Around this time, after some resorts dumped waste directly into the water, officials started warning tourists against swimming in the polluted bay. Acapulco's international reputation was suffering. In 1994, just 15 percent of Acapulco's tourists were foreigners, and in 2006 the number fell all the way to 1.5 percent.

In a sure sign of its waning popularity with Americans, the international brands retreated. After a decades-long stint by Westin International Resorts, La Brisas is once again in the hands of a Mexican company. This trend repeats across the bay and in Diamante. In previous decades, Marriott, Hyatt, and Fairmont all ran hotels here. None do today.

This had all come to pass by the time the drug violence revved up. Blaming new dangers for Acapulco's falling out of favor with foreigners doesn't add up, especially given similar problems in other Mexican resorts that remain popular. In at least one recent year, Los Cabos had a higher murder rate than Acapulco, yet the crowds from up north keep coming. And of course, proclaiming Acapulco over just because the Americans are no longer coming disregards the resort's continuing popularity with Mexicans.

Before I head out of town, I stop at the Villa Vera, where Tony Rullan got his start and which I'm surprised to find is still in business—none of the many people I've met here recommended I check it out, including Tony. Unlike Las Brisas, it's not what it once was. Unlike Los Flamingos and El Mirador, it hasn't managed to trade on its history with nostalgia seekers. I walk into reception, a drab room the size of a Manhattan bedroom, where a kid who can't be more than twenty explains in Spanish that I can't come onto the property because they're hosting a private event that day for some visitors from Mexico City.

In Slim Aarons's photographs of Villa Vera from the 1960s, the crowd seems perpetually to be gravitating toward the swim-up bar. Not a single woman has gotten her hair wet. They look happy to be idle, lounging halfway in the pool. They look great doing it, and seem aware of this fact. The late afternoon sun gives them a backlit glow. They probably think Acapulco will be just like this forever.

TWELVE

UP TO HERE

Miami Beach

Every time I come to Miami Beach, on the barrier island just offshore from the city of Miami, I'm surprised anew to find that I like it. What should be an exercise in irritability, given my long-standing aversion to aggressive oceanfront development and extortionate pricing and crowds, becomes something else. In Miami Beach these common vacationland nuisances rearrange themselves alongside manifold delights, until everything vulgar takes on a disarming charisma. I boil it down to the simple fact that I like Miami Beach because I've always liked places that feel like places and not categories: This destination off the southeastern coast of Florida is identifiably Miami Beach, even if it is also identifiably a beach resort, and in this way it stands in contrast to so many other well-known oceanfront destinations. Its artificiality possesses clear notes of authenticity. It is somehow a living locality despite existing to serve tourists.

Much of its appeal, of course, derives from the famous Art Deco streetscapes. But I also love the beach itself, wide and swimmable and dotted with those brightly painted lifeguard towers. I love the particular brand of spectacle here, in evidence one evening when Scott and I take a nap, then go to the Fontainebleau Hotel at midnight, where I order an old-fashioned and observe the nightlife scene like a movie villain, detached and with an imagined shrewdness. Being here feels like a reality show in the flesh—so many shiny fabrics, on men and women alike, and I love it. Next to the sparkly stuff lies a defiant grittier side—dive bars from another era, neglected blocks a couple of streets in from the beach, even some of the best Art Deco buildings that have yet to be reimagined for today's glamorous scene, and I love that, too. I love how on this particular trip, all the guys working the bar at my hotel have what Scott takes to calling the Mike Patton, after the Faith No More singer: shaved underneath and long enough for a ponytail up top. I like the fact that, if you are from New York, you are bound to know someone else visiting Miami Beach at the same time you are. This time around, it's a friend in town for a conference, who treats us to drinks on his expense account.

One afternoon, I walk up to the entrance of Gianni Versace's former mansion between 11th and 12th Streets, now the $750 per night Villa Casa Casuarina, where a woman with a clipboard runs down the order of operations for me. First, buy a drink at the bar. Only then can I walk around taking pictures of the place where Versace lived and was murdered. Later I'll read that the murder took place not inside the mansion but on the very doorstep where I am making the inquiry. Of his visit to the mansion, the writer Geoff Dyer remembered that his girlfriend "took a picture of me with the disposable camera we had bought in Nassau. Until we had done this we found it difficult to tear ourselves away from the spot, the spot where people were having their pictures taken, the spot where Versace had been gunned down." Miami Beach's lurid undertones bring out the same in its visitors. This too is part of the draw.

The delight I experience during a few days spent in Miami Beach contrasts distinctly with the coverage it receives in the press. I read article after article that opens with the reporter wading through a flooded Miami Beach street. But I don't see any of that. Unlike tourists, these reporters are chasing the climate catastrophe, while the rest of us chase the sunshine. When the biggest problems I encounter during a stay are the attitude wafting my way from the odd hotel staffer at the beach club, or the single sprawling cloud that's suddenly taken up residence between the sun and myself, or the parking that generally costs more per day than a steak dinner, climate change can start to present as an abstract concept.

The reports are right, though. Widely shared affinity for Miami Beach tends to obscure certain hard truths about the very viability of the place and complicates dispassionate conclusions over what to do about it. We as tourists may not see it with our own eyes when we come here for a blissful few days in January, when both rainfall and the tides are at low points, but that doesn't change the fact that Miami Beach is drowning. It is not projected to begin drowning fifty years down the line if worst-case scenarios for sea level rise come to fruition. It is drowning already.

The question that remains: How much sense does it make to spend hundreds of millions of dollars to preserve a barrier island that didn't have any business going into the beach business in the first place?

BEFORE THE ATLANTIC BEACH HOTEL OPENED IN 1915, THE SPIT OF LAND just off the southeastern tip of Florida's mainland went through only a couple of iterations. There's evidence of at least temporary habitation by Native Americans, but when the first permanent structure went up here in 1875, the sandbar was devoid of human activity, if lousy with mosquitos, rats, and crocodiles. That first structure, a house of refuge for shipwrecked sailors, contained enough provisions, clothes, and first-aid supplies to last until help came from the mainland.

The first efforts to tame the place came in 1882, when a group of businessmen bought up the land cheap and set about turning it into a coconut plantation. As work got under way, "it became more and more obvious that if this beach had been a good place to plant things, someone would have done so long ago," wrote Polly Redford in her 1970 history of Miami Beach, *Billion-Dollar Sandbar.* Yet the men continued, bringing in more investors as funds ran low. One of those investors was John S. Collins, who today lends his name to Miami Beach's most famous street. Collins invested $5,000 in the plantation sight unseen, but in the early 1890s headed down to find out for himself how things were going. The answer was evident: not well. But Collins became intrigued by the sandbar, and even though the coconut project had failed, he was interested in cultivating it somehow. By 1907 he'd taken over and started an avocado farm, which would also fail.

Collins and his family hailed from New Jersey, where they were well familiar with the success of the Jersey Shore resorts. His kids and their spouses convinced him to pivot once again and pursue what they saw as the only viable future for Collins's weird property off the coast of Miami—an Atlantic City of the south. As part of the effort, Collins started building a wooden bridge to the mainland in 1912, with an eye toward bringing in day-trippers, but ran out of money before it was finished.

Carl Fisher, the Indiana multimillionaire who founded the Indianapolis 500 and had recently purchased a home in Miami, stepped in with funding to finish the bridge. The deal introduced Fisher to a peninsula that was more mangrove than solid ground (Miami Beach would become an island only in 1917, with the creation of the Baker's Haulover Inlet at its northern end), but where others saw folly, he saw a challenge. In an alternate history, the sandbar may have been left to do what it did best: serve as a protective barrier between the tumult of the ocean and the fledgling city of Miami on the mainland. Instead, its destiny could have provided the plotline for an early Werner Herzog movie, with fantastical engineering projects and pie-in-the-sky heroics. There would even be an elephant helping out at Fisher's hotels, once things really got going.

In the summer of 1913, Fisher and two other early developers, brothers John and James Lummus, began a $600,000 (more than $15 million today) fill project, dredging 6 million cubic yards of gunk from the bottom of Biscayne Bay. With it, they would create 1,000 new acres of land on the bay side of the peninsula where before had been only impenetrable mangrove swamp a mile wide at some points. To make way for the fill, all that mangrove was cleared away. Then, to keep the new land in place, Fisher built a dike along the new perimeter; workers plunged pilings into the bay floor, then secured timber to them with steel cables. Only then did the dredging machine get revved up.

After the fill was done, Fisher left it alone for six months while it dried into hard, white, sandy dirt. Topsoil from the Everglades was then hauled in to cover it. The project remade the geography of Biscayne Bay, with the *Miami Metropolis* reporting later in 1913 that "[i]t took faith to undertake the job of making the waste of sand and the mangrove swamp into an attractive and habitable place, but faith marches at the head of progress, and there are now few doubters as to the ultimate outcome." Fisher, Collins, and other developers began bringing their vision of a beach resort to life on a slice of land that was roughly half man-made.

It was in a precarious position from the start. A category 3 hurricane in 1926 nearly ruined it all just as it was getting going, depositing two feet of sand onto Collins Avenue, blowing windows out and roofs off. After surveying the damage, Fisher wrote that the buildings that fared best were "those we purchased from Sears, Roebuck." The hurricane served as the first indication that Miami Beach's relationship with nature might not be a smooth one. In addition, the storm shook investors' and visitors' confidence, sending the newly created city into an economic tailspin.

But by the 1930s, Miami Beach had rebuilt and, unlike most other parts of the United States, continued building throughout the Great Depression, just as the Art Deco architectural style jumped the

Atlantic. Miami Beach's version was simpler than what originated in Europe—elaborate decorative details gave way to a more streamlined look that dovetailed perfectly with American desires to set trends, pursue modernity, and build economically at the same time. Hundreds of Deco buildings went up over the course of the decade and proved immediately popular. Not even the Depression slowed business down.

WHEN I SPEAK OF THE MIAMI BEACH I'M TAKEN WITH, I AM REALLY SPEAKing of South Beach, where the Art Deco buildings from this era are concentrated. From our own hotel, a minor Deco relic called the Redbury at 18th Street, we head out onto Collins Avenue, where the sun is shining and the holidaymakers are wandering from restaurant to bar to hotel. Up here the hotels are a little taller, ten or so stories on the oceanfront, and they're almost all slim and elegant and painted white, with carefully chosen decorative flourishes at the entrance or perched on top. I especially love the entrance to the Shelborne, where a circular overhang is held up by three elongated diamond columns, and the sign atop the Delano, with its enormous eagle wings comprising each of four corners. This is high Art Deco, a category I just invented.

For the most part, the original plots along the ocean have never been combined, a fact that helps distinguish South Beach from other beach resort towns, where the norm is for a single large hotel to inhabit a wide swath of the beachfront. As a result, the hotels here conform to the city's fabric rather than obliterating it. There's a pedestrian culture here, with one of the joys of a visit being a wander from one magnificent hotel lobby bar to the next. Above the streets of the 20s, Miami Beach squanders some of this charm as the hotels become larger and the street life sparser. Up here Miami Beach is more like any other overdeveloped beach resort. This is thanks to the footprints left by Millionaire's Row, the sprawling estates once

The Art Deco Sagamore, National, and Delano hotels
along Collins Avenue in Miami Beach.

belonging to prominent names from industry and finance. The basic property lines those estates created still stand, in many cases. The 1,500-room Fontainebleau, for example, was built on the site of the former Firestone estate.

As we wander into the heart of Miami Beach's Art Deco District below 14th Street, things get less towering and more confectionary, with all the colors of nonseriousness and birthday parties. Like the Midcentury Modern phase that would follow it, the lines are clean, the surfaces smooth, the shapes unembellished. But the attitude is all different. Instead of asking to be taken seriously, Art Deco just wants you to enjoy yourself.

The strip along Ocean Drive looks wonderful taken in from Lummus Park across the street; up close, it's a tourist dystopia, with the customary gaudy menus and restaurant employees trying to woo you in from the street. One such employee stands at the edge of the sidewalk with a cigar tray hanging from her neck. Ancillary sales, I guess. Tables and canopies mostly obscure the sidewalk, a relatively recent development—before the current millennium, some of the buildings' front terraces were barely used. In September 2019, the city officially acknowledged the nuisance of the hawkers, enacting a law imposing increasingly steep penalties for "solicitation" from restaurants and cafés. In the law's first two months on the books, eighteen restaurants received citations. A month and a half after that, I stroll down Ocean Drive and sidestep any number of additional infractions in the making.

Stroll even farther south and you're in a mostly artificial landscape, with everything west of Washington Avenue originally either part of the bay or a mangrove swamp. Above 5th Street, the original footprint widens just a bit, but the western half of the island is still man-made. Fisher, as could be expected, built his new Miami Beach land only as high as it needed to be at the time. Today some of it already sits below sea level.

Miami Beach has become well known in recent years for its "sunny-day flooding," or flooding that occurs on cloudless days with mild weather. This comes thanks to a geological trait that renders all of southern Florida uniquely ill-fated. In addition to lying barely above sea level, the region's bedrock is composed of porous limestone—it's often likened to Swiss cheese or a sponge. When the water table rises, there is no way to keep water from seeping up. If the tide is high enough, which it increasingly is, Miami Beach floods not from the sides but from below. Between September and November, record-breaking high tides have become the norm, and so has flooding.

The hotels, at least the nicest ones, ended up on the higher land just behind the beach. But in addition to the transient population occupying the island's 215 hotels on any given day, more than 90,000 people call Miami Beach home, and they tend to live on Fisher's man-made land, which, unsurprisingly, receives the worst of the flooding.

Since 1994, the average sea level here has risen about six inches, twice as much as the global average. For an island that lies, on average, just four feet above sea level, every inch counts in a big way. Sea levels here are projected to rise between 21 and 54 inches by 2060, from 2000 levels. By the end of the century, if left to its own devices, nature will have undone Carl Fisher's hard work and returned all that land to Biscayne Bay.

THE FRONT ENTRANCE TO THE DELANO HOTEL ON COLLINS AVENUE AND 17th Street stands hidden behind a hedge as tall as the ranch house I lived in as a kid. Above it, the accordion-like angles of the façade give the impression of a building that is folding open. Walking past the hedge and onto the property feels like stepping through C. S. Lewis's wardrobe. Entering the hotel is itself an event, an experience leaving so powerful an impression that once you've had it, you might feel as though you could skip the rest of the trip and still have had a fabulous time.

On this, my fifth or so time coming here for a drink over the years, the effect hasn't diminished. The ceiling is somewhere up there, so far up that I don't recall ever having noticed it. Yet from it, waves of sheer white fabric hang strategically among swollen white columns to create a central aisle, or a catwalk, or a procession. An occasion. That these two elements—simple fabric and simple columns—can create such drama speaks to some secret sauce of design that the French architect Philippe Starck perfected in this lobby. Past the columns on either side, nooks showcase exaggerated, off-kilter furniture. This is very 1990s but also unique to the Delano. It's all so moody, the opposite of Instagram-friendly.

Earlier in the day, I read a 1994 *Times* article covering plans for a future South Beach hotel in which the hotelier Ian Schrager explains the milieu in which he and his partner, Starck, are working as "not a time for one-upmanship and three-legged chairs." Partway through the lobby, I come upon a gold three-legged chair displayed more or less as a piece of art. Times have once again changed, Schrager might say.

Scott and I walk out back and to the bar at the far end of the pool, where the table and chairs positioned *in* the infinity pool remain one of my favorite-ever design touches, with the optical illusion created of their floating on the water, when in reality they are positioned at the exceptionally shallow end of the pool. But the outdoor bar is too crowded for comfort, even on this windy evening. We opt for the Rose Bar, just off the lobby.

There's no overstating the extent to which the Delano redefined what a beach resort can be. That it was able to do so had everything to do with the time and place from which it emerged. Miami Beach had begun to fall seriously out of fashion in the late 1960s. For a new generation, Miami Beach was that kitschy place their parents had once enjoyed. All those Deco baubles transitioned from hotels to down-market apartments for retirees. Then, in the 1970s, drugs, crime, and refugees from Cuba poured into Miami and Miami Beach, an influx the cities were unprepared to handle. The government exacerbated the problem by declaring South Beach blighted, part of a plan to raze the entire neighborhood and lure a major redevelopment. A developer didn't materialize, and the condemned buildings languished. The streets grew unkempt and menacing. By 1981, a *Time* magazine cover story titled "South Florida: Trouble in Paradise" noted that the area had the highest murder rate in the nation.

But in a twist no one anticipated, Miami Beach was saved by those same hotels. In 1979, South Beach's Art Deco architecture was placed on the National Register of Historic Places, bringing publicity to the derelict district. In the eighties, the local government would bestow on the buildings enforceable landmark protections. Then in 1984, the TV show *Miami Vice* premiered, giving viewers a perspective on the city that mostly didn't really exist, with Don Johnson and Philip Michael Thomas taking on the illegal drug industry in Italian suits and six-figure cars. In doing so, it exhibited the Deco buildings in a way that emphasized the aesthetic appeal of Miami's Beach's artificial landscape. The show would run for five seasons, portraying a Miami—and a Miami Beach especially—where danger, glamour, bikinis, and intrigue commingled as the norm. Even locals looked at their city in a new light.

In the late eighties, fashion photographers started taking advantage of the great light and the clean Deco backdrops, and before long South Beach had become a winter mecca for models. The South Beach fashion effect reached its zenith in 1992 when Gianni Versace bought a mansion on Ocean Drive. By the time Schrager and Starck came to the Delano in the early nineties, the buzz was there, even if a lot of the hotels were still a dated mess. In other words, perfect timing.

THE HISTORIC DESIGNATION AND THE MUSIC VIDEO TREATMENT COIN-cided with a long overdue restoration of the beach itself. Beach erosion has been a problem for Miami Beach since its 1926 hurricane. The significant sand loss from that storm resulted in the installation of sheet piling and wooden groins meant to keep it in place going forward. Instead these structures interrupted the natural flow of the sand and ultimately made the erosion worse. By the 1950s, more than half the island had no beach at high tide. In subsequent years, many hotels hovered directly over the back edge of the beach. Some, like the Deauville, which opened on Collins Avenue and 67th Street in 1957 and hosted the Beatles for their legendary *Ed Sullivan Show* performance, built their hotel structures out onto the sand itself.

In 1966, Congress authorized the U.S. Army Corps of Engineers to develop a solution to Miami Beach's erosion problem. This centuries-old agency of the Defense Department is tasked with, among other things, reducing risk to Americans from natural disasters. Because of this, it spearheads shoreline protection and restoration projects that will make communities more resilient. Its headquarters, as luck would have it, stand in Norfolk, Virginia, one of the American cities most vulnerable to flooding from sea level rise.

In the late 1970s, the Corps of Engineers installed a shoreline levee along Miami Beach to protect buildings and infrastructure. That soon failed, leading the Florida Department of Environmental Protection to receive a state grant in the mid-1980s to install the more resilient vegetated dunes you see there today. Miami Beach received its first major beach nourishment in six phases between 1975 and 1980, with almost 14 million cubic yards of sand dumped along 10.5 miles of shoreline, dredged from offshore supplies at a cost of $56.8 million (about $240 million accounting for inflation). As is standard in Army Corps projects, the federal government footed half the bill, the state of Florida paid for 37.5 percent, and Miami-Dade County chipped in the remaining 12.5 percent via a bond issue that voters passed in 1972. Since the initial renourishment, sand has been added to stretches of Miami Beach on an as-needed basis, the most recent being a $16 million project in 2020 that brought in 61,000 tons of new sand. In addition, three breakwaters were eventually installed near 32nd Street, a particularly problematic spot.

The renourishment project proved more effective than expected, likely thanks to Miami Beach's peculiar geological situation, protected from the full force of the ocean first by a barrier reef a couple of miles offshore, but more significantly by the Bahama Banks, those massive limestone plateaus around the Bahamas that lie as close as fifty-five miles from Miami Beach. Waves that do make their way to the shore here generally form west of the Bahamas, without the headway to gather much force. If Miami Beach has any natural advantage over other beach locations around the world, this is it.

On the other hand, the same traits that protect the beach also mean that Miami has had few offshore sand reserves from which to draw when it's time to build the beach back up. Its sand comes not from a larger ocean system but from the breakdown of shells and coral already present—an extremely slow process. Today the offshore sand is gone, finally used up in the years preceding Hurricane Irma, which proceeded to wash away 170,000 cubic yards of sand from Miami Beach.

Miami Beach, if it is to maintain its appeal, must now bring sand in from elsewhere. The obvious place to get more of it would be in the nearby Bahamas, with their abundance of sand compatible with Miami Beach's own. But U.S. beaches are prohibited from importing sand unless they can first prove they have been unable to source it domestically (or unless they want to pay for it without the help of the federal government). Florida senator Marco Rubio has twice introduced legislation that would amend the Water Resources Development Act of 1986 to allow the importing of sand, but it has stalled in Congress both times, at least in part thanks to lobbying by the domestic industry.

If the law were to change, mining sand in the Bahamas would present yet another set of potential problems. As the coastal geologist Orrin H. Pilkey points out in his book *Sea Level Rise: A Slow Tsunami on America's Shores*, the Bahamas' sand is generally so fine that it would cause excess sediment in the water off Miami Beach, which can kill off filter-feeding organisms. In addition, the sand would introduce nonnative species to Miami Beach. In the Bahamas, meanwhile, changes in the land from sand removal could affect the way waves break, and could also lead to increased flooding and damage from storms.

BY OUR CURRENT CENTURY, MIAMI BEACH HAD LONG BECOME A DRIVER of its entire metropolitan area's economy. Today profit is coursing through the island. In 2018, 23 million visitors to Miami-Dade County created an $18 billion economic impact and generated $1.25 billion in tax revenue. Miami Beach's real estate was worth $37.4 billion in 2018. A lot of people with a lot of resources have a lot of incentive to keep it viable.

As a result, Miami Beach benefits both from a political will and an availability of economic resources with which to engage in the fight against climate change. In a World Bank study of the world's 136 largest coastal cities' vulnerability to flood damage, Miami ranks second, but when expected flood damage is measured against that city's GDP, it falls out of the top ten.

The local and regional governments here are taking climate change seriously in a state that often hasn't. In 2010, four counties—Miami-Dade, Broward, Palm Beach, and Monroe—formed the Southeast Florida Climate Compact, a body intended to provide recommendations for dealing with climate change. It has no regulatory power, but both the Miami Beach city government and the Miami-Dade county government use the compact's sea level rise projections and other guidance in their planning.

When I talk to Miami Beach's director of environment and sustainability, Elizabeth Wheaton, we of course discuss the city's $600 million flood mitigation project, a multipronged undertaking that started in 2015 when Miami Beach raised the first of an eventual 60 percent of its streets. At the same time, it began installing water pumps that would send water away from land and into the bay during flooding events, adding new drainage pipes, and installing check valves in the storm drains so that water would not be able to flow up through them.

The flood mitigation project receives a lot of attention for several reasons—its ambition and sheer scale; because it's funded completely by the city itself, largely via a steep increase in stormwater fees; because it shows a willingness to experiment with new solutions that make Miami Beach a laboratory for the rest of the world. And because of pushback from the local community, who not only voice concern about what the raised streets will do to their properties' values, but also have complained that the streets previously served to channel water away from their properties—now, they say, the higher streets merely dump floodwater into them.

The flood mitigation project is just one part of the city's overall strategy, however. Over the course of our conversation, Wheaton mentions no fewer than six additional initiatives currently under way. There's the 100 Years Visioning Plan in partnership with Florida International University, and another partnership with the University of Miami to create an artificial reef just offshore. There's a partnership with Columbia University's Resilience Accelerator to enhance resilience planning. Perhaps most significantly in the short term, in 2018 the city brought in the Urban Land Institute to review its resilience program, which led to the hiring of Jacobs Engineering to advance the city's water management plan.

There's also the enlisting of progressive design firm Schulman + Associates to produce options for the preservation of Miami Beach's historic buildings, which include raising buildings 10 inches or 14 inches, individually or all at once. Officials are currently considering the recommendations. To preserve the fabric of the historic district, the entirety of the buildings would need to be lifted up in tandem. Others are proposing that new beachfront hotels be built with an especially tall first-floor ceiling, so that as water encroaches, the floor of the lobby can be raised and remain a welcoming place.

"Here in Miami Beach we're moving forward but we're also evaluating and refining our strategies to make sure that we're moving forward with the best approaches in the existing projects," Wheaton says, "because we don't have an answer today of exactly how you should be addressing the challenges." In other words, the city is ready to try new solutions, but dogged in evaluating their efficacy.

MIDAFTERNOON, WE WANDER TOWARD THE OCEAN, ONTO THE BEACH walk and over the dunes, then onto the sand itself, where we claim the two loungers included with our room. In one of Miami Beach hotels' more irritating quirks, the loungers are included in hotels' resort fees, but if you want an umbrella, it will run you twenty-five dollars.

Lucky for us, it's in the low seventies and we've applied sunscreen. The beach is wide, with fine sand. On this afternoon at least, the acoustics of it are weirdly muffled, like I am wearing noise-canceling headphones but playing no music.

Miami Beach's system of dunes between the hotels and the sand protects the properties from storms but obscures their views of the ocean. In Miami, no matter how prime your hotel's property, it's impossible to walk straight out of it and onto the sand. It wasn't always this way. In the 1940s, the pools of hotels like the Raleigh and the Delano opened directly onto the narrow sand beach. Today the pools are self-contained spaces, as is the beach.

I decide to have a swim. The water remains a shade of shallow jade for hundreds of feet out; underneath it, the bottom is perfectly sandy. Except during inclement weather, the water doesn't produce much in terms of waves. It's great for swimming, in fact—the perfect temperature for a plunge.

Of course the water is warm. That's one of the problems. The average water temperature off southeast Florida's coast has always been warm, partially thanks to the Gulf Stream, the major current running up from the Caribbean that brings water in from even hotter points on earth and which, historically, pushes a lot of warm surface water into the depths of the ocean. William Sweet, an oceanographer with the National Oceanic and Atmospheric Administration (NOAA), told me that the faster sea level rise in Miami may come partially thanks to a slowing of the Gulf Stream. As it slows, more of the warm water remains closer to the air.

Warmer surface temperatures mean more intense storms and hurricanes, thanks to a couple of factors. Heat is energy, and warmer waters serve up more of it to developing storms, which means their maximum wind speeds are increasing. Warmer air temperatures assist by causing more water to evaporate from the ocean. The air then holds on to more of that water than cooler air would, to be unleashed all at once when a hurricane makes landfall. There aren't necessarily more storms developing as the planet warms, but those that do develop are showing themselves to be more destructive. The one-two-three punch of Hurricanes Harvey, Irma, and Maria in 2017 caused record damage. In 2019, Hurricane Dorian became arguably the strongest hurricane in history to strike land when it devastated much of the Bahamas.

As water heats up, it also expands, causing sea level rise. And the warmer the water to begin with, the more it expands. "Warmer water that warms will expand more than colder water that warms the same amount," Sweet tells me. "So forty-degree water that warms by one degree versus eighty-degree water that goes from eighty to eighty-one—the expansions [with the 80 degree water] are a bit more." At certain times of year, the water is already becoming too warm for the finicky reef two miles offshore.

DIRECTLY ACROSS THE STREET FROM MY OWN HOTEL, THE RALEIGH HOTEL has been shuttered since Hurricane Irma. In early 2019, its group of owners, which included the fashion designer Tommy Hilfiger, sold the property to the developer Michael Shvo for $103 million, or $1.24 million per room. Soon after, Shvo and his partners went into contract on the two hotels next door to the Raleigh, the Richmond and the South Seas, for an additional $87.85 million and $52 million, respectively. Shvo conditioned completing his purchases on the city passing an ordinance that he himself proposed and which would allow him to skirt former regulations on building heights in this district—in addition to combining the three historic hotels into one property, Shvo's plan involved putting up a 200-foot-high tower behind the Richmond and South Seas.

In July 2019, the Miami Beach Historic Preservation Board conducted a hearing for the proposed ordinance. The most skeptical of the board members, Nancy Liebman, pointed out that the stretch of Collins Avenue under consideration is the most photographed in all of Miami Beach and called the proposed ordinance "another assault on historic preservation." I agree—one thing that makes South Beach so special architecturally, and sets it apart from other beachfront resort areas—is that it *hasn't* allowed its historical properties to be combined. Nevertheless, the board recommended approval of the ordinance, followed by the Miami Beach City Commission. Its approval in September 2020 capped the new tower at 175 feet. By the time you read this, construction will likely be under way, with a scheduled opening date of June 2023.

Shvo's proposal is the latest and perhaps most galling example of the city's impending doom doing absolutely nothing to deter developers. A new hotel's payback period, or time before the initial investment is paid off, usually runs somewhere in the range of five to fifteen years. By that metric, hotel developers in Miami Beach might figure that for now, profit can still be made, provided that Miami Beach remains viable for the next few decades. Most of the island will likely be underwater by century's end, but in the meantime, real estate developers today are set up for success. "The greater fools theory fully comes into play in commercial real estate," Jan Freitag, senior vice president of Lodging Insights for STR, a market data firm for the hotel industry, says. "You can always find a greater fool. [The developer's] hold is not seventy years . . . unfortunately, that speaks to a short-term horizon in hotel development, which means they think, 'If it's good for five years, I can make my money.'"

Richard Stockton, the CEO of Braemar Hotels & Resorts, which owns the Ritz-Carlton on St. Thomas, provided some insight into another buffer for developers when he was unusually candid after the resort suffered extensive damage from Hurricane Irma. "It's no different if a hurricane hit the property or it didn't," Stockton is quoted as saying in *Bloomberg*. "The reality is it's inconsequential to us from a financial perspective." The insurance payout likely equaled the revenues, in other words. The Ritz-Carlton St. Thomas remained closed for more than two years. During that time, it happened to turn some of the needed repairs into fortuitous improvements. With a robust insurance policy, then, a resort can turn a hurricane into an opportunity to upgrade its offerings in a trend-driven market.

This kind of nonchalance toward extreme weather works only as long as the insurance policies that enable it remain affordable. Signs are emerging to indicate that they may not, even in the medium term. Since 2015, insurance premiums have risen steeply for resorts, thanks to an onslaught of hurricane activity in the United States, plus typhoons in Japan and even the wildfires in California and Australia. The collapse of the Champlain Towers South condo building in Surfside in 2021, mere feet from the town's border with Miami Beach, initiated a new era of insurance hikes for oceanfront properties. At the same time, the tragedy highlighted the challenge of maintaining buildings that contend with rising seas, salty air, and more intense storms.

Still, the hotel and insurance industries are only beginning to grapple with new risks from climate change. Experts aren't sure where the tipping point is, but most agree one exists at which beachfront hotels in many locales will become so-called uninsurable. Alex Kaplan, executive vice president for alternative risk at Amwins, a company that sells specialty insurance products, sees the problem coming to a head down the line. "I think [beachfront hotels] will be theoretically insurable for a long time, but it's a question of how much are people willing to pay," he says.

For potential buyers of Sandals Resorts, the widespread Caribbean all-inclusive chain, the answer already seems to be, not *that* much. Sandals put itself up for sale in September 2019, but as of this writing no buyers have stepped up, with speculation emerging that concerns over insurance costs have been the chief roadblock.

In its 2020 annual report, the Australian insurance giant QBE acknowledged the eventual "uninsurable" issue, writing that "over the longer-term, climate change will impact our customers and the communities that we serve. This may cause insurance premiums to become unaffordable, especially for customers in areas more exposed to weather-related events." The report indicates that the company generally expects this to happen sometime after 2050.

As for Michael Shvo's four-building beachfront development, one has to conclude that its insurance policy will safeguard his investment regardless of hurricanes and sea level rise, at least for the next couple of decades.

FOR NOW, THE OCEANFRONT HOTELS THAT RELY SO HEAVILY ON THE beach for the success of their businesses aren't being asked to contribute to its maintenance. This holds true in most locales, and Miami Beach is no exception. "Until something is impacting their financial bottom line, they're not too involved. [The hotels] are very supportive of the city of Miami Beach and all the efforts we're taking, obviously, because the majority of our hotels are located directly on the beach," Matt Kelly, Miami Beach's director of culture and tourism at the time, tells me. "But in terms of environmental and sustainability initiatives, we more pass information along to them more than they're interested in being at the table at the beginning." The hotels aren't going to meddle with a system that shoulders the expense of resilience for them.

Publicly funded beach resilience projects serve a public good, on one hand, in that they maintain a public beach for everyone's enjoyment. On the other hand, those who benefit most are the already affluent beachfront home and hotel owners, whose property values are propped up by government-funded beach renourishment projects. Then again, those who own the beachfront property typically provide a large percentage of a locality's tax base, based on a property tax in Miami Beach of $5.88 per $1,000 worth of property (it should be noted that this is a lower-than-average property tax). Shvo's $103 million Raleigh Hotel should bring the city of Miami Beach more than $600,000 per year in property taxes. Leaving such properties to ruin and driving them out doesn't feel like an option. At the same time, $600,000 doesn't necessarily feel like enough.

Guests of the hotels pay a collective 7 percent of their booking fee for various taxes, but currently the hotels themselves are not required to contribute directly in the same way. Again, there are early signs that this might be changing in Miami Beach. In 2016, four Miami-Dade County commissioners put forward a proposal to consider the implementation of "impact fees," which would require developers to pay for some of the costs required to maintain infrastructure when they build on land vulnerable to sea level rise. Such a fee would be related to the common "polluter pays" principle, which holds that those companies responsible for pollution should also be responsible for its cleanup and management.

If seas rose not at all in the next hundred years—a zero probability scenario—the barrier island would still be facing flooding, sand erosion, and the periodic category 5 hurricane. The city would still be investing hundreds of millions of dollars to raise streets and install water pumps. It would still have run out of more sand to pump in.

For the foreseeable future, the economic windfall from Miami Beach outweighs the substantial cost of maintaining the place. Miami Beach is an especially fascinating study because it has both an enormous challenge ahead of it and enormous wealth with which to take on the challenge. I recall something that the coastal geologist Robert Young told me, in response to a question about the future of Miami Beach: "I just don't see them being able to cost-effectively maintain robust beaches along all of South Florida," adding, "There may be some places where the economy is so powerful that they'll be able to pay whatever it takes to barge sand over from the Bahamas or something like that. Those places are going to be rare, but maybe South Beach will be one of them."

How do we reconcile the likelihood of four feet of sea level rise in the coming decades with an island that's an average of four feet above sea level? Orrin H. Pilkey, the coastal geologist who has been sounding the alarm on sea level rise since the 1980s, puts it bluntly: Miami will disappear. Those with skin in the game—residents and investors, among others—choose a more optimistic prognosis. A common refrain holds that humans will have invented something thirty years from now that we haven't thought of at all yet, and with it they'll save places like Miami Beach at the eleventh hour. But even some local politicians concede that Miami going under is a matter of when, not if. To preserve what's already there is one thing. To develop new neighborhoods, new high-rises, new hotels, seems like pure folly.

RETURN TO RAILAY

I decide to go back to Railay, the peninsula in Thailand, almost exactly ten years after my first trip there, an experiment to see if the beach where I found my beach will still provide it. The context is different now. Last time I'd been fleeing my daily life, for one, while this time I'm homesick for it. I've seen more of the world now and suspect that the threshold for being impressed has risen. Would it have changed, would I still love it, or would it be like rereading *Catcher in the Rye* fifteen years after first encountering it as a teenager?

I fly into nearby Krabi, but by the time I reach the ticket office for boats, I've missed the last one to Railay and have to charter my own. Today I can throw money at a problem like this—ten years ago I'd have been stuck on the mainland for the night. The "captain" doesn't help me in or out of the boat, and I have to wade over to it myself; he says he's taking me to Railay East, where I'm staying, but drops me off at Railay West. Fine. I jump out of the boat and wade onto shore with my suitcase on my head.

I've booked ahead, as I do these days, so this time I know my destination once onshore. I get to my hotel, for which I've prepaid $110 or so per night, then sit down at its al fresco restaurant. A local guy is playing the guitar and singing Western hits. I text with Scott while I eat my dinner, and even send him a video of the musician. Even this far from home, I'm no longer as far from home as I used to be.

I'm looking forward to another early morning swim, but don't wake up until 9 a.m., and don't make it to the beach until 11, by which time the undulating crowds have already descended. Jet lag, like other things in life, can't be relied on to stay the same over the course of a decade.

The little differences: The handwritten signs advertising snorkeling trips have been replaced by slick printed ones. It's more crowded, but should I attribute this to March instead of April or a general growth in popularity? The water doesn't feel almost-too-warm in the afternoons, it feels just right. There are more bars, more restaurants, but they're in the same mold as the ones I remember. The cliffs, if anything, are more spectacular.

On my second evening, I watch the sunset at the Tew Lay Bar, located outside of town along a rocky shore, another new addition. I sit on a wooden platform built over the water and sip a mojito from an elaborate metal bowl. To my left, another solo woman is doing the same. To my right, a guy in a white linen shirt waits for his massage from one of the Thai women performing them all in a row just beyond the bar. I swear my cocktail is weak until a pleasant buzz takes hold as I near the bottom of it. At the moment the sun sets, the enormous bats of my last trip take to the sky, in the distance this time. After dark, I walk over to Railay West for a swim. The bioluminescence is still there, but not as bright as before.

The next morning I make coffee and watch a pack of monkeys hop around on a cliff a thousand feet above my terrace. I take a swim in the pool. I didn't think I'd care to have a pool at my hotel in Railay, so perfect are the beaches for swimming, but the direct access from my own terrace has changed that equation. Later I walk up the same old jungle path in search of the awful cabana of ten years ago. It's easy to find, part of a property most recently called the Railay Cabana Garden Bungalows, but currently not called anything because it's abandoned. Aside from the overgrown brush, the cabins hardly look worse than when I stayed in one of them. On the way back down, I check out a well-appointed resort next door that I am sure was not there last time. Back in town, I can't find the other hotel I stayed in, and conclude that it no longer exists.

Finally, on day three, I wake up in time for the early morning swim. I walk down to the beach in a weird mood, happy but also wary of getting too close to a fond memory. I am beat to the shore only by a woman being photographed at the water's edge in her yoga poses by both her boyfriend *and* her mother. I walk down the beach to have a stretch of sand to myself. Monkey tracks are already running down the beach; they've finished with their breakfasts and gone.

The sun is up, but the water is shaded thanks to the cliffs. Later, even the shade will be too hot. The water is something like sensory deprivation, the same temperature and texture as my own skin. The reds and browns and grays of the cliffs contrast with the pastel green of the water, as calm as that of some small Alpine lake. What a glorious swim I have. And what a relief that instead of tinkering with my memory of Railay, it reinforces it.

Later, I sit at a spot called the Jamaica Bar in the 95-degree afternoon heat, where the young Thai Rasta guys are still at it, though probably a new generation of them. In 2019, the bar's hippie vibe presents as almost a throwback, at odds with the blond wood and poured concrete that generally stand in for eccentric lifestyles these days. I get to chatting with the couple sitting next to me, honeymooners from Seattle. I wonder if two cool German guys would still be chatting me up if they were the ones sitting there. Either way, the acquaintances I make are Westerners, a fact that annoyed me not at all ten years ago, but does now.

Once I'm home I find that memories from my recent trip don't supplant the older ones. When my thoughts wander to Railay, they still wander to 2009. The best swim of my life remains the one I took at 6 a.m. in April 2009, despite the identical one in March 2019. Still, Railay holds up. I loved it there again. Maybe I did once entertain the possibility that *I don't like the beach*. But as Wallace Stevens wrote, the sea is a form of ridicule. It has not easily accommodated my efforts to dismiss it.

THIRTEEN

A BETTER WAY

Tioman Island (Malaysia)

My first morning on Malaysia's Tioman Island, twenty miles off the country's mainland in the South China Sea, I wake to a fervent downpour. Outside, the sooty gray sky sits in proportional opposition to the life-affirming blues that engulf the island when the sun's out. The rain is so heavy that Alvin Chelliah, the program manager at a nongovernmental organization called Reef Check Malaysia, with whom I'm scheduled to meet in half an hour, messages me to stay put. I oblige, and breakfast on a protein bar while staring out my second-floor window, at eye level with the raindrops working the palm fronds like they're piano keys. It's an inauspicious start to what will turn out to be an illuminating day.

The rain finally lets up in the late morning and I walk the twenty or so minutes from Air Batang—the village colloquially known as ABC—to Tekek, the main village and one of only two on the island with roads that can accommodate cars. As I stroll along ABC's main street, which is no wider than a sidewalk, the sea is on my right, and out there somewhere lie the coral reefs that draw divers from far and wide. Each side of this little street is flanked by small, family-run hotels, some with huts opening directly onto the beach, many with air-conditioning. They're joined by the occasional restaurant or convenience store or dive center or, somewhat surprisingly, recycling bins made of chicken wire. Every so often, a motorbike approaches and I step off the concrete to let it pass.

Tioman has relied on its beach resorts and dive centers since the 1990s, when the Malaysian government designated the surrounding waters a Marine Protected Area and began promoting tourism here. Today almost all of the island's population has abandoned fishing to work in tourism, with the exception of a few rubber farmers over on the east coast. A few high-end resorts welcome affluent foreign travelers farther south, in places accessible only by boat, but for the most part, the island's 52 square miles remain a backpacker's and diver's paradise, the domain of small hotels owned and run by the locals. Thanks partially to the lack of commercial flights, more than 80 percent of its 230,000 annual tourists come from elsewhere in Malaysia via the frequent ferries from the mainland. It's also popular with residents of nearby Singapore.

Reef Check Malaysia launched on Tioman in 2007 after a local dive shop owner, Julian Hyde, helped get the organization registered as a nonprofit in the country. The umbrella Reef Check organization maintains a global reef-monitoring network run by local citizens, precluding the need for stationed scientists. Initially, its objective on Tioman was narrow in scope—the reef monitoring itself, plus some educational programs with the local schools to get the next generation of Tioman Islanders thinking about the future of their reefs.

But then Alvin Chelliah came along. He began volunteering with Reef Check while working on his master's degree, came to work full time with the organization in 2011, and has been living on Tioman since 2014, when the organization concentrated its efforts more heavily on the island. Having grown up about thirty minutes outside of Kuala Lumpur and obsessed with scuba diving, Chelliah is a natural fit for this work. He wanted to become a dive instructor, but his parents insisted that he go to university. Marine science seemed like the area of study closest to diving, so he chose it and then realized he found it fascinating.

Alvin picks me up on his motorbike at the edge of Tekek. Like many on Tioman, this motorbike is fitted with a sidecar, which I hop into. We go to the Reef Check office, where Alvin tells me how the organization's purview has expanded well past the reefs themselves. "The plan was to identify all the local threats to coral reefs and find simple, realistic solutions," he says. But working on the ground, Alvin quickly understood that he was dealing with an ecosystem, and to save one part of it—the reefs—he had no choice but to address the other elements as well. Tourism activities became a major focus. "With tourism, there's three main issues," Alvin tells me: "snorkeling, diving, and the hotels themselves." He got to work making all three more sustainable.

The list of small victories for Chelliah on Tioman Island is so long, it almost feels unfair that I should have to remember them all: water refill stations at hotels and other businesses, easing the demand for bottled water; a program to train snorkel guides in first aid and ecologically sound practices; an island-wide recycling program for plastic, aluminum, and cardboard; implementation of the UN's Green Fins sustainable certification program for dive centers, a third of which have so far qualified. Reef Check Malaysia has started its own certification program for sustainable hotels, and six so far have passed. They've also started recycling the endless discarded fishing nets that wash up onshore.

Most recently, Alvin has been making inroads toward getting the locals to stop building on top of the sand itself, which happens around the island but is a particular problem in the village of Paya, where entire buildings have gone up on concrete piles driven into the beach—a terrible practice not only for the beach health, but for the aesthetics of a place that's advertised as paradise. Alvin says a law is in place to prevent such construction but has never been enforced. The week before my arrival, and thanks to his prodding, for the first time the local land office sent out letters to those whose construction violated the law, warning them that the offenses needed to be corrected.

From his office, Alvin takes me around to a few of the resorts in Tekek that he's been working with, and it's here that I'll see the most startling of all the small victories. At one of the resorts, we meet Sham, a local guy with a round face and big smile, who says he knows I am American just by observing my facial expressions. Since he is right, all I can do is offer him a grin, another signature American facial expression, which he finds hilarious. Sham runs Tioman Cabana Village. Like many of the locally owned resorts on Tioman, this one started out small, with a beach bar, then expanded bit by bit with private rooms and dorms for backpackers.

Alvin and Sham show me the room next to reception, a workshop where a couple of guys are busy with various projects. Next to one wall, a tall, slim machine sits propped on a plastic bucket. When the machine is turned on, Sham can feed an empty beer bottle into the opening at the top of it, and moments later, sand pours out the bottom into the bucket.

Sham then shows me the newest addition to his resort, a building directly across the dirt road from where we are standing, built with concrete that was mixed with sand that Sham made himself, using the machine in his workroom and the discarded beer bottles of a thousand tourists.

I can't get over it. Two major problems of beach tourism have just been solved with one stone. Tourism-generated waste—the beer bottle—has been turned into sand to make concrete, eliminating the need to buy sand expensively from elsewhere, or mine it illegally, as happens on a small scale here on Tioman. I wonder what Nias, the island in Indonesia where I witnessed so much illegal sand mining, might be able to accomplish with one of these machines.

Alvin purchased this machine through Reef Check Malaysia for 25,000 ringgit, including shipping from New Zealand, or about

This machine on Tioman Island, Malaysia, converts used
beer bottles into sand that can be used to make concrete.

$6,000 US. One of his primary goals with Reef Check is to eventually hand its initiatives off to be run by locals. Once Sham showed an interest in the machine and Alvin became confident that he'd use it productively, he gave it to him, no strings attached. Now people from around the island bring their glass bottles to him, and in return he gives them sand.

Beach resorts can create a never-ending supply of problems. Constructed too close to the water, importing the majority of their food and drink, replicating the comforts of home at the expense of a unique experience, touting their sustainability even as they encourage long-haul flights. Overdeveloped shorelines dot the globe, their immovable high-rise hotels eroding beaches, sometimes beyond the point of return. But the sand-making machine showed me that with the right combination of local knowledge, local buy-in, and modest funding, positive change can happen.

Can we do beach resorts, but better? I came across one small machine at the edge of a room on Tioman Island that inspired optimism. Over my years of traveling to beaches around the world, it was the single most exciting achievement I encountered, the elegance of the solution a match for the complexity of the problem. In the spirit of this optimism, I've put together here a list of the best cases and suggestions I've come across, in no particular order, to serve as a foundation for a more durable and inclusive industry.

REIN IN LONG-HAUL FLIGHTS

The airline industry today is responsible for more than 2 percent of all carbon emissions, a number that is expected to increase with the growing middle class's appetite for travel. While its per-flight carbon footprint has improved with technological advances, we are still many years away from sustainable commercial airplanes. Until then, no resort in the Maldives, or Hawaii, or the Seychelles, nor most other global beach destinations, will run sustainably, all claims aside. To become environmental allies, beach resorts need to address the problem of air travel.

The answer for now is to discourage long-haul flights.

At Finland's soon-to-open Arctic Blue Resort, guests will be able to lower their final bills by lowering the carbon footprint of their vacations, earning discounts by choosing locally sourced meals or minimizing water usage, for example. Mode of transportation to the resort would be a great addition to this model. Beach resorts could discount room rates for guests flying fewer than 500 miles, for example, or taking a train instead of a plane, depending on the location. A twist on the Arctic Blue Resort's scheme might involve resort brands reorganizing their marketing efforts by region, with the goal of attracting guests to the resort closest to their homes.

In reality, a few resorts today are urging guests to buy carbon offsets for their flights, but otherwise they have not engaged further on the issue. This leaves it to governments and governmental bodies, which are beginning to compel change. The most far-reaching of the new regulations, if also the least stringent, is the UN's Carbon Off-setting and Reduction Scheme for International Aviation (CORSIA), enacted in 2016. The program will eventually require airlines to offset all their international flight emissions over a 2019 baseline. CORSIA started its pilot phase in 2021, and in 2027, it will become mandatory for all UN member countries. More than seventy countries are vol-untarily participating from the outset.

CORSIA is a good start, although critics rightly point out that the program won't motivate airlines to bring emissions below their 2019 levels. Other entities are beginning to increase the pressure. The United Kingdom's Committee on Climate Change commissioned a report in 2019 that recommended doing away with frequent-flyer programs, which reward travelers for boarding planes more often and over longer distances. In an earth-friendly world, incentives should do the opposite. The report also recommended taxing flyers on miles flown past a certain amount every year.

In Europe, Germany, France, and Sweden have already intro-duced flight taxes intended to hold the high-polluting industry ac-countable and raise funds for more efficient solutions. In Sweden, home of Greta Thunberg, "flight-shaming" has become such a potent cultural force that in 2019 the number of people passing through its airports actually decreased by 4 percent. The same year, nine member countries appealed to the EU to enact a flight tax across Europe. In the summer of 2020, Austria implemented a minimum airfare price of 40 euros in order to discourage the proliferation of routes from low-cost airlines where train routes already exist. In April 2021, France approved a ban on domestic flights for trips that could be made by train instead in under two and a half hours. It's a matter of time be-fore flight taxes and other regulations on flying become a ubiquitous tool in the battle against climate change, which should have travelers prioritizing beaches closer to home.

SOURCE LOCALLY AND REGIONALLY

Over the past couple of years, I've ordered French wine at a resort in Indonesia, and Kentucky bourbon at one on the French Riviera. Most of the food these drinks are accompanying has been shipped in from elsewhere. Despite general culinary trends toward local ingredients, resorts continue to import most of their food, sometimes because of unavailability in the local market, but sometimes simply because resorts want to serve their guests food with which they are familiar.

It doesn't have to be this way. As a chef in a Barbados resort put it in *Behind the Smile*, "We could be using our own black-belly sheep instead of New Zealand lamb." Fiji should source its wine from New Zealand and Australia. Mexican resorts should source theirs from California, and so on. Food and beverage should be sourced locally whenever possible. This should be made a feature of the menu, and a part of the travel experience.

Any resort that doubts the promotional potential of locally sourced cuisine need only take a look at the line of people angling for a table at Tulum's Hartwood on any given night. The seminal restaurant offers a proof of concept for the all-local destination meal, even if it does come with a generous side of self-satisfaction. The changing daily menu exclusively uses ingredients available in the region, and the chefs use this as their point of differentiation. The result has many travelers making the trip to Tulum specifically to eat at Hartwood.

BUILD MORE SENSIBLY AND FLEXIBLY

In a sense, this one is simple: Developers need to stop building with concrete next to beaches. They especially need to stop building highrises, which block the flow of sand, inevitably causing beach erosion. Once sand erodes, building owners are faced with a series of choices, each less appealing than the next: build a seawall to secure the land the building sits on, continually replenish the beach, or abandon the building. Instead, resorts should be set back from the beach, built as a series of smaller buildings rather than a single immovable one, using materials and techniques that make them flexible both in terms of potential relocation and for repairs after storms.

This has been well understood at least since the seawalls went up in Waikiki in the early twentieth century. "[Oceanfront] communities that have a lower density of development are certainly going to have a lot more flexibility than communities that have a lot of high-rises," says Robert Young, the coastal geologist at Western Carolina University. In the early twenty-first century, some developers are finally taking heed.

Andrew Thomson, the Fijian hotel manager, predicts that soon, new resorts will no longer go up just behind beaches. Instead they'll be built farther back or, ideally, atop hills or cliffs overlooking the sand. Only the beach club and maybe a restaurant will directly overlook the beach. Before its tourism industry ground to a halt in 2017, Nicaragua offered a glimpse of what this might look like. The country's law dictates that no buildings can go up within 50 meters of the high-tide line, so developers have taken advantage of the mountainous terrain behind the Pacific coast beaches, building high above the water. What they lose with direct access to the beach they make up for with sweeping views and pleasant breezes.

Maderas Village was built with new best practices in mind, featuring multiple small cabanas placed up the hill from the shore and constructed using indigenous wood and palm fronds, which regenerate quickly. It has endured a couple of hurricanes so far with minimal damage. But even if damage had been more extensive, the resort would have been able to quickly acquire the materials to rebuild. In the future, expect more new resorts to look like Maderas Village and fewer to look like a twenty-story all-inclusive in Cancún.

A DIFFERENT KIND OF ALL-INCLUSIVE

We take it as a matter of fact that exclusivity is intrinsic to the beach resort. The idea that a resort might be built for both visitor and local runs counter to its working definition. In their moves to exclude local communities, new resorts are only replicating the established model of similar successful properties the world over.

I've never visited a resort that intentionally caters to locals, especially if those locals aren't as wealthy as the typical overnight guest. But I recently encountered an example of one that did in the unlikeliest of places, on a trip to New York City's Museum of Modern Art, where I viewed the exhibit "Toward a Concrete Utopia: Architecture in Yugoslavia 1948–1980."

Eastern European socialist architecture might be the last place I would have looked for beach resorts done right, and yet there they were, in these captivating wall-size photos of hotels hugging the Adriatic Coast that prioritized sensible integration into the environment and practiced inclusivity instead of exclusivity—the resorts were built to be part of the local communities and embraced a diverse clientele, both ethnically and economically.

As Justin McGuirk wrote in a review of the MoMA exhibit in the *New Yorker*, the resorts were "open and free-flowing," a design strategy that presented them as part of the surrounding environment, rather than separate from it. The beach resorts of communist Yugoslavia begin to make sense as products of the time's politics—this was an attempt by the government to create a society without class divisions. They strived not to have an elite segment of society, so why would they create resorts that catered to one class.

The success was short-lived—as Westerners began to pour into these Adriatic resorts, they drove prices up to a point at which Yugoslavs could no longer afford them. Today, long after the fall of Yugoslavia, many of those resorts, now in Croatia, sit abandoned. But they proved for a moment that a more inclusive form of beach tourism might be possible.

BREAK THE PALM TREE HABIT

Scientists believe that the coconut palm existed originally in just two parts of the world: India and the Malay Peninsula in Southeast Asia. From there it eventually fanned out to every self-respecting tropical resort the world over. It's not clear why the palm tree became the most recognizable symbol of beach culture, but by the twentieth century, the association had taken root.

It was a terrible choice. Palm trees provide little shade, require huge amounts of water, have shallow root systems that don't do much to prevent erosion, and don't absorb carbon as effectively as other trees can.

Many types of canopy tree thrive with fewer resources and provide protection from the heat of the sun. As temperatures continue to rise, shade increasingly becomes an amenity unto itself. In some areas, the move away from the palm tree is already under way. In West Palm Beach, Florida, where the palm tree is so iconic that the place is named after it, new regulations require trees in parking lots; 75 percent of those must be shade producing, not palms. Similar moves are being considered in Los Angeles and San Diego. Where municipalities are heading, resorts could follow.

RESORTS SHOULD PAY FOR THAT FROM WHICH THEY PROFIT

On the afternoon that I visit La Croisette, the famed avenue running parallel to the shore in Cannes, on the French Riviera, the markers of a cosmopolitan beach experience are all there—Louis Vuitton and Valentino shops, the convention center that hosts the annual film festival, grand old hotels. What's missing is the beach itself, which isn't visible until I descend a set of stairs from the street into one of the sequestered beach clubs. At this point, a beguiling white stretch of sand presents itself. This is by design. Unlike the majority of beaches in the world, here private enterprises control 21 plots of sand in the heart of the tourist area.

The one on which I'm currently taking a seat is run by the Croisette Beach Hotel. The hotel's managing director, Michel Chevillon, has just arrived to have a drink with me. The hotel secured a plot in 2002, with a fifteen-year lease. When that was up in 2017, Chevillon applied to renew it. He secured another twelve years on the condition that the hotel adhere to new regulations. These stipulated that no part of the beach club could be housed in a permanent structure (with the exception of the restaurant's utilities and kitchen, which lie behind the beach and under La Croisette).

"Concrete and everything had to be destroyed completely," says Chevillon. "This cost us two million euros to destroy and rebuild." Of that amount, half a million went toward replenishing the sand itself, and this is where the Cannes version of beachfront preservation gets interesting.

Whereas in Miami Beach and the Riviera Maya and the Caribbean and Hawaii, the government pays for the bulk of beach maintenance and renourishment, here in Cannes—one of the French Riviera's only sand beaches, and in fact one that is entirely manmade—the responsibility falls largely to the hotels themselves.

Chevillon complains of the endless red tape involved in running a beach concession in Cannes. Some does seem like overreach—the beach clubs are required to be open for eleven months of each year, which means operating an open-air beach restaurant in the winter months. And every day the beach club is open, the owner must pay for a lifeguard to be on duty.

Even with these requirements, though, Cannes beach clubs manage to absorb the expenses and remain profitable, not surprising when you consider that entry to the club for the day costs 41 euros (for nonguests), or that for the ten days of the Cannes Film Festival in May, studios and other movie industry players pay a base rate of $100,000, food and drink not included, to rent out a beach club such as that of the Croisette Beach Hotel.

The idea that the beach resorts should contribute to the maintenance of the very resource from which they profit is one that deserves wider attention. Versions have been floated in the United States. In Miami, county commissioners proposed an "impact fee" that would require resorts to shoulder some of the cost of the strain they place on infrastructure. In 2016, two Georgetown University scholars suggested that municipalities begin charging developers "climate exactions," fees determined at the time of development that "can put a price on the carbon emissions from new development and also on development that reduces the natural resiliency of the jurisdiction to the effects of climate change, such as sea level rise." In other words, they pay for the damage they do to the environment. In addition to funding repairs, such fees may encourage developers to build in less damaging ways in the first place.

REPLACE THE GREEN CERTIFICATION RACKET

I attended the 2019 Asia-Pacific Sustainable Tourism Conference in Chiang Mai, Thailand, expecting a charity-oriented gathering looking to make tourism a more earth-friendly enterprise. It was organized by the Global Sustainable Tourism Council (GSTC), which was created by the United Nations, which seemed promising. I attended several thought-provoking panels, but as they wore on, I started to glean that the whole thing was organized around GSTC's core mission of establishing standards for sustainable certification, and that this was a moneymaking operation.

GSTC's system is meant to offer an alternative to the likes of

LEED, the best-known green building certification in the world, which certifies only the building itself, while GSTC joins existing certification bodies like Green Key and Green Seal in auditing hotels' and resorts' operations as well. This could result in a more complete measure of sustainable practices.

But none of these bodies are doing the work for free. LEED certification can be exceedingly expensive, with fees for a large resort often surpassing $1 million. Certification is big business and has conflict of interest built into it: those applying for green certification are paying the certifier.

GSTC adds another layer to the system, creating and enforcing standards for for-profit companies that pay an annual fee to remain GSTC accredited. Hotels then pay those companies to audit them and, assuming they pass, provide certification. In most cases, hotels need to recertify every year or every other year, which means paying an annual fee in perpetuity. At the conference, it wasn't at all clear to me which problems GSTC is solving within this system.

Alternatives to pay-to-play certification do exist. Since 2004, the U.S. Environmental Protection Agency's Energy Star program has included certification for commercial buildings, including hotels. Unlike most of the others, Energy Star certification is free, although the applicant does have to pay for an independent engineer or architect to conduct an audit. Energy Star says this cost usually runs between $1,000 and $1,500—a chunk of change, but nothing like what other certification bodies charge. And on a small scale, Reef Check Malaysia does it as well, with its free sustainable hotel certification for Tioman Island's accommodations.

Moving away from the certification model altogether, governments are again stepping up. California is aiming to bring emissions from its buildings below 1990 levels by 2030. In 2019, New York City enacted a law capping the carbon emissions of all buildings over 25,000 square feet. When buildings are required by law to go green, certifications become redundant.

EMPOWER LOCAL COMMUNITIES

The sand-making machine on Tioman Island would not have happened without Alvin Chelliah's long-term commitment to understanding the needs and challenges of the island. He had to first overcome locals' suspicion of outsiders, even a fellow Malaysian from the mainland. There's only one way to accomplish this: spend time, lots of it, years probably, living in the community.

In the beginning, Chelliah says, "We were always talking to the locals about the environment and the reefs. But they've got their own set of issues that they are interested in. And if you don't sort their issues out, then they've got no time for yours, you know?"

In the case of the sand-making machine, Alvin knew that locals were frustrated with the worsening trash situation on the island. He also understood that in Malaysia, silica (the main compound used to make glass) was cheaper than recycled glass. While they are able to sell plastic, aluminum, and cardboard off the island for recycling, that approach wouldn't work with glass. He bought the machine as an alternative and started running it at Reef Check. At the same time, Alvin got to know Sham, who had "shown a lot of interest," and who was "doing a lot of eco-friendly stuff." It made sense to give him the machine. And now the glass-to-sand machine is built into the fabric of the community.

None of it would have been possible without Chelliah's extended effort to understand the island and its community. Herein lies one of the major challenges of conservation and sustainability: No two places have the same environmental challenges, nor the same cultural systems influencing them, so their solutions must always be tailor made. Each location needs an Alvin Chelliah, who understands both the global, scientific concerns and the needs and concerns of the locals.

Beach resorts are in a position to fill this role. Nihi Sumba in Indonesia sets a great example. Its founders spent decades living in the area, gaining a comprehensive knowledge of the local culture, and were then able to improve Sumbanese lives in quantifiable ways based on that knowledge. Hotel managers should note that Nihi Sumba's owners report that the philanthropic efforts have been great for business at the resort itself.

LIMIT TOURIST NUMBERS

Two hundred and twenty miles off the coast of Brazil, a collection of twenty-one islands known as Fernando de Noronha rivals any location in the world for its exquisite beachfront landscapes. It has all the elements that people look for when they head to the beach: gorgeous blue-green waters, incredible diving and snorkeling, killer surfing, dramatic volcanic landscapes, the whitest of sand beaches, average temperatures that hover around 80 degrees year-round, and the highest concentration of dolphins in the world.

These features remain intact not because Fernando de Noronha is a freak of nature, which it is, but because its local government has seen fit to limit tourism development and redirect existing tourism revenues toward waste treatment, careful infrastructure maintenance, and conservation efforts. Every visitor pays a $14-per-day environmental fee (which increases steeply per day after ten days, encouraging tourists not to overstay their welcomes), plus a one-time park fee of $41 US.

Strict laws allow for only 420 visitors to enter the archipelago each day—in total, about 100,000 make it to the island each year. These low numbers have provided enough revenue to increase standards of living for the islands' 3,000 residents, with basic infrastructure, incomes, and the supply chain for food and other products vastly improved. At the same time, the limits have enabled authorities to conserve the natural elements that make Fernando de Noronha special in the first place.

Nature, not the tourist, takes priority in Fernando de Noronha. There are no large hotels or resorts. On arguably its best beach, Baía do Sancho, humans are banned altogether from 6 p.m. until morning during the turtle nesting season.

Fernando de Noronha is not the only beachfront destination to have limited tourist numbers. The Cinque Terre in Italy, Ecuador's Galapagos Islands, Lord Howe Island in Australia, and the Seychelles, off the coast of mainland Africa, have all moved to limit tourists, while others, like Maya Bay in Thailand and Boracay in the Philippines, have temporarily closed to tourism altogether in an attempt to save them from ecological ruin. Unlike most of the above locations, Fernando de Noronha enacted its limit before the damage was done, an approach that more up-and-coming destinations should consider. Brazil's president, Jair Bolsonaro, has pledged to open the islands to mass tourism development, but so far, resistance to his plan has held up.

STOP BUILDING GOLF COURSES

Despite their long-standing association with beach resorts, golf courses are an enemy of beachfront health. A single golf course uses hundreds of thousands of gallons of water *every day*, often in a place where water supply is a problem. Remember that when the Four Seasons' golf course opened on Nevis, it used more water than the Caribbean island's main town. In addition, at courses near a beach, the fertilizer used to keep the greens so very green inevitably runs off into the nearby ocean, the nitrogen and phosphorous contained in it causing algae blooms that smother coral reefs, cause coral disease, and wreak havoc on the ecosystem.

A typical course takes up something in the range of 100 to 150 acres of land. In places where beachfront space is limited, this can seem like an egregious misuse to those who live nearby, as expressed by the jet-ski operator in Barbados who saw the golf courses as a major reason locals were being squeezed out.

As the Earth continues to get warmer, many popular beachfront vacation spots will become so hot that a round of golf will no longer be a comfortable proposition. This is a particular concern in places like Portugal's Algarve, with its dozens of golf courses, and Spain's Costa del Sol, with sixty or so. Both popular beach destinations are warming faster than the global average, exacerbating the issue.

For all of the above reasons, resort areas should reconsider giving coveted acreage over to golf, a sport which by many indications is already on the decline.

DEEMPHASIZE BEACHES

Officials in beach destinations are beginning to understand that relying completely on their vulnerable shorelines for tourism revenue may spell economic disaster down the line. St. Kitts, as we've seen, is emphasizing cultural tourism alongside its beaches, in a departure from the Caribbean norm. And in Portugal, despite the 500 miles of shoreline that currently serve as the country's key tourism magnet, current official promotion focuses on inland destinations.

At the GSTC conference in Chiang Mai, I met Joseph Waleanisia, an official from the Solomon Islands who has been involved in the Pacific island nation's nascent efforts to develop its tourism industry. He says that for his small country, tourism is embraced only so far as it can be "commensurate with cultural preservation." Tourism must fit around the culture, not vice versa. Waleanisia says that in practice this might mean using a shoreline as a cultural attraction at certain times of year when tourism won't interfere with a tribe's rituals, rather than as a traditional beach leisure area.

Bottom line: Diversification of tourism offerings in beachfront areas eases the stress on beaches in ways that are positive for both the environment and local communities.

DISRUPT THE TOURISM LIFE CYCLE

In R. W. Butler's Tourist Area Life Cycle, local communities and visitors alike generally express satisfaction with an emerging destination as it moves through the Exploration and Involvement stages. With only a few adventurous travelers making their ways to a place, and local businesses cropping up to accommodate them, local stakeholders are benefiting directly from and exerting considerable control over tourism. Environmental issues also remain at a controllable level, the local community tends to view interactions with visitors favorably, and tourists feel they are experiencing an authentic place.

But as an area moves into and through the Development Stage, locals begin to feel squeezed out, while the first tourists begin to reminisce about how much better the place used to be. Early signs of environmental degradation emerge. International companies move in.

It would be better, then, if beach resort areas could find a way to freeze things in the Involvement Stage. Limiting tourists, as Fernando de Noronha has, is one way to accomplish this. Others might include zoning restrictions on beachfronts that limit both the number of total resorts and the number of rooms within each resort, and infrastructure improvements that encourage better tourism, not just more of it.

For the latter, Tioman Island again provides a useful example. Alvin Chelliah is sure that tourism has maintained manageable numbers here only because attempts to build an airport that can accommodate large planes have so far failed. While some on the island would like to see the increased business from a bigger airport, others understand that overdevelopment would inevitably follow. That is the point: Without deliberately imposed limitations, the overdevelopment always follows, and overdevelopment leads to decline.

SAVE THE CORAL REEFS

Just south of Miami Beach, Virginia Key sits comfortably off the tourist path. It boasts a couple of nice beaches used mostly by locals, the Miami Seaquarium, and the University of Miami's campus for the Rosenstiel School for Marine and Atmospheric Science, where I'm meeting Dalton J. Hesley, a senior researcher on a team working furiously to save the only coral reef in the continental United States before it's too late. Running from southeast Florida and down the Florida Keys, the Florida Reef a few decades ago enjoyed 40 percent coral cover—a term that refers to the amount of a reef made up of the all-important stony coral, upon which the entire ecosystem relies. Recently that number has dropped to 3 or 4 percent.

To clarify: It's very nearly too late. "We are precipitously close to losing our reefs entirely," Hesley says. "The issues around coral reefs are alarming and we don't feel like we have fifty years to figure this out."

In terms of tourism, coral reefs provide an attraction in and of themselves. They also serve as a crucial first line of defense against storms for many beaches around the world, breaking the power of waves as they move over them. And in fact, the white sand common to tropical beaches is most often composed of broken-down coral. Lose the reefs, lose the sand, too.

Helsey describes the calcium carbonate comprising the stony corals as a stable but fragile material that requires specific conditions to thrive. "Corals are kind of divas," he says. As the oceans absorb increasing amounts of carbon dioxide, CO_2's reaction with salt water creates carbonic acid. In this acidic seawater, corals can dissolve and be damaged by excess algae growth. Coral also doesn't do well when the water rises above 80 degrees, a threshold the waters of the Florida Reef are flirting with. Adding to these problems, in 2014 the little-understood stony coral tissue loss disease emerged in the waters just off Virginia Key, relentlessly killing off stony coral. In 2017,

Hurricane Irma added insult to injury, bringing further damage to an already weak reef.

To save it, the Lirman Lab launched on this campus in 2007. The first five years, Helsey says, were dedicated to figuring out how to collect corals and grow them in captivity. He shows me a large room full of white tubs stacked three levels high, all of which house growing coral reefs that will hopefully be relocated to the ocean. This lab in fact comprises a small portion of the total being cultivated. Most are in two coral nurseries on the seafloor nearby. Corals grow slowly—only by a few centimeters per year—so patience is necessary, but when they're ready, scientists transplant them from the nurseries to existing reefs. "It went from transplanting a few hundred per year to a few thousand per year, to now we can do tens of thousands per year," Helsey says. "That's actually an ecologically significant scale, where you can see the difference."

Researchers are learning a lot about corals along the way. By simulating conditions in nature, they've determined which corals do better in acidic water, or in higher temperatures. They're even breeding new hybrids—one coral that's, say, resistant to bleaching crossed with another that's less susceptible to disease. "We're actually building coral reefs of the future rather than trying to build the ones that have declined," Helsey says. With continued support for programs such as that run at the Lirman Lab, he believes the world's coral reefs can be saved.

REGROW MANGROVES

Many of today's popular beach vacation shorelines were once lined with mangroves, those large woody shrubs that thrive in the shallow, salty, coastal waters. They were removed for aesthetic reasons, or because experts believed that opening up the land to the sea breeze would make populations healthier. But it turns out that mangroves provide wonderful natural protection to coastlines against storms and erosion. Patrick Nunn, a geographer and geologist who spent much of his career researching the effects of sea level rise on Fiji, told me that on one Fijian island he studies, just two of the twenty or so waterfront villages never cleared their mangroves. "Of course those two communities are the ones that aren't having any problems with shoreline erosion or coastal flooding," he says.

In some places, including Fiji, efforts are under way to regrow the mangroves. Newly planted mangroves take around twenty-five years to mature into true protective buffers, and some long-term-oriented beach resorts are warming up to the idea of them. Six Senses, for example, is developing a couple of new resorts with plans to feature just a small beach surrounded by a big swath of mangroves.

The ultimate success of new mangrove forests at beach resorts will depend on a reimagining of what we consider to be an ideal beach, and that shift should be encouraged now, as we wait for newly planted mangroves to mature.

BACK ON TIOMAN ISLAND, THE WORK CONTINUES FOR ALVIN CHELLIAH and Reef Check. It's been a long road, but among the many small victories there has been a major one. The reefs around Tioman suffered their first major bleaching event in 2010, when 90 percent of the island's surrounding coral reefs turned white, a major warning sign that coral is in danger of dying, and that is usually caused by warming waters. They slowly recovered, and the reefs in the water off Tioman Island have actually seen an increase in coral cover since 2013, a rare event in a world where coral cover has declined by somewhere between 30 and 50 percent since the 1980s. "I will not say it's because of our own work, because we don't know for sure," Chelliah tells me. He lets a *however* hang in the air, unspoken.

FOURTEEN

SANDS OF TIME

The Future of the Beach Resort

Nearly three hundred years after Brighthelmstone shortened its name to Brighton and became one of the world's first seaside resorts, I go for a drink in the town's old North Laine section. I arrive early to the pub where I'm meeting an acquaintance of Scott's who lives here, order a beer, and sit down to the background din of conversation and the Smiths. Nothing elicits in me a sense of rusty English city life like the music of the Smiths, the Manchester band who so perfectly encapsulated the postindustrial urban ennui of the eighties. This is not beach vacation music. It's the first moment of many this evening indicating that Brighton today is no longer a resort first; it is a city.

Back in the 1960s and 1970s, after English travelers began skipping over Brighton in favor of beach destinations farther afield and farther south, the town entered a classic Decline stage. Counterculture swooped into the hole left behind and Brighton soon became known as a freethinking alternative to London, with the country's most visible LGBTQ population. The vibe endures today. Walking around, I keep feeling like I'm in San Francisco circa the 1990s.

But among the markers of Brighton's city life, the imprints of its resort history remain. At the eastern end of the old town, the 123-year-old Palace Pier continues to host a few million visitors every year, the vast majority of them day-trippers. It's Brighton's enduring down-market seaside attraction, famous for its amusement park rides and video arcade. Less than a mile along the boardwalk, the melancholy shell of the West Pier stands in front of Regency Square, with its terraced townhouses on three sides, the fourth left open to showcase the sea. Starting in 1866, the West Pier stretched more than a thousand feet into the water, festooned with elaborate gas lamps and a concert hall. Today it's mostly gone, the eerily photogenic metal beams of its frame all that remain after decades of neglect, an emblem of past glories. At its base stands the regrettable British Airways i360 Viewing Tower, a controversial observation deck opened in 2016 in an effort to reinvigorate tourism.

Between the two piers, the Grand Brighton Hotel stands facing the sea, its eight stories of Italianate grandeur looking much as it did

The remaining shell of Brighton's West Pier is today an emblem of the resort's past glories.

when it opened in 1864. On either side of it, other hotels, including the Hilton Brighton Metropole from the nineteenth century and the Old Ship from the eighteenth, today recall a scruffier Cannes.

Look out from these hotels, though, and the future of this shoreline stares down its history. Ten miles into the English Channel the horizon is interrupted by the 116 turbines of the Rampion Offshore Wind Farm, which provides clean electricity to hundreds of thousands of homes in England and obliterates our sense of the ocean's infinity. Here is something the Romantics didn't anticipate when they conceived of the sublime (imagine Friedrich's *The Monk by the Sea* with a farm of wind turbines breaking up the horizon), that Butler didn't think to include in his stages of the tourism cycle. Nowhere in the accepted narrative of the beach resort have we allowed for the possibility that we can no longer entertain the paradise fantasy. Not when we have to harness the resources of the world in new ways that won't destroy it. Brighton has adapted to this new reality, as all beach resorts must.

IN SOME CASES, ADAPTING WILL MEAN DISAPPEARING. EVEN IF THE changes recommended in the previous chapter come to fruition and nations collectively bring global emissions down drastically, some resorts we know and love today will be gone in a few decades. As sea levels rise between one and three feet by century's end, and as storms cause increasing damage to waterfront properties, authorities will be forced to choose the survivors. It's been estimated that without intervention, for example, between $15 billion and $23 billion of Florida real estate will be underwater by 2050. In all likelihood, only the most profitable of that will make it through to the other side.

Already in the Florida Keys, the government is wrestling with difficult decisions over which of its low-lying roads to maintain. On Sugarloaf Key, the most recent indication was that the $75 million required in the near term to safeguard three miles of road serving about twenty homes would not be worth it. In a similar situation in North Carolina's Outer Banks, local governments are trying to raise property taxes as much as 50 percent in order to pay for maintenance of the road onto the islands, as well as periodic renourishment of the beaches. Residents are resisting furiously. The impasse will end when the funds run out, or when it becomes more economical for the government to buy property owners out of their holdings than to maintain their access to them.

In some parts of the world, shorelines have already been shaped by such decisions. On the coast by Sitges, a popular resort town twenty-five miles southeast of Barcelona, jetties, breakwaters, and sand replenishment have ensured the continuing attractiveness of crowded beaches in town. But immediately beyond the last jetty at the municipal border, the coast becomes an unsightly seawall fronted by stones and pebbles. On this coast, we now already know which beaches will be saved.

For those that endure, more and more frequent beach nourishment will become necessary, and even then, things could become untenable for resorts, for one because the world is running short of sand with which to replenish the beaches, but also because at some point the replenishment will stop working. Of Waikiki, Chip Fletcher, the coastal geologist at the University of Hawaii, told me, "I would guess that at one foot of sea level rise, and certainly at two feet of sea level rise, we're looking at a beach which is becoming very difficult to hold in the same footprint."

A plan from one of Fletcher's doctoral students, Shellie Habel, has all hotels along the Waikiki shoreline being lofted in the future. Their first floors would be emptied out, allowing water to take up residence as necessary, and their lobbies relocated to the second floors. To the as-yet-unconcerned ear, it's a proposal that sounds overly dramatic, but it likely aligns well with future realities. Of course, we still have to gauge travelers' appetites for a hotel with no beach, or a beach *behind* the hotel itself.

One way or another, resorts of the future will look different than they do today. Their grounds will feature fewer palms, which will be replaced by shade-providing trees, and a return to indigenous flora and recultivated mangroves. Grass lawns will phase out (along with the grass swaths of golf courses). Some resorts are already heading in this direction. Jeff Smith, the vice president of sustainability at Six Senses, explained to me why the brand is going for unconventional but more natural landscapes. "From an ecological point of view and also from just an aesthetic and style point of view, we like to have vegetation as a buffer. So you see beach and natural vegetation and then the villas are tucked back behind the vegetation. It gives our villas a little more privacy. It also means that when you are walking along the beach you have the feeling of being on a deserted island."

Resorts' architecture will also change as we reconsider the wisdom of building as close to the shore as possible. Robert Young, the coastal geologist, pointed out that high-density beach resort areas will face particularly daunting challenges. "If what you're doing is looking fifty years down the road, then communities that have a lower density of development, where the oceanfront is made up primarily of single-family homes or duplexes, are certainly going to have a lot more flexibility than communities that have a lot of high-rises or shorelines that are heavily urbanized," Young told me. The Miami Beaches and Waikikis and Acapulcos might be the last of their kind.

As the Fijian hotel manager Andrew Thomson predicted, many new resorts and new resort areas will be built on higher ground and/or set back from the shoreline, with a beach club as the only structure near the beach itself. This approach incidentally will mark a return to the layout of nineteenth-century resorts like the Hotel du Cap on Cap d'Antibes in France and Congress Hall in Cape May, New Jersey. It has already been adopted in several countries where laws require new developments to be set back a specified distance from the high-tide line. Nicaragua, for example, has implemented such a law successfully, with resulting shoreline aesthetics that differ from those in older resort areas where buildings crowd the sand.

Some resorts will depart even more significantly from the familiar beach resort template, with techniques designed to overcome new geographical challenges. They, too, will have precedents to build on: Remember that overwater bungalows originally became popular as a way to monetize shorelines with no beaches. And already in 1988, a floating hotel opened on the Great Barrier Reef, off Australia's eastern coast. The seven-story, 200-room Four Seasons Barrier Reef Resort was financially challenged from the outset. It lasted only a year there before relocating to Vietnam for a decade and then, finally to North Korea, where it continues to languish today.

More recently and perhaps more auspiciously, Qatar is building 16 floating, movable hotels near Doha in the Persian Gulf in anticipation of hosting the 2022 FIFA World Cup. Each one will feature 101 rooms and be located—for now—near popular beaches. In the future, they can be relocated to any location where the water is at least 13 feet deep. (Cruise ships, by comparison, typically require depth of 30 or so feet.)

Looking forward, architecture and design firms are experimenting with prefab and modular hotel rooms and villas that can be relocated as needed. A young company called Nomadic Resorts particularly caught my attention with its customizable tents and pods, already in use by the luxury Wild Coast Tented Lodge in Sri Lanka. Nomadic Resorts' founder, Louis Thompson, started thinking about resort structures that could be easily moved after the 2004 tsunami destroyed both his housing and the resort where he was working in the Maldives. He teamed up with architect Olav Bruin, using cutting-edge materials and low-emission construction techniques to reimagine accommodations for high-end resorts.

Thompson sees the direction of resort design being dictated by advances in building materials. "We work in one of the areas where the performance of building materials is constantly improving," he says. As one example, he talks about the future of solar energy. "In ten years' time, your tent itself will be a solar collector. [Today], solar power is laminated onto the membrane. In the future the solar panel will *be* the membrane." Other new materials could include tents made of "invisibility" fabric that can seamlessly blend into their environments. Nomadic Resorts also envisions creating high-end inflatable tents—like a bounce house for kids, but fancy—that could be even more portable than their current designs. "There are certain organizations in the world that are doing things that are so freakishly alien to traditional construction methodology," says Thompson. At the most freakish end of this spectrum, "living" materials used to build resorts would actually respond to and interact with their environments.

Increasingly, Nomadic Resorts is receiving requests to supply pop-up resorts with which developers might either create seasonal resorts or "on-demand" resorts in remote locations. In practice, this could mean relocating the entirety of a resort's structures before, say, hurricane season arrives, or rearranging the structures on a property as sections become flood-prone with rising seas—a more reliable approach, perhaps, to increasingly unreliable coastlines.

For now, innovative sustainable solutions like those coming from Nomadic Resorts are being embraced almost exclusively by the high end of the resort market. Because of their high costs, this will likely remain the case for some time. And it in part explains why regions developing new beach tourism industries have shown a preference for catering to the high-end traveler. They've seen from the examples set by others that doing so will allow them to maximize revenue while minimizing negative local impacts.

Growing demand for sustainable tourism is just one factor that could push the global beach tourism industry out of reach for the middle market, as its reliance on mass consumption and low margins proves untenable. The growing scarcity of good beach areas, coupled with the ballooning ranks of the middle class, will cause prices to go up as demand outstrips supply. In addition, resorts themselves will face new and greater basic costs. They will increasingly be required to contribute to the enormous cost of keeping the beaches from which they benefit viable. A 2018 study of beach areas in Veracruz, Mexico, for example, found that proximity and access to the beach led to a 57 percent higher room rate for hotels. Some of that extra revenue will need to be redirected toward preserving the beaches. In Waikiki, resorts have already contributed directly to beach nourishment. Also, remember that in Miami, officials have proposed impact fees, which would require developers to shoulder some of the cost of infrastructure maintenance.

Then there's the matter of insurance. In 2019, the Federal Emergency Management Agency, which runs the National Flood Insurance Program in the United States, announced that flood insurance rates would begin increasing to align with the snowballing risk from climate change—one of the goals being to discourage development along at-risk shorelines. Despite some political pushback, the first rate increases went into effect in October 2021. Private insurance premiums for beach resorts have likewise risen dramatically since 2017's hurricane season, the costliest ever in terms of property damage. Eventually the flood insurance reckoning will arrive, and none but the best-financed resorts will be able to afford coverage.

WHEN COVID CLOSED DOWN THE TOURISM INDUSTRY IN THE SPRING OF 2020, we didn't know yet if it would change beach travel in permanent ways. On one hand, the year-long global quarantine revealed just how badly people want to get to the beach. Many beach resorts provided the one thing that made a place viable during the pandemic—wide-open spaces with a consistent breeze. Especially given the image hit suffered by one of beach tourism's biggest rivals, the cruise industry, they seemed primed to welcome socially distanced crowds. Sometimes, not so socially distanced: As the pandemic was taking hold, college students defiantly flocked to their spring breaks. As summer arrived, a wide swath of the population insisted on beach outings, myself among them. Scott and I sat in beach chairs near the back of the sand one July afternoon in Rockaway, awed by the sight of this perfectly arranged, socially distanced collection of humans enjoying their lives. I felt in that moment that the beach held a unique power to create this experience.

As time went by, it indeed became clear that beach tourism would return, but it wouldn't look exactly the same after all was said and done in the pandemic. Often, it was small things—the buffet meal has gone the way of the flip phone, for one. Other changes have been more fundamental.

Business travel, especially, seems unlikely to return to previous levels, and if large-scale conferences don't return in force, locations like Miami Beach and Cannes that cater to them will look to fill the void, possibly with a new class of working traveler.

Enter the workcation. In the wake of the work-from-home year of 2020, many companies had the epiphany that *it could have been an email*. In response, they untethered employees from their cubicles. The British banking company Revolut made an official policy of allowing all of its 2,000-plus employees to work from abroad for two months out of every year. Twitter announced that all of its 5,200 employees could now work from anywhere. REI and Target gave up their primary headquarters, anticipating an increase in employees working away from the office. Ford Motor Company announced that 30,000 of its workers can now tailor their work locations to their needs. This sea change means that working for a month in Hawaii, or Bali, or anywhere with competent Wi-Fi will be an option for a sizable slice of the working population going forward.

Locations are already competing for these workers' business. Anguilla, Bermuda, Dubai, and others have created a new class of visa aimed at remote workers. Individual beach resorts are shifting their offerings to accommodate them. The Hilton in Aruba offers private office space to guests for an extra $50 per day. At the ultra-luxury

Nautilus in the Maldives, a new workcation package includes dedicated workspace, a personal assistant, fax and wireless printing, and a dedicated phone line, in addition, of course, to high-speed internet. Other resorts are offering a third week free on two weeks booked, anticipating the demand for longer-term stays. We can expect sections of beach resorts to start resembling coworking spaces. We can expect a greater availability of on-site childcare during working hours.

The COVID era also saw sharp limits placed on international travel, leading those who did vacation to rediscover their own regions. While international travel picked up as vaccine rollouts accelerated in the wealthy countries that most tourists come from, the short-haul trip remains newly desirable. Even as the COVID pandemic fades, growing environmental concerns may reinforce the newfound reluctance to take long-haul flights. If wealthy travelers find the carbon footprint required to reach far-flung beach destinations harder to justify, certain locales will automatically suffer, most notably island locations with little or no regional tourist base to draw on.

Other localities are reconsidering how heavily they want to rely on beach tourism for their economic well-being. As we saw in chapter 7, Portugal's takeaway from the pandemic is that diversification of its economy away from tourism is essential. Over in the Caribbean, the International Monetary Fund advised countries in early 2021 to take urgent steps toward economic diversification in the face of long-term strains on tourism. Even the president of the Maldives, a remote island nation whose economy relies almost completely on beach tourism, indicated in a CNBC interview that the country would be diversifying into fishing and agriculture and beefing up its public service sector.

AT ITS ROOT, THE HOLD THAT THE BEACH RESORT HAS ON US IS A SOCIAL construct, kept in place by the cultural forces that shape our desires and behavior. In the short term, the beach vacation looks to remain as popular as ever, but who's to say that our love affair with the water will continue forever? As sea levels rise and the ocean becomes a constant source of peril, perhaps we'll learn to again regard it warily. If wind turbines rob the sea of its infinite wonder, we may no longer find it so intriguing. If feet in the sand become passé on Instagram, the beach vacation will surely suffer.

So many resorts have already disappeared. I think of the 150 major resorts that once lined New England's shores, almost all of them gone. I think of Baiae, down there on the floor of the Bay of Naples. I think of Long Branch, once the "American Monte Carlo" and now a nondescript commuter town in northern New Jersey. I think of other places that have become lesser versions of their former beguiling selves: Atlantic City, Bali, Skegness, Spain's Costa del Sol. I think of the Royal Hawaiian, gamely keeping the high-rises around it at bay even as the beach in front of it threatens to disappear. I think of the abandoned resort on Nias, the one in Fiji, the one in Railay. I think of the swath of empty beachfront in Rockaway that once hosted the country's toniest resorts. I think of Phuket, the beach tourism juggernaut in Thailand, with its emptied-out storefronts in the wake of the pandemic. I think about these places and I know that no resort is permanent, no matter how deeply it has embedded itself into the popular imagination.

There will be others, whose names we don't yet know, that rise up to replace the resorts we lose. Some will take extreme measures to exist at all. They'll spend millions hauling in sand from somewhere far away. They'll wrestle shorelines into place with sandbags, seawalls, jetties, and breakwaters. They'll wait out hurricanes, then survey the damage, then watch to see what happens to their insurance premiums in the aftermath. As they adapt, they'll stop looking like the beach resorts we recognize today.

What will the resort of last resort look like? It will be farther away from the equator, and farther back from the shoreline. It will forgo palm trees in favor of those that provide shade. For many of us, it will be prohibitively expensive. It will cater to Chinese and Indian tourists as much as to Western ones. It will be portable. It may even be intentionally temporary. It might not be at the beach at all, as long as there's a killer pool to lounge around.

Or it could look like a hotel in Brighton, reoriented once again toward the water, as southern England's temperatures by century's end become more like the French Riviera's today. The future English tourist, in fact, may no longer see much reason to flock south for her vacation.

For now, though, English beachgoers are down in Spain while I'm spending a few bracing October days on the east side of Brighton's Regency Square at the Hotel Una, a boutique accommodation spanning two former houses, and which in character aligns more closely with hip, design-driven hotels in a Kyoto or Nashville than it does with your typical oceanfront resort. A block off the square, Preston Street boasts a multicultural restaurant row. I order a latte at a new café there, then wait for a friend to arrive on the train from London for one night of my stay. We wander the town. We check out some pubs. We eat vegan pizza for lunch. I take her to the Colonnade Bar, which Scott's acquaintance had introduced me to a couple of nights ago, where we have a nightcap, talk about real estate, talk about wind energy, argue about the ethics of foie gras.

What we don't do, at this seminal eighteenth-century beach resort, is go to the beach.

ACKNOWLEDGMENTS

For a seemingly solitary project, this book came together thanks to an entire global community. First and foremost, *The Last Resort* never would have happened had my partner, Scott Rosenstein, not dragged me to all the surf breaks that piqued my initial fascination with beach culture. He also offered consistent logistical and creative support over the years it took to complete this project. We joke that he's my research assistant, but the real joke is that he's been far more than that for this book.

Along with Scott, Sacha Philip Wynne and Micilin O'Donaghue knew before I did that *The Last Resort* would be a book and served not only as insightful early readers, but as contributing architects. Micilin also translated documents from French that proved integral to the section on Senegal, while Sacha's knowledge of and ties to St. Kitts were crucial to the section on that island.

Nicola Thomson took an early interest in my research and connected me to her large network in Fiji. One of those people was Andrew Thomson, who helped me understand not only the beach resort industry in Fiji, but around the world. Michelle Alves de Lima read news articles in Portuguese to keep me updated on the situation in Fernando de Noronha. Erum Naqvi and Jack Woods helped me more firmly grasp philosophical concepts, especially the sublime. Mark Cammack and Stepany Tambunan helped me understand important elements of Sumatra's and Nias's culture (thanks to an introduction from Derek and Jessie). Feifei Yang reached out to her friends and family back home in China to give me insight into the perspective of today's international traveler from that country. Pam Bristow introduced me to James McBride, who facilitated my visit to Nihi Sumba in Indonesia, and Claude Graves sat with me for as long as I needed to grasp the full history of that resort. Matt Dickinson was unremittingly open in relaying his experience running a resort in Nicaragua. Hoa Nguyen likewise shared his successes and frustrations in pioneering beachfront tourism in Central Vietnam. Antonio B. Gilkes, Paula Phillips, and another local Bajan named Donovan were gamely forthcoming about their experiences dealing with tourism and tourists in Barbados.

Thank you to the scientists and scholars who have made a life out of studying the oceans and beaches, and then on top of that put their complex findings into terms I could understand: Chip Fletcher, Dalton J. Hesley, Robert Young, Patricia Beddows, Patrick Nunn, Barbara Davidde, and William Sweet. Apisalome Movono was exceedingly generous with his research on Vatuolalai and the Naviti Resort in Fiji.

Thanks to friends and family whose beachgoing experiences and observations appear in or inform the book: Tyler Gore, Leah Flax, Lionel Beehner, Steve Ruddy, Ed and Sue Stodola, Anya Khait, and Yael Friedman.

Many people around the world who didn't need to take the time to help me navigate a particular locale did so anyway: special thanks in this regard to Hazel Williams in St. Kitts, Chris Clark in Fiji, Alvin Chelliah on Tioman Island, John White in Brighton, Mark

Flint on Nias, and Sarah Schacht in Barbados. Madji Sock offered her logistical and scholarly support in Senegal from afar. Malou Morgan put me in touch with local Bajans who were willing to speak candidly with me.

Thank you to the members of my writing group—Douglas Belford, Matthew Gilbert, Greg Wands, Tyler Gore, Erum Naqvi, and Sacha Philip Wynne—who have helped keep writing fun for all these years.

My editors at Ecco, Denise Oswald and Norma Barksdale, shepherded the manuscript with a sharp intelligence, applied to finer points and overarching concepts alike with remarkable ease. They are so good at what they do. My agent, Matthew Elblonk, understood my vision for this book from the beginning and remained protective of it to the end.

Finally, I am indebted to the authors of literature and scholarship related to the beach that came before *The Last Resort* and upon which I was able to build.

NOTES

One: I'm Never Coming Home: Thailand and England

13 Dr. Robert Wittie came to Scarborough to start a resort: Lena Lencek and Gideon Bosker, *The Beach: The History of Paradise on Earth* (Penguin Books, 1999), p. 68.

13 William Clarke's letter about his time at the seaside: Fred Gray, *Designing the Seaside: Architecture, Society and Nature* (Reaktion Books, 2006), p. 17.

14 Design of the earliest seaside resort hotels: Ibid., pp. 22–23.

18 Henry James on the seaside town of Hastings: Henry James, *Collected Travel Writings: Great Britain and America* (Penguin Putnam, 1993), pp. 225–26.

Two: Where All Passions Combine: Monte Carlo, the Jersey Shore, and Cap d'Antibes

20 I owe much of the history of Monte Carlo recounted here to: Mark Braude, *Making Monte Carlo: A History of Speculation and Spectacle* (Simon & Schuster, 2016).

20 The 1852 guidebook noting Monte Carlo's sad state: *Handbook for Travellers in Northern Italy*, 4th ed. (London: John Murray, 1852), p. 75.

21 Venice's Ridotto and its eventual outlawing of gambling: David G. Schwartz, *Roll the Bones: The History of Gambling*, second printing (Winchester Books, 2013), pp. 97–98.

21 Germany bans gambling in 1872: David Clay Large, *The Grand Spas of Central Europe: A History of Intrigue, Politics, Art, and Healing* (Rowman & Littlefield, 2015), p. 200.

22 Early-nineteenth-century Nice accommodations and English Quarter: Mariana Starke, *Travels in Europe between the Years 1824 and 1828* (London: John Murray, 1828), p. 117.

23 The "fine sandy beach" that once graced the bay in Monte Carlo: Georges Vigarello, "The Bathing Resort in Monaco," from *Monacopolis: Architecture, Urban Planning, and Urbanisation in Monaco: Projects and Constructions, 1858–2012* (Nouveau Musée National de Monaco, 2013), p. 576.

23 François Blanc took over the Monte Carlo casino in 1863: Ibid., p. 579.

24 François Blanc's improvements to Monte Carlo: Ibid., pp. 579–80.

24 The railroad reached Nice in 1864: Mary Blume, *Cote d'Azur: Inventing the French Riviera* (Thames & Hudson, 1994), p. 37.

25 The year after the train to Monte Carlo began service, overnight visitors shot up to almost 170,000, with 345,000 visits to the casino: Bernard Toulier, "Monaco: Inventing a World-Class City-State by the Sea," from *Monacopolis: Architecture, Urban Planning, and Urbanisation in Monaco: Projects and Constructions, 1858–2012* (Nouveau Musée National de Monaco, 2013), p. 556.

26 The origins of the phrase "a sunny place for shady people" in reference to the French Riviera: This phrase is usually attributed to W. Somerset Maugham, who used it in his book *Strictly Personal*, published in 1941. A quick search of Google Books confirms that writers were using it already in the early twentieth century. And anyway, the full sentence that Maugham writes is, "The Riviera isn't only a sunny place for shady people."

28 Pleasure and even hedonism took over at the seaside in Monaco: Vigarello, "The Bathing Resort in Monaco," p. 583.

31 At Cape May, a slope "so regular that persons may wade out at a distance. It is the most delightful spot the citizens can retire to in the hot season": Charles A. Stansfield, *Vacationing on the Jersey Shore: Guide to the Beach Resorts, Past and Present* (Stackpole Books, 2004), p. 14.

31 Cape May's first hotel opened by Elgin Hughes: Emil R. Salvini, *The Summer City by the Sea: Cape May, New Jersey, an Illustrated History* (Rutgers University Press, 1995), p. 8.

31 Early history of Congress Hall: Jack Wright and Curtis Bashaw, *Tommy's Folly: Through Infernos, Hurricanes and War: The Story of Congress Hall, America's Oldest Seaside Hotel* (Exit Zero, 2016).

32 The Mount Vernon Hotel's demise: Ibid., p. 28.

32 Sources on the early history of Cape May include *The New Jersey Coast in Three Centuries*, written by William Nelson and published in 1902; *The First Resort*, written by Ben Miller and published in 2010; and *Cape May* from the Images of America series, written by Joseph E. Salvatore, MD, and Joan Berkey, and published in 2015.

32 The very early history of Long Branch: *Entertaining a Nation: The Career of Long Branch*, a publication by the Writer's Project, Works Projects Administration, State of New Jersey, 1940.

33 "much and fashionable company" at Long Branch: from *Gordon's Gazetteer* in 1834, as quoted in *Entertaining a Nation*.

33 Several books offer good histories of Long Branch and the Jersey Shore resorts in general, notably *The Jersey Shore: The Past, Present & Future of a National Treasure,* by Dominick Mazzagetti; *Entertaining a Nation: The Career of Long Branch*, commissioned and published by the Federal Writers' Project, Works Progress Administration in 1940; and *The New Jersey Coast in Three Centuries*, written by William Nelson and published in 1902.

33 Long Branch was the most popular resort in the United States: "Seeking Comeback: Long Branch Hopes to Regain Some of the Glamour of the Old Days," *New York Times*, June 4, 1961.

33 Long Branch as favorite watering hole in the United States: "Long Branch: The Season at Its Height," *New York Times*, July 13, 1870, p. 4.

33 Long Branch as "the American Monte Carlo": Chas. Sydney Clark, "The Strange Holy City of New Jersey," in *The Wide World Magazine*, January 1900, p. 496.

33 Nahant as an early summer resort: Bryant F. Tolles Jr., *Summer by the Seaside: The Architecture of New England Coastal Resort Hotels, 1820–1950* (University Press of New England, 2008), pp. 89–90.

34 On the Black experience in Atlantic City: Nelson Johnson, *Boardwalk Empire* (Nelson Press, 2010), pp. 35–53.

34 African-American coastal land ownership in the American South after the Civil War: Andrew W. Kahrl, *The Land Was Ours: How Black Beaches Became White Wealth in the Coastal South* (UNC Press Books, 2016), p. 7.

39 John Dos Passos on Gerald and Sara Murphy: Calvin Tomkins, "Living Well Is the Best Revenge," *New Yorker*, July 28, 1962.

39 In Antibes in the summer, the movie theater opened once per week and telephone service shut down at 7 p.m.: Amanda Vaill, *Everybody Was So Young: Gerald and Sara Murphy, a Lost Generation Love Story* (Houghton Mifflin, 1998), p. 122.

40 When Gerald Murphy got to La Garoupe, the seaweed was four feet deep: Tomkins, "Living Well Is the Best Revenge." (This profile provides a lot of key information about the Murphys' time in Antibes.)

41 The beach is the modern picnic: As described by my friend Steve Ruddy.

41 The renovated casino in Juan-les-Pins: Mary Blume, *Cote d'Azur: Inventing the French Riviera* (Thames & Hudson, 1994), p. 90.

Three: Among the Very Tall: Waikiki

44 Oahu's 27,000 hotel rooms: Numbers reported by the Hawaii Tourism Authority.

44 The Hawaiian Islands' $18 billion tourism industry: Hawaii Tourism Authority's 2018 statistics.

45 The beach of Waikiki was originally a barrier island, with wetlands taking up the area between it and mainland Oahu: Robert L. Wiegel, "Waikiki Beach, Oahu, Hawaii: History of Its Transformation from a Natural to an Urban Shore," *Shore & Beach* 76, no. 2 (2008), p. 3.

46 A thirty-one-year-old Mark Twain stayed in Hawaii for four months reporting on the islands for the *Sacramento Union*: James Mak, "Creating 'Paradise of the Pacific': How Tourism Began in Hawaii," working paper written for the Economic Research Organization at the University of Hawaii, February 3, 2015, p. 5.

46 Queen Lili'uokalani "living very quietly at a little place called Waikiki": "Hawaiians Want a Monarchy," *New York Times*, November 30, 1893.

47 "What I have always longed for was the privilege of living forever away up on one of those mountains in the Sandwich Islands overlooking the sea": Mark Twain, *Roughing It in the Sandwich Islands* (Mutual, 1990), p. xxiv.

49 "Waikiki as it exists today is generally a keen disappointment to the visitor": "Honolulu Beaches Will Be Improved," *New York Times*, October 29, 1928.

49 By around 1930, eleven groins had been constructed on the Waikiki beaches: Tara L. Miller and Charles H. Fletcher, "Waikiki: Historical Analysis of an Engineered Shoreline," *Journal of Coastal Research* 19, no. 4 (Fall 2003), p. 1027.

53 In Waikiki, "a $1.5 million restoration and expansion is in the works":

Nathan Eagle, "Save Beaches or Property? Climate Change Will Force Tough Choices," *Honolulu Civil Beat*, July 28, 2017.

54 In 1885, a round-trip ticket on a steamship between San Francisco and Honolulu cost $125: Mak, "Creating 'Paradise of the Pacific,'" p. 16.

55 Commercial air travel from the continental United States arrived in Honolulu in 1936: Rebecca Maksel, "Hawaii by Air," *Air & Space Magazine*, October 2014.

55 A ticket on the first flight from California to Hawaii in 1936 cost $3,000: David Romanowski, "The First Transpacific Passenger Flight," Smithsonian Air & Space Museum website, July 14, 2014.

55 Silent film star Dorothy Mackaill died in her room at the Royal Hawaiian in 1990: "Dorothy Mackaill, Actress, 87," *New York Times*, August 16, 1990.

56 More than 3 billion people in the global middle class: Homi Kharas, "The Unprecedented Expansion of the Global Middle Class: An Update," Brookings Institution working paper, February 2017.

57 Sea levels are rising faster in places losing the gravitational pull of the Greenland Ice Sheet: Elizabeth Gudrais, "The Gravity of Glacial Melt," *Harvard Magazine*, May-June 2010.

57 The Ala Wai Canal was created to catch the overflow of water in Honolulu and direct it toward the ocean: Katie Okamoto, "Honolulu Might Be Sunk Due to Climate Change," *Newsweek*, May 1, 2016.

57 The groundwater in Honolulu is rising: "As sea level rises, much of Honolulu and Waikiki vulnerable to groundwater inundation," Phys.org, March 28, 2017.

58 Since 1960, sea level has risen between two and six inches in the Hawaiian Islands: "What Climate Change Means for Hawaii," Environmental Protection Agency, August 2016.

58 In April 2017, Waikiki experienced its highest-ever tide: Catherine Toth Fox, "Our Waikīkī: King Tides, Beach Erosion and Water Pollution— Can Waikīkī Be Saved?" *Honolulu Magazine*, February 12, 2018.

59 Waikiki's 2012 beach renourishment funding: "2012 Waikīkī Beach Maintenance," Hawaii Department of Land and Natural Resources, July 2013.

Four: Into Far-Flung Places: Fiji

62 Fiji's pre–World War II tourism in Suva: Nicholas Halter, "Tourists Fraternizing in Fiji and the 1930s," *Journal of Tourism History* 12, no. 1 (2020), pp. 27–47.

63 Pan Am's first transatlantic direct flight: Elizabeth Becker, *Overbooked: The Exploding Business of Travel and Tourism* (Simon & Schuster, 2016), p. 9.

64 The French received guaranteed paid vacation time in 1936: Ibid., p. 52.

64 Between 1940 and 1970, U.S. GDP rose 10 times over: United States Bureau of Economic Analysis statistics.

65 The world's first overwater bungalows: Mark Ellwood, "The Story Behind the World's First Overwater Bungalows," *Condé Nast Traveler*, August 11, 2017.

65 Growth in international tourist arrivals since 1950: "UNWTO Tourism Highlights: 2017 Edition" and the UNWTO Tourism Dashboard.

65 Airline passengers increased tenfold between 1950 and 1970: Hans-Liudger Dienel and Peter Lyth, eds., *Flying the Flag: European Commercial Air Transport Since 1945* (Palgrave Macmillan, 1988), p. 16.

65 Tourism is now the third-largest export globally: "UNWTO Tourism Highlights: 2017 Edition."

66 Tourism became Fiji's biggest industry: Apisalome Movono, "Conceptualizing Destinations as a Vanua: The Evolution and Resilience of a Fijian Social and Ecological System," in *Tourism Resilience and Adaptation to Environmental Change* (Routledge, 2017), p. 291.

68 Bill Clark coined the term *bure*: Colin Taylor, "Revive the History of the Tropics," *New Zealand Herald*, July 4, 2008.

68 The Korolevu Beach Hotel size by the 1970s: Unheadlined article, *Sydney Daily Telegraph*, May 28, 1974.

71 A report on the Denarau development from the time: Rowan Callick, "Tourism Project Puts Fiji on EIE's Map," *Financial Review* (Australia), November 9, 1989.

72 Tourist accommodations "reifying and aestheticizing regional differences": David Bennett and Sophie Gephardt, "Global Tourism and Caribbean Culture," *Caribbean Quarterly* 51, no. 1 (March 2005), p. 15.

73 The history of the village of Vatuolalai and the Naviti Resort, and the evolution of Vatuolalai's culture, comes from Apisalome Movono's extensive research on the topic, relayed to me in interviews and published in the following journal articles: Apisalome Movono, Heidi Dahles, and Susanne Becken, "Fijian Culture and the Environment: A Focus on the Ecological and Social Interconnectedness of Tourism Development," *Journal of Sustainable Tourism* (August 17, 2017): 451–69; Apisalome Movono and Susanne Becken, "Solesolevaki as Social Capital: A Tale of a Village, Two Tribes, and a Resort in Fiji," *Asia Pacific Journal of Tourism Research* (2018): 146–57; and Apisalome Movono, "Con-

ceptualizing Destinations as a Vanua: The Evolution and Resilience of a Fijian Social and Ecological System," in *Tourism Resilience and Adaptation to Environmental Change: Definitions and Frameworks* (Routledge, 2017), ch. 17 (no page numbers).

74 The *magimagi* building technique in Fiji: A good explanation of the technique can be found on the website of the Museum of New Zealand: collections.tepapa.govt.nz/topic/1116.

77 That sea walls cause beach erosion was well understood by the 1970s: Orrin H. Pilkey and Howard L. Wright III, "Seawalls Versus Beaches," *Journal of Coastal Research*, Special Issue No. 4. The Effects of Seawalls on the Beach (Autumn 1988): 41–44.

79 "Runoff from the resort and its golf course had served as a fertilizer to an ocean algae": Apisalome Movono, Heidi Dahles, and Susanne Becken, "Fijian Culture and the Environment: A Focus on the Ecological and Social Interconnectedness of Tourism Development," *Journal of Sustainable Tourism* (August 17, 2017): 462.

80 The construction of a concrete walkway and decline of fishing in Vatuolalai: Ibid.

80 The ecological changes to Vatuolalai by 1998: Ibid., 458–59.

Five: New Frontiers, Precarious Business: Nicaragua and Senegal

86 Nicaragua's low crime rate: "A Surprising Safe Haven," *Economist*, January 28, 2012, p. 43.

86 Growth in international arrivals to Nicaragua: Matthew L. Fahrenbruch and David M. Cochran Jr., "Waiting for the Wave: Assessing the Vulnerability of Tourism in San Juan del Sur, Nicaragua, to Tsunamis," *Journal of Latin American Geography* 13, no. 3 (2014): 31.

88 The Sandinistas' appropriation of land and property: Mark A. Uhlig, "Nicaragua Victor Plans to Return Some Land Seized by Sandinistas," *New York Times*, March 3, 1990, sec. 1, p. 1.

88 Daniel Ortega taking a high-end property in Managua for himself: Larry Rohter, "A Tug-of-War in Nicaragua Over Seized Property," *New York Times*, March 2, 1997, sec. 1, p. 8.

88 The Somoza estate from which Anastasio fled: Howard LaFranchi, "Former Somoza Estate Calls Tourists, but Only a Few Echos Are Heard," *Christian Science Monitor*, January 22, 1997.

88 The Sandinistas turned Montelimar into a resort: Stephen Kinzer, "Nicaragua's Ideology of Sun and Surf," *New York Times*, November 23, 1988, sec. A, p. 3.

88 Half of Nicaraguans in poverty in the early nineties: World Bank International Development Association Report: "Nicaragua: Supporting Progress in Latin America's Second-Poorest Country."

89 Nicaragua minister of tourism on promoting tourism in Nicaragua: Larry Rohter, "Nicaragua on the Mend," *New York Times*, February 16, 1997, sec. 5, p. 10.

90 Bands recording at Maderas Village's studio: Julia Eskins, "Two Nights in Maderas: Plugging into Nicaragua's Most Magnetic Village," *Suitcase*, April 21, 2017.

92 "My bathing suits, even when I hung them out to dry": Adapted from my own work, "Shocks of Beauty and Mildew, 50 Meters from the Ocean," *Flung Magazine*, February 27, 2017.

93 Nicaragua's tourism industry represents 12.7 percent of GDP in 2017: "Travel and Tourism Power and Performance Report," World Travel & Tourism Council, 2018, p. 5.

93 The causes of 2018 unrest in Nicaragua: Richard E. Feinberg, "Nicaragua: Revolution and Restoration," paper published by *Foreign Policy* and the Brookings Institution, November 2018, p. 7.

94 Nicaragua tourism after the April 2018 uprising: Al Emid, "Nicaragua's Political Impasse," *Global Finance*, July/August 2019.

94 Nicaragua's economy in 2019 and 2020: The Economist Intelligence Unit's "Nicaragua: Country Outlook," December 2019.

94 Loss of tourism employment after protests in Nicaragua: Tom Phillips, "Ghost Resorts: Nicaragua Crisis Ravages Nascent Tourism Industry," *Guardian*, August 8, 2018.

98 In the early 1970s, the Senegalese prime minister made a speech on tourism development, among other topics, at the Plaza hotel: Robert J. Cole, "Senegal to Base Her Future on Broad Diversification," *New York Times*, October 21, 1970, p. 65.

99 Senegal's tourism peaked in the 1980s and then began a steady decline: Phil English, "Senegal: A Service Economy in Need of an Export Boost," WIDER Working Paper, No. 2016/150, United Nations University World Institute for Development Economics Research, 2016, pp. 4–6.

99 Hotel nights in Senegal declined over the first decade of the twenty-first century: "Senegal Update: Learning from the Past for a Better Future," World Bank Group, December 2014, p. 32.

100 Saly's beach resorts lost their beaches: Ibid.

101 Government changes to encourage tourism after Sall became president: "Race to the Next Income Frontier: How Senegal and Other Low-

Income Countries Can Reach the Finish Line," International Monetary Fund, 2018, p. 345.

104 Reasons for the high cost of hotels in sub-Saharan Africa: "Tourism in Africa: Harnessing Tourism for Growth and Improved Livelihoods," World Bank, 2013, p. 46.

105 Factors hindering air travel in Africa: Julian Hattem, "Why Is African Air Travel So Terrible?" *Bloomberg*, November 21, 2017.

105 More liberal aviation policy in Africa would lead to lower fares: "Africa Would Benefit from Liberalization," International Air Transport Association, October 9, 2014, accessed at https://airlines.iata.org/analysis /africa-would-benefit-from-liberalization.

106 Senegal's difficult bureaucratic and judicial system for businesses: "2020 Investment Climate Statements: Senegal," U.S. State Department, Bureau of Economic and Business Affairs.

106 Only a quarter of Senegal's population can read and write in French: Leigh Swigart, "The Limits of Legitimacy: Language Ideology and Shift in Contemporary Senegal," *Journal of Linguistic Anthropology* 10, no. 1 (June 2000): 95.

Six: Paradise Lost (to Overdevelopment): Tulum, Ibiza, and Cancún

112 Lionel Beehner's experience in Tulum: Lionel Beehner, "From Beach Bungalows to Artisanal Dinners, A Tulum Postmortem," *Flung Magazine*, May 8, 2015.

115 Early days of Ana and Jose in Tulum: Susan Spano, "Yucatan Journey, by VW Beetle," *New York Times*, December 19, 1993, sec. 5, p. 6.

116 Tulum's landfills can't handle the trash: Reeves Weideman, "Who Killed Tulum?" *New York*, February 20, 2019.

122 Butlin took Henry Ford's approach to carmaking: David Harrison and Richard Sharpley, eds., *Mass Tourism in a Small World* (CABI, 2017), p. 98.

123 Club Med as "a haven of informality and escape": Grace Lichtenstein, "Does Club Med Live Up to Its Titillating Legend?" *New York Times*, January 1, 1972.

124 Trigano explaining Club Med's appeal: Flora Lewis, "Smile! It's Profitable for Club Med," *New York Times*, October 10, 1976.

124 The Situationists' Club Med slogan: *Screaming for Change: Articulating a Unifying Philosophy of Punk Rock* (Lexington Books, 2010), p. 69.

124 By 1972, there were sixty-four Club Meds: Lichtenstein, "Does Club Med Live Up to Its Titillating Legend?"

124 In 1992, 23 percent of warm-weather vacation bookings were for all-inclusives: Betsy Wade, "Counting Costs at All-Inclusives," *New York Times*, April 19, 1992, sec. 5, p. 3.

124 Growth of the all-inclusive market between 2014 and 2019: Lebawait Lily Girma, "Why the Business of All-Inclusive Resorts Will Never be the Same," *Skift*, March 3, 2021.

128 History of spring break: The 2016 documentary *Spring Broke* provides a great overview of spring break's evolution.

129 The building of a road along the Caribbean coast of the Yucatan Peninsula: Paul P. Kennedy, "Jungle Road Deep in Mexico," *New York Times*, July 7, 1963.

129 The city built alongside the Cancún resort: Robert J. Dunphy, "Why the Computer Chose Cancun," *New York Times*, March 5, 1972, accessed online.

132 Cancún had 35,024 hotel rooms as of 2017, the most recent data available from Mexico's Secretariat of Tourism.

Seven: A Global Juggernaut: Vietnam and Portugal

136 The rise of the Chinese middle class as "one of the most fascinating human dramas of our time": Cheng Li, "Introduction: The Rise of the Middle Class in the Middle Kingdom," in *China's Emerging Middle Class: Beyond Economic Transformation*, ed. Cheng Li (Brookings Institution Press, 2010), p. 3.

136 Size of the Chinese middle class: Homi Kharas and Meagan Dooley, "China's Influence on the Global Middle Class," Brookings Institution, October 2020, p. 2.

136 In 2009 the Chinese government dropped its tightest restrictions on overseas travel: Elizabeth Becker, *Overbooked: The Exploding Business of Travel and Tourism* (Simon & Schuster, 2016), p. 296.

136 On the growth of Chinese international travel: Oliver Smith, "The unstoppable rise of the Chinese traveler—where are they going and what does it mean for overtourism?" *Telegraph*, July 2, 2019.

136 Chinese share of the global tourism market: "China and the World: Inside the Dynamics of a Changing Relationship," McKinsey Global Institute, July 2019, p. 102.

137 Annual growth of the global middle class: Homi Kharas, "The Unprecedented Expansion of the Global Middle Class: An Update," *Global Economy and Development at Brookings* (February 2017), p. 13.

137 The reshuffling of the geography of the global middle class: Ibid., pp. 11–14.

137 Obtaining tourist visas as an Indian citizen: "How This Indian Couple Navigated Visas to Travel the World," Nomadic Matt, December 4, 2019.

141 Vietnam's growing tourist arrivals, especially from China: "UNWTO Tourism Highlights: 2018 Edition," p. 16.

141 Tourism's share of Vietnam's economy: World Travel & Tourism Council data.

141 4 million Chinese visitors to Vietnam: "China and the World," p. 105.

143 Factors in the erosion of Cui Da beach in Vietnam: An Thinh Nguyen et al., "Tourism and Beach Erosion: Valuing the Damage of Beach Erosion in the Hoi An World Heritage Site, Vietnam," *Environment, Development, and Sustainability* 21, no. 1 (March 2018).

145 "Leakage" in Vietnam's tourism industry: "Taking Stock: Recent Economic Developments of Vietnam, Special Focus: Vietnam's Tourism Developments: Stepping Back from the Tipping Point—Vietnam's Tourism Trends, Challenges, and Policy Priorities," report from the World Bank, July 2019, p. 43.

146 Since 2015, the Chinese company Fosun International has owned Club Med: Dominique Vidalon, "Chinese-owned Club Med to Open 15 New Resorts by 2019," Reuters, January 26, 2017.

146 Club Med catering to Chinese guests: Kevin Chan, "Western Brand, Chinese Characteristics: Club Med in Guilin," *Chicago Tribune*, August 25, 2017.

149 McKinsey's surveys on Chinese consumer behavior: "China and the World," p. 98.

149 Special lanes for Chinese tourists at Thailand's airports: "Special Lanes Open for Chinese Tourists at 5 Airports," *Bangkok Post*, August 4, 2018.

149 The most popular international destination for Chinese tourists: "Guidelines for Success in the Chinese Outbound Tourism Market," World Tourism Organization, 2019, p. 14.

152 90 percent of international tourists to Portugal come for coastal tourism: "Tourism Statistics at the Regional Level," report published by Eurostat, March 2020, p. 8.

153 2008 financial crisis effect on Portugal: Paul Hockenos, "Portugal Has Emerged as Europe's Booming Anti-Germany," *Foreign Policy*, December 28, 2017.

153 The arrival of low-cost airlines in Portugal: "Low-Cost Airlines:

Bringing the EU Closer Together," report by the Centre for European Policy Studies, 2018, p. 20.

153 Emergence of big-wave surfing in Portugal: Patrick Kingsley, "This Town Once Feared the 10-Story Waves. Then the Extreme Surfers Showed Up," *New York Times*, November 11, 2018.

154 International tourism down 72 percent in the first ten months of 2020: Data from the World Travel & Tourism Council.

154 Portugal's tourism revenues crashed during 2020: Catarina Demony, "Portugal must diversify tourism-dependent economy after pandemic, government official says," Reuters, November 23, 2020.

155 Economic impact of foreign versus domestic tourists in Vietnam: "Taking Stock," pp. 36 and 43.

155 Portugal's changing climate is more extreme than the global average: Anabela Carvalho et al., "Climate Change Research and Policy in Portugal," *Wiley Interdisciplinary Reviews: Climate Change* 5, no. 2 (2013).

155 Portugal may soon have two separate seasons as July and August become too hot: Camelia Surugiu et al., "Climate change impact on seaside tourism—Portugal and Romania: Two different case studies with strong particularities," *Revista Economica*, January 2011, p. 126.

155 Richard Tol on northern Portugal as a safer real estate bet than southern Portugal: Brad Amburn, "Warm New World," *Foreign Policy*, October 26, 2009.

156 The ripple effect of climate change and climate migration: Abrahm Lustgarten, "The Great Climate Migration," *New York Times Magazine*, July 23, 2020.

Eight: The Long Haul to the High End: Sumba (Indonesia)

165 Carbon footprint of a trip from the United Kingdom to Croatia: "Calculating the Carbon Emissions of Vacations—Key Findings," results of study commissioned by Responsible Travel published at: responsiblevacation.com/copy/carbon-emissions-of-holidays.

165 Per capita CO_2 emissions by country: Data by country is available on the World Bank's website.

166 Transport to hotels accounts for more carbon emissions than hotels themselves: "OECD Tourism Trends and Policies 2018," p. 71.

166 The development of electric and hybrid planes: Chris Baraniuk, "The Largest Electric Plane Ever to Fly," BBC, June 17, 2020.

166 The development of biofuels for aviation: David Hitchcock, "Ready for

Takeoff? Aviation Biofuels Past, Present, and Future," report produced by the Atlantic Council, January 8, 2019.

173 Patients treated in the Sumba Foundation's health clinics: The Sumba Foundation Year End Report 2018, p. 8.

Nine: Beyond the Sea: Barbados and St. Kitts

178 Growth in tourism to Barbados from 1955 to 1980: R. B. Potter, "Tourism and Development: The Case of Barbados, West Indies," *Geography* 68, no. 1 (January 1983): 46.

179 The early decades of British Barbados: Simon P. Newman, *A New World of Labor: The Development of Plantation Slavery in the British Atlantic* (University of Pennsylvania Press, 2013), pp. 55–59.

179 Sugar cultivation and slavery both took hold in Barbados in the 1650s: Dr. Karl Watson, "Slavery and Economy in Barbados," *BBC History*, most recently updated February 17, 2011.

180 Mark Carey on historical European and American views toward the Caribbean climate: Mark Carey, "Inventing Caribbean Climates: How Science, Medicine, and Tourism Changed Tropical Weather from Deadly to Healthy," *Osiris* 26, no. 1 (2011): 129–41.

181 Black Barbadians purchased land with money earned working on the Panama Canal: Christine Barrow, "Ownership and Control of Resources in Barbados: 1834 to the Present," *Social and Economic Studies* 32, no. 3 (September 1983): 96.

188 Barbados's western shoreline has been eroding since the 1960s: J. Brian Bird et al., "Coastal Subsystems of Western Barbados, West Indies," *Geografiska Annaler. Series A, Physical Geography* 61, no. 3/4 (1979): 221–36.

189 The sewage spill on Barbados's south coast in 2018: "Barbados's Mucky Election: Polluted Politics," *Economist* (online), May 24, 2018.

194 Growth of St. Kitts and Nevis's tourism industry in 2019: "Travel and Tourism: Global Economic Impact and Trends 2020," World Travel & Tourism Council, p. 6.

197 The Four Seasons' golf course on Nevis used up more water than the island's main town: Carol McCabe, "Small Is Beautiful: On the Island Nation of St. Kitts & Nevis, the Clock Stands Still and Tourists Are Sparse," *Los Angeles Times*, October 20, 1991.

Ten: A Tale of Two Islands: Bali and Nias (Indonesia)

207 The Dutch were intrigued by the Hindu religion on Bali: Adrian Vickers, *Bali: A Paradise Created* (Periplus Editions, 1989), p. 12.

208 Bali's slave trade: Ibid., p. 14.

208 In 1914, the tourist bureau in Batavia extended its scope to Bali: Michel Picard, "Cultural Tourism, Nation-Building, and Regional Culture: The Making of a Balinese Identity," in *Tourism, Ethnicity and the State in Asian and Pacific Societies* (University of Hawaii Press, 1997), p. 190.

208 Opening of the Bali Hotel in Denpasar: Michel Picard, *Bali: Cultural Tourism and Touristic Culture*, translated by Diana Darling (Archipelago Press, 1996), p. 24.

209 Number of tourists visiting Bali in the 1930s: Ibid., p. 25.

210 The Dutch program of "Baliseering," or the Balinization of Bali: Picard, "Cultural Tourism, Nation-Building, and Regional Culture," p. 186.

210 Niassans traded slaves for gold with the Achenese: Andrew Beatty, *Society and Exchange on Nias* (Oxford University Press, 1992), pp. 3–4.

210 The Dutch took an interest in Nias beginning in the 1660s: Ibid., p. 3.

210 The 1693 agreement between the Dutch East India Company and Nias chiefs: Bente Wolff, "Extending the Self: Otherness in Cosmology and Consumption in a Nias Tourism Area" (PhD diss., National Museum of Denmark, May 1999), p. 38.

210 Dutch fort on Nias destroyed by flood in 1861: Ibid., p. 39.

211 The Dutch took control of Nias in 1906: Beatty, *Society and Exchange on Nias*, p. 4.

211 Mabel Cook Cole writing about Nias in 1931: Mabel Cook Cole, "The Island of Nias, at the Edge of the World," *National Geographic*, August 1931, pp. 201–24.

211 "Primitive Nias . . . rivals Bali for strange customs, royal processions and festive dress": "Random Notes for Travelers," *New York Times*, October 20, 1935, p. 193.

211 The *Times* again promoted a cruise to Nias: "Notes for the Traveler," *New York Times*, November 28, 1937, p. 203.

211 The ring road built on Nias in the 1930s: Alain Viaro, "Road Development and Tourism in Nias, Indonesia," TU Vienna, ASSIP Project, 2016, p. 54.

212 In the 1950s, Bali had very little tourism: Adrian Vickers, *Bali: A Paradise Created* (Periplus Editions, 1989), p. 182.

212 In 1989, two underwater cables brought electricity from Java to Bali: Anto Mohsin, "'Lighting 'Paradise': A Sociopolitical History of Electrification in Bali," *East Asian Science, Technology and Society: An International Journal* (2016): 3–4.

212 Bali hotels in the 1960s: Vickers, *Bali: A Paradise Created*, p. 184.

212 Bali's tourism development in the 1970s with a World Bank loan: "Project Completion Report: Indonesia: Bali Tourism Project," World Bank, June 5, 1985.

213 Bali's own government was not involved in the tourism plan for the island: Picard, "Cultural Tourism, Nation-Building, and Regional Culture," p. 182.

213 Growth in foreign tourists on Bali: Data from Badan Pusat Statistik Provinsi Bali (Bali's statistics agency).

214 Problems on Nias with Dutch shipping line KPM ceasing operations in Indonesia: "Indonesia's Economic Dilemma," *Far Eastern Survey* 29, no. 4 (April 1960): 59.

216 The reemergence of surfing at Kuta Beach in the 1960s: Scott Laderman, *Empire in Waves: A Political History of Surfing* (University of California Press, 2014), p. 66.

217 Javanese taking the best jobs on Bali and tourism increasing inequality: Picard, *Bali: Cultural Tourism and Touristic Culture*, pp. 62–63.

218 Locals grew suspicious of motives behind Nias airport plan: Wolff, "Extending the Self," p. 36.

218 The 2004 earthquake was the strongest in forty years and longest in recorded history: "Analysis of the Sumatra-Andaman Earthquake Reveals Longest Fault Rupture Ever," National Science Foundation website, May 19, 2005.

220 Bali's trash problem: Fiona MacGregor, "Bali Fights Back as Tons of Plastic Threaten to Spoil Once-Pristine Paradise," NBC News, August 23, 2019.

221 Bali's per capita GDP is over $17,000 US: From statistics provided by the Indonesian government's statistics bureau, translated for me by Fiona Chandra.

221 The non-Balinese development of Bali tourism: Graeme MacRae, "If Indonesia Is Too Hard to Understand, Let's Start with Bali," *Journal of Indonesian Social Sciences and Humanities* 3 (2010): 19.

223 Just 3,143 foreign tourists came to South Nias in 2016: Anggreani Dachi et al., "Tourism Village Development Pattern in Bawomataluo Village, South Nias Regency, Indonesia," *International Journal of Research* 6, no. 3 (March 2019): 295.

223 South Nias GDP and poverty level: From statistics provided by the Indonesian government's statistics bureau, translated for me by Fiona Chandra.

223 Nias poverty and income levels: From statistics provided by the Indonesian government's statistics bureau, translated by Fiona Chandra.

Eleven: Ghosts in the Machine: Baiae, Rockaway, and Acapulco

226 The size and position of Baiae's ruins: *Nero's Sunken City*, documentary that aired on PBS, March 29, 2017.

228 The layout of ancient Baiae: Lawrence Keppie, "'Guess Who's Coming to Dinner': The Murder of Nero's Mother Agrippina in Its Topographical Setting," *Greece and Rome* (Cambridge University Press; second series), vol. 58, no. 1 (April 2011): 37.

229 The concrete dome of the Temple of Mercury: *Nero's Sunken City*.

229 The large freshwater cistern in Baiae: Ibid.

230 Horace writing about Baiae: Fikert K. Yegul, "The Thermo-Mineral Complex at Baiae and *de Balneis Puteolanis*," *Art Bulletin* 78, no. 1 (March 1996): 137.

231 No public buildings have been uncovered in Baiae: *Nero's Sunken City*.

231 Nero's murder of his mother at Baiae: Keppie, "'Guess Who's Coming to Dinner.'"

231 Vice and scheming at Mar-a-Lago: Isaac Arnsdorf, "The Shadow Rulers of the VA," *ProPublica*, August 7, 2018. Sean Illing, "Why Trump's Mar-a-Lago Is a Magnet for Grifters," *Vox*, August 25, 2020. Don Sider, "Party Time at Mar-a-Lago," *South Florida Sun Sentinel*, June 28, 1995.

231 Baiae land falling and rising due to bradyseism: *Nero's Sunken City*

235 On the early history of the Rockaways: Alfred Henry Bellot, *History of the Rockaways from the Year 1685 to 1917* (Bellot's Histories Inc., Far Rockaway, 1918).

236 The scene at the Marine Pavilion hotel: Benjamin F. Thompson, *History of Long Island* (E. French, 1839), p. 359; "Manners, Customs, Amusements and Characteristics at Rockaway," *New-York Daily Times*, August 10, 1853, p. 2.

236 Early Rockaway tourism centered on the peninsula's eastern end: Vivian Rattay Carter, *Images of America: Rockaway Beach* (Arcadia, 2012), p. 7.

236 Far Rockaway's status with elite New York in the mid-nineteenth century: "Far Rockaway. A Once Fashionable Sea-Side Resort," *New York Times*, May 31, 1874, p. 9.

238 Rockaway's bygone hotels: Emil R. Lucev Sr., *The Rockaways* (Arcadia, 2007).

238 Arverne's golden age at the end of the nineteenth century: "Arverne Urban Renewal Project: Cultural Resources Survey," report prepared for Dresdner Associates by Historical Perspectives in 1986.

239 Rockaway Beach Hotel details: "Rockaway Beach Hotel. A Description of the Mammoth Summer Inn Which Is Almost Ready for the Public," *New York Times*, July 9, 1880, p. 5.

239 Rockaway neighborhoods were among the hardest hit from COVID in spring 2020: Michael Schwirtz and Lindsey Rogers Cook, "These N.Y.C. Neighborhoods Have the Highest Rates of Virus Deaths," *New York Times*, May 18, 2020.

241 Over 100 hotels in Rockaway in the 1930s: Lawrence Kaplan and Carol P. Kaplan, *Between Ocean and City: The Transformation of Rockaway, New York* (Columbia University Press, 2003), p. 72.

241 Rockaway hotels at the end of World War II: Ibid., p. 82.

241 48 million visitors to Rockaway in the summer of 1950: Carter, *Images of America: Rockaway Beach*, p. 9.

241 Rockaway's falling summertime population in the midcentury years: Kaplan and Kaplan, *Between Ocean and City*, p. 38.

241 The failed attempts to modernize Rockaway as a resort: Kaplan and Kaplan, *Between Ocean and City*, p. 76.

242 The train to Rockaway becoming part of New York City transit: Carter, *Images of America: Rockaway Beach*, p. 93.

242 The Jacob Riis parking lot was built for 9,000 cars: Robert Caro, *The Power Broker* (Vintage Books, 1975), p. 508.

242 Cutting "Rockaway Special" train service: "Rockaway Special Cut to Weekends," *New York Times*, July 17, 1959, p. 21.

242 New York City's plan to relocate welfare recipients to Rockaway: Kaplan and Kaplan, *Between Ocean and City*, p. 57.

243 The substandard welfare housing in the Hammels section of Rockaway: Ibid., pp. 62–63.

243 Robert Moses's plan for new apartment buildings in Rockaway: "Housing to Erase Rockaway Slums in Hammels Area," *New York Times*, November 13, 1956, p. 1.

243 The Rockaways' disproportionate amount of Queens public housing: Kaplan and Kaplan, *Between Ocean and City*, p. 130.

243 More than 4,000 structures razed in Rockaway's Edgemere and Arverne: Mark Sherman, "City Opens Its Biggest Plot, in Arverne, to Development," *New York Times*, March 11, 1984, sec. 8, p. 7.

246 Staying at the Hotel Las Brisas in 1981: Alan Riding, "What's Doing in Acapulco," *New York Times*, February 8, 1981, sec. 10, p. 13.

248 The first flights to Acapulco in 1934: Stephen R. Niblo and Diane M. Niblo, "Acapulco in Dreams and Reality," *Mexican Studies* 24, no. 1 (Winter 2008): 35.

249 The earliest hotels in Acapulco: Andrew Sackett, "Fun in Acapulco?" In *Holiday in Mexico: Critical Reflections on Tourism and Tourist Encounters* (Duke University Press, 2010), pp. 172–73.

249 There were four hotels in Acapulco in 1933: Ibid., p. 164.

249 Mexico's promotion of Acapulco in the 1930s: Ibid., pp. 164–65.

249 Farmers kicked off their land for Acapulco tourism development received no compensation: Niblo and Niblo, "Acapulco in Dreams and Reality," p. 40.

250 The Mexican government's forceful expropriation of beachfront Acapulco land: Sackett, "Fun in Acapulco?," p. 170.

253 Flights available to Acapulco from New York City in 1981: Riding, "What's Doing in Acapulco," p. 13.

253 The anarchic nature of Guerrero in the early twentieth century: Niblo and Niblo, "Acapulco in Dreams and Reality," p. 33.

254 Teddy Stauffer attacked by gunman at his hotel: Teddy Stauffer, *Forever Is a Hell of a Long Time* (Henry Regnery, 1976), pp. 246–48.

254 Overdevelopment in Acapulco: Roger Joseph Bergeret Munoz et al., "Complexity of Acapulco Evolution as a Tourist Destination," *Journal of Intercultural Management* 9, no. 3 (September 2017): 16.

254 Cancún overtook Acapulco with foreign tourists: Michael Clancy, "Mexican Tourism: Export Growth and Structural Change since 1970," *Latin American Research Review* 36, no. 1 (2001): 135.

254 The decline of international visitors to Acapulco: Munoz et al., "Complexity of Acapulco Evolution as a Tourist Destination," pp. 17–18.

Twelve: Up to Here: Miami Beach

257 Geoff Dyer on visiting Miami Beach: "The Despair of Art Deco," *Threepenny Review*, Spring 2002.

259 History of the pre-tourism days of Miami Beach: Polly Redford, *Billion-Dollar Sandbar: A Biography of Miami Beach* (Dutton, 1970), pp. 70–71.

260 The creation of artificial land on Miami Beach: Ibid., pp. 70–71.

260 "[i]t took faith to undertake the job of making the waste of sand and the mangrove swamp into an attractive and habitable place": This passage from the *Miami Metropolis*'s January 10, 1913, edition is quoted on page 14 of the city of Miami Beach's "Ocean Beach Historic District Designation Report" in 1995.

260 For a wonderful accounting of the projects that have added to Miami Beach's total acreage: Carolyn Klepser, *Lost Miami Beach* (History

Press). Specifically, see the section titled "Reconfiguring the Land," beginning on page 22 of the 2014 paperback edition.

260 On the 1926 hurricane: Redford, *Billion-Dollar Sandbar*, pp. 173–74.

263 Miami Beach's anti-hawking regulation: Susan Askew, "Sidewalk Café Hawking Violations and Appeals Mounting," *Re: Miami Beach*, November 30, 2019.

264 Numbers on global sea level rise and Miami-area sea level rise: These were provided to me by Dr. William Sweet at the National Oceanic and Atmospheric Administration (NOAA).

264 Projected sea level rise in southeast Florida: "Unified Sea Level Rise Projection Southeast Florida: 2019 Update," report published by the Southeast Florida Regional Climate Change Compact, p. 9.

264 On the plans for the Delano Hotel in 1994: Timothy Jack Ward, "Remaking a Hotel, the Un-Miami Way," *New York Times*, August 4, 1994, sec. C, p. 4.

265 The abandoned plan to raze many blocks of buildings in South Beach: Gregory Jaynes, "In Decaying Southern Miami Beach, the Elderly Huddle in Frailty and Fear," *New York Times*, October 28, 1982, sec. A, p. 18.

265 In 1981, Miami had the highest murder rate in the country: Kelly, James, "Paradise Lost?," *Time*, November 3, 1981.

266 History of Miami Beach's beach erosion and replenishment efforts: Miami-Dade County Beach Erosion Control Master Plan, 2006.

267 Vegetated dunes were installed on the Miami Beach shore in the 1980s: City of Miami Beach Dune Management Plan, January 2016.

268 Hurricane Irma Washed Sand from Miami Beach: "Replacing Miami's beach sands costs millions. Here's how Congress could make it cheaper," *Miami Herald*, October 24, 2017.

268 Miami-Dade County Economic benefit from tourism: William D. Talbert III, "Greater Miami has worked hard to become a top tourist destination, and it shows," *Miami Herald*, October 24, 2019.

268 Miami Beach's real estate was worth $37.4 billion in 2018: "Miami Beach, Florida: Stormwater Management and Climate Adaptation Review." Report from the Urban Land Institute Report. April 2018, p. 20.

269 On the check valves installed in Miami Beach's drainage pipes: Jeff Goodell, *The Water Will Come: Rising Seas, Sinking Cities and the Remaking of the Civilized World* (Little, Brown and Co., 2017), p. 235.

272 Michael Shvo bought three hotels in South Beach: Katherine Kallergis,

"Here's How Much Michael Shvo and Partners Paid for Their South Beach Hotels," *Real Deal*, August 5, 2019.

272 Michael Shvo conditioned his purchase of the Richmond and South Seas hotels on the passing of a new zoning ordinance for the properties: Susan Askew, "Approval of Additional Oceanfront Height Opens Door for New Development," *Re: Miami Beach*, August 3, 2019.

273 A $100 million renovation of the Ritz-Carlton St. Thomas was "substantially funded by insurance proceeds": "Braemar Hotels & Resorts Reports Fourth Quarter and Year End 2019 Results," *Bloomberg*, February 26, 2020.

274 On Sandals Resorts not selling: Josh Kosman, "Caribbean Hurricanes Scaring Sandals Resorts Bidders," *New York Post*, November 13, 2019.

276 Miami-Dade's proposed impact fees for developers: Jessica Lipscomb, "Miami-Dade Could Ask Developers to Pay for Climate Change Costs," *Miami New Times*, July 6, 2016.

Thirteen: A Better Way: Tioman Island (Malaysia)

287 Prices based on carbon footprint at the Arctic Blue Resort: Company press release, accessed at http://arcticblueresort.com/ArcticBlueResort _PR_EN_V3.pdf.

288 The British report that recommended abolishing frequent-flyer programs: Laurie Clarke, "Here's How a Frequent Flyer Tax Could Help Cut Airline Emissions," *Wired*, October 16, 2019.

288 Passengers flying via Sweden's airports decreased 4 percent in 2019: "Sweden Sees Rare Fall in Air Passengers, as Flight-Shaming Takes Off," BBC, January 10, 2020.

291 Westerners drove up prices at Yugoslavia's Adriatic resorts: Rory Yeomans, "From Comrades to Consumers: Holidays, Leisure Time, and Ideology in Communist Yugoslavia," in *Yugoslavia's Sunny Side: A History of Tourism in Socialism (1950s–1980s)* (Central European University Press, 2010), pp. 93–94.

292 Coconut palms native to India and the Malay Peninsula: Lucas Brouwers, "Coconuts: Not Indigenous, but Quite at Home Nevertheless," *Scientific American* (online), August 1, 2011.

292 West Palm Beach requires trees other than palms: Kimberly Miller, "Oaks Instead of Palm Trees? Florida's Iconic Palms Don't Cut It with Climate Change," *Tampa Bay Times*, November 26, 2019.

294 Miami-Dade's proposed impact fees for developers: Lipscomb, "Miami-Dade Could Ask Developers to Pay for Climate Change Costs."

294 The argument of climate exactions: J. Peter Byrne and Kathryn A. Zyla, "Climate Exactions," *Maryland Law Review* 75, no. 3 (2016).

298 Golf course fertilizer kills coral reefs: Emily M. Bock and Zachary M. Easton, "Export of Nitrogen and Phosphorus from Golf Courses: A Review," *Journal of Environmental Management* 255 (February 1, 2020).

303 Coral reef cover has declined between 30 percent and 50 percent since the 1980s: Melissa Gaskill, "The Current State of Coral Reefs," PBS, July 15, 2019.

Fourteen: Sands of Time: The Future of the Beach Resort

306 Between $15 billion and $23 billion of Florida real estate will be underwater by 2050: "Risky Business: The Economic Risks of Climate Change in the United States," report published by the Risky Business Project, June 2014, p. 24.

306 Some of the Florida Keys will not be saved: Alex Harris, "At $60 Million a Mile, the Keys May Abandon Some Roads to Sea Rise Rather than Raise Them," *Miami Herald*, December 5, 2019.

307 Property tax hikes in the Outer Banks: Christopher Flavelle, "Tiny Town, Big Decision: What Are We Willing to Pay to Fight the Rising Sea?" *New York Times*, March 14, 2021.

311 Beach proximity increases room rates in Mexico: Gabriela Mendoza-Gonzalez et al., "Towards a Sustainable Sun, Sea, and Sand Tourism: The Value of Ocean View and Proximity to the Coast," *Sustainability* 10, no. 4 (2018): 1012.